D1015089

SIX SIGMA
TEAM DYNAMICS

SIX SIGMA
TEAM DYNAMICS

The Elusive Key
to Project Success

GEORGE ECKES

JOHN WILEY & SONS, INC.

Published by John Wiley & Sons, Inc., Hoboken, New Jersey.
Published simultaneously in Canada.

For general information on our other products and services please contact our Customer Care Department within the U.S. at (800) 762-2974, outside the United States at (317) 572-3993 or fax (317) 572-4002.

Wiley also publishes its books in a variety of electronic formats. Some content that appears in print may not be available in electronic books.

Library of Congress Cataloging-in-Publication Data:

Eckes, George, 1954–
    Six sigma team dynamics : the elusive key to project success / George Eckes.
      p. cm.
    Includes bibliographical references and index.
     ISBN 0-471-22277-1 (CLOTH : alk. paper)
     1. Teams in the workplace.   2. Project management.   3. Leadership.
    I. Title.
HD66 .E324   2002
658.4′04—dc21

                        2002006584

10 9 8 7 6 5 4 3 2 1

To my dear Uncle Joseph Della Malva,
it has been an honor being a part of your "team."
And to the memory of my sister, Adrienne.
You left our "team" too soon.

Foreword

As the Business Leader for Household Retail Services, I have become keenly aware of the impact Six Sigma, as a management philosophy, can have in managing a business. Both in my current responsibilities and in my previous career at General Electric, I have seen the power of Six Sigma firsthand in helping my organization improve both its effectiveness and efficiency.

We have embraced Six Sigma at Household Retail Services since early 2001. Having worked with George Eckes at General Electric, I knew he had a results-driven approach. Since Household Retail Services contracted with Eckes and Associates Inc., we have had impressive success.

A key ingredient in our success was embracing Six Sigma as a management strategy. Beginning in the spring of 2001 we created our Six Sigma Business Process Management System. My management team and I aligned our core and subprocesses to our business objectives and began to collect data on measures of both effectiveness and efficiency. By the summer of 2001, we had selected nine low-performing, high-impact projects for improvement. Over the course of the next six months, George Eckes and his staff trained our project improvement teams to apply Six Sigma tactically. By year-end 2001, we were celebrating our first round of successes. These successes included reducing dispute resolution from an average of 38 days to less than 3, and dramatically reducing incidences of fraud.

Which brings me to the topic of George's third book on Six Sigma, *Six Sigma Team Dynamics: The Elusive Key to Project Success*. The tools and techniques of Six Sigma at the tactical level are relatively simple to use once a team gains some experience in their application. Of much greater difficulty is managing the team and its interactions. When managed properly, team dynamics can result in a significant increase in Six Sigma project success. When ignored, they can result in the failure of the project team to meet its goals and objectives.

As he did in his first two books on Six Sigma, *The Six Sigma Revolution: How General Electric and Others Turned Process into Profits* and *Making Six Sigma Last: Managing the Balance Between Cultural and Technical Change,* George communicates the key concepts of managing Six Sigma team dynamics in easy to understand language.

In Chapter 2, he begins with an explanation of the roles and responsibilities of a Six Sigma team. Included in this discussion are the roles of the business leader, the project sponsor (also known as the Project Champion), the team leader, and team members. In pragmatic fashion, George lays out eleven action items the Project Champion should address even before the project team meets for the first time. In subsequent chapters (Chapters 5 and 7), George discusses what a good Champion should do during the project and describes the responsibilities of the Champion after the team disbands.

Good Six Sigma team dynamics requires a combination of preventions and interventions. As the saying goes, "An ounce of prevention is worth a pound of cure." In Six Sigma, the modified version of the adage rightfully states, "An ounce of prevention is worth a pound of intervention." This adage is directly applicable to Six Sigma teams and their dynamics. In Chapter 3, George lays out detailed, common sense preventions that can dramatically increase the achievement of the Six Sigma team's goals and objectives. They include how to create meaningful agendas so that teams break down their project work into bite-sized pieces. Suggestions on which tools to use to address each agenda item are given as well as suggestions on the importance of providing time limits to achieve goals. Another prevention included is how to set meaningful ground rules for each Six Sigma meeting. Ground rules are one element of facilitation that are intended to help prevent maladaptive behaviors from interfering with the work of achieving Six Sigma improvement. They are conventions that assist a team in establishing a set of acceptable and unacceptable behaviors so that the work of the team is not detoured by maladaptive behaviors.

Despite the best efforts of any team to prevent maladaptive behaviors, they will occur. In Chapters 4, 6, and 7, George provides specific suggestions as to how to deal with those behaviors, including how a team member should handle minor disruptions to the more severe situation of how the team Champion must handle an intransient resistor.

The ability to utilize project management tools is often a missing ingredient in Six Sigma teams. Simple but effective tools like Work Breakdown charts, Linear Responsibility charts, and Activity Reports can dramatically improve the effectiveness and efficiency of the time a Six Sigma team devotes to their project. These tools address the common complaint from teams that they don't have the time for Six Sigma. Understandably, this complaint is often voiced by more disorganized teams that waste valuable time between training sessions. In Chapter 5, George addresses how to use a sample of project management tools to expedite a Six Sigma team's work.

George takes a unique approach in his third book by combining detailed information on Six Sigma team dynamics through a *fictionalized* financial services organization. This fictionalized organization, Alpha Omega, is easily recognized as a representation of any organization that you may encounter.

Like his first two books, each chapter ends with a list of Key Learnings. A new addition to his third work is three appendices that I found particularly valuable. Appendix A includes the templates used by the fictitious call center team that attempted to improve effectiveness and efficiency at Alpha Omega. Of particular value is Appendix B where George provides 95 questions good Champions should ask their teams during the Define, Measure, Analyze, Improve, and Control stages of the improvement process. Appendix C is the list of specific responsibilities of the Project Champion. These include detailed action items to use *before* the Champion forms the team, *during* the team's four- to six-month existence, and *after* the team disbands.

Six Sigma, as a management philosophy, can be a major factor in achieving your business objectives, but only if done right. *Six Sigma Team Dynamics: The Elusive Key to Project Success* can help you get there.

Sandra Derickson
Managing Director and CEO,
Household Retail Services

Preface

Joseph Della Malva was born on July 13, 1917, to Italian immigrants. His father Michael was born in Rodi Garganico on the Adriatic coast of Italy and settled in Hoboken, New Jersey, when he came to this country in 1906. A widower with a six-year-old son, Michael married Assunta De Felice, also from Rodi, in 1916. They moved to West Hoboken, where Joseph was born the next year. The Della Malva family, which by then included two daughters, eventually moved to Jersey City.

Joseph Della Malva was a bright, inquisitive young man who led an amazingly diverse life, that included acting on Broadway in the late 1930s. As a result of his high school studies, he was fluent in several languages, leading to a job as a translator in New York City. However, in spite of remarkable life experiences, nothing could have fully prepared him for the world events of the early 1940s.

At the age of 23, Joseph volunteered for military service. He was stationed in the Philippines in December 1940. In February 1941, he was transferred by secret orders to Military Intelligence in Manila, with the rank of special agent. As a special agent, he conducted investigations of Nazis, fascists, and subversive activities in the Philippines. On November 28, 1941, Joseph transferred to Sea Coast artillery on Corregidor, the fortified island opposite the Bataan peninsula.

The Philippines became engaged in hostile actions against Japanese forces on December 8, 1941. Ultimately, after fighting against overwhelming odds, the American and Filipino defenders on Bataan surrendered to the Japanese on April 9, 1942. Corregidor fell 28 days later, on May 6th. Joseph Della Malva became a prisoner of war, and was held captive for the next three years and four months, until liberation in September 1945.

Six months after his initial capture, he was transferred by prison ship (which was barely missed in a torpedo attack by a U.S. submarine) to Japan, where he did hard labor at locations throughout Japan. He was a railroad freight yard worker in Osaka, a construction worker for a dry-dock in Tanagawa, a graphite factory worker in Naru, and finally, during the last five months of the war, as a stevedore on the docks of Tsuruga, a seaport on the west coast of Japan. Unlike POWs in Europe, POWs in Japan were as likely to die on Japanese soil as they were to return to the United States.

There were a host of reasons why Joseph Della Malva survived. He had tremendous emotional strength, which was instilled in him during his youth. He learned at his father's knee the importance of being strong. Being an Italian immigrant in the early twentieth century meant being ridiculed and harassed. He learned early to withstand the taunts of those who were less intelligent than he was and to face adversity with stoicism and endurance.

He faced much adversity while a POW in Japan. Harsh work conditions, uncertainty of survival, and physical abuse were high on the list of adversities. In the barracks where he and his fellow prisoners existed, evening conversations were centered around memories of their favorite meals back home. While his friends reminisced about thick-cut, medium-rare steaks, Joseph Della Malva mused about a simple treat he had first enjoyed as a small boy.

His fellow prisoners were regaled by Joseph's vivid description of his mother's homegrown tomatoes, resting on a bed of Italian bread, drenched in olive oil, and sprinkled with oregano, topped with a thick slice of provolone cheese. The prisoners' obsession with food was all encompassing and, sadly, nearly a losing battle.

It was only through circumstance and guile that malnourishment did not take his life. That, and the fact that Joseph Della Malva was a thief. As well documented in recent years, the Japanese did not passively house their prisoners. They forced them to work. One day while working in a warehouse that was crammed full of burlap bags, Joseph discovered that one of the bags was damaged. He slit it open and discovered it was filled with soybeans. Driven by his hunger, he shoved handfuls of the beans into his mouth. Deliberately, he chewed them until they were a milky pulp that could be swallowed. He continued this for months, until his carelessness eventually led to being caught by a guard.

The guard who caught Joseph stealing, along with another guard, dragged him unceremoniously to the commandant's office.

The Japanese commandant ordered the guards to beat Joseph. And they did, with fists, open palms, and a chair. His head and face were bruised and swollen, and one eye was damaged, along with his hearing. Meanwhile, in the compound, the camp's ranking noncommissioned officer had ordered all of the men on Joseph Della Malva's work detail, 50 in all, to assemble and stand at rigid attention. Enraged, the officer shouted at the prisoners, claiming that he knew two other men besides Joseph Della Malva had stolen soybeans, and they were to step forward. At that moment, Joseph was marched in front of the 50 prisoners, barely able to stand. Gasps were heard from the ranks.

Again, the guilty prisoners were ordered to step forward. Without prompting and in military unison, all 50 men took one step forward. Visibly stunned by this symbol of team strength, the Japanese sergeant in command ordered each prisoner to be slammed once, with rifle butts, by the guards.

This dramatic, subtle but convincing show of team strength was a tribute to Joseph Della Malva that day. When the prisoners returned to their barracks, they did not discuss what had happened. They didn't have to. It was a different time and a different generation. Years later, thankfully, Joseph Della Malva did share this story with his nephew, and it was from this story that his nephew learned the importance of teams. The Key Learning—Teams can accomplish what no one individual can accomplish alone.

His nephew never forgot the importance of team solidarity. Years later, when he began his career as a Six Sigma consultant, he would see teams attempt to achieve improved business performance, without the kind of results seen by his Uncle that day in the prison camp. While today's business culture doesn't face the kind of life-threatening challenges that occurred in the Japanese POW camp, businesses are increasingly attempting to use teams to achieve improved business performance. In recent years, Six Sigma teams have taken on the challenge of increasing productivity, and gaining greater effectiveness and efficiency in the way things get done.

Sometimes these teams succeed. Many times they fail. This book is aimed at helping you achieve greater team effectiveness. While you will not experience the profound closeness of those POWs, possibly some of the tools and techniques in this book will help you achieve greater team effectiveness—something Joseph Della Malva's nephew believes is the *elusive key to Six Sigma success.*

Joseph Della Malva's nephew, George Eckes

Acknowledgments

My deepest thanks to the staff of John Wiley & Sons for publishing my third book on Six Sigma. To Matthew Holt for his encouragement, support, and suggestions to make this and my other books so successful. To the staff of Publications Development Company of Texas for their editing and production support. And to my book agent, Lisa Swayne, I am thankful that you are part of my literary team.

Thank you, Uncle Joe, for sharing your memories from years past while you were a prisoner of war in Japan. Thanks to my staff whose skills have helped make this text come alive. Specifically, thanks to Dr. Susan Ayarbe who has provided support, loyalty, and friendship during my most difficult days. You will always have a special place in my heart. To David Schulenberg for his humor and professionalism. You are my "clean-up" hitter. To Robyn Holley, my assistant, you have exceeded all my requirements and surprise me every day with your intelligence, hard work, honesty, and encouragement. Your future is unlimited ("LINE 2!"). To all my other associates for their hard work, dedication to their craft, and patience. To Carmen Danielson, my legal counsel, you negate every lawyer joke ever told. Thank you for your support in all my legal matters. To Mike Mutter who personifies the values of Notre Dame (win, lose, or ty). To Fran Goss, for her travel assistance and taking care of Lucy. To Teresa, Robert, Claudia, Evelyn, and the entire crew at the Superior Safeway for showing customer focus in all you do. To Rod Smith, for his assistance in making this a better book. To Ross Leher, the person who makes me think long after our dinners.

To Joe and Temo—you continue to amaze me as your father. In the final analysis, your review is the only one I treasure. To Dave, you will always be NHL caliber with me. To Dad, for aging so productively. To Herb, for his ability to sit in the rain for over three hours (welcome to the subway alumni). To Charlotte, whose maternal approval I value. Finally, to Debbie, may we always be the team we committed to be in 1986.

G.E.

Contents

All truths pass through 3 stages:

First, it is ridiculed,
Second, it is violently opposed, and
Third, it is accepted as being self-evident.

Arthur Schopenhauer

SIX SIGMA
TEAM DYNAMICS

Chapter 1

Six Sigma Team Dynamics

The Elusive Key to Project Success

"Only those who dare to fail greatly can achieve greatly."

John F. Kennedy

This book is like no other book on Six Sigma. While much has been written on the topic of this predominant management philosophy that has swept the globe in recent years, much is still a mystery for those organizations attempting to achieve results similar to organizations such as General Electric and AlliedSignal.

Six Sigma is first and foremost a management philosophy. As such, it begins with the strategic component. In our first Six Sigma book, *The Six Sigma Revolution: How General Electric and Others Turned Process into Profits,* the strategic component was covered in Chapters 2 and 9. We discussed the importance of linking process identification with the Strategic Business Objectives of the organization. We addressed the importance of management beginning data collection on key processes, how to create and maintain a Business Quality Council to sustain Six Sigma as a true management strategy, and how to select high-impact projects. The rest of that book discussed improvement methodology at the tactical level, explaining the techniques a project team must use to achieve the type of successes most commonly associated with Six Sigma.

In our second book, *Making Six Sigma Last: Managing the Balance Between Cultural and Technical Change,* we addressed the cultural component of gaining acceptance to Six Sigma. We discussed how to

1

create the need for Six Sigma and deal with the four major types of resistance to Six Sigma. We also reviewed how to create an organization's Six Sigma vision and how to modify and measure the Six Sigma culture so that Six Sigma is more than just a cost savings initiative.

In this, our third book, *Six Sigma Team Dynamics: The Elusive Key to Project Success,* we return to the tactics of Six Sigma, but with a key difference that has not been addressed by any other Six Sigma text: How teams work together to achieve Six Sigma improvement.

In our previous books, we explored the reasons that project teams fail. Data collected by Eckes and Associates has documented that the majority of the time project teams fail, the primary root cause is poor team dynamics. Although conducting multiple regression analysis or determining the F ratio for the statistical significance of a process variable may be difficult to learn the first time it is attempted, these skills can be honed in a relatively short period. A more common stumbling block is how a team conducts its work, and the dynamics of the team. Thus, it is our hope that we can review the keys to improving what, for many, is an elusive target—having groups of individuals work together to achieve what they could not achieve alone.

These team dynamics are not necessarily technical in nature. They include knowing the responsibilities of each member of the project improvement team, including the team leader (known as either the Black Belt or Green Belt), the internal consultant (known as the Master Black Belt), the team members themselves, as well as the project sponsor (known as the Champion). In addition to team responsibilities, team dynamics include knowledge and application of basic facilitation skills. While there are many books on facilitative leadership, our third book focuses on facilitation using a Six Sigma approach.

In addition to team responsibilities and facilitative leadership skills, project management skills are another factor affecting the team dynamics of Six Sigma teams. We address these project management skills and the importance of using them as teams progress through the Define, Measure, Analyze, Improve, and Control (DMAIC) methodology.

Many teams have participants who exhibit maladaptive behaviors. Later chapters address this problem and how to reduce or eliminate these behaviors. Specifically, we focus on the importance of the Champion and the various responsibilities this pivotal role has in Six Sigma team dynamics. As we have done in both previous books, we finish with a chapter on the pitfalls to avoid as teams seek to improve their team dynamics.

■ WHAT ARE TEAM DYNAMICS?

One definition of a team is: *two or more individuals associated in some joint action.* In the business world, these joint actions should have some mission or objective that achieves results. Most business-related teams, however, reflect the dictionary definition of a group—any collection of or assemblage of persons or things. This is even more so with the host of teams attempting to achieve Six Sigma improvements through the use of the Process Improvement methodology (DMAIC), or the Process Design methodology, Define, Measure, Analyze, Design, Verify (DMADV). Many groups of individuals who call themselves a team end up failing miserably using either the DMAIC or DMADV methodology. Often, the reason behind their failure is poor team dynamics.

For our purposes, a team is defined as *a group of two or more individuals engaged in some joint action with a specific mission or goal.* Team dynamics are defined as *the motivating and driving forces that propel a team toward its goal or mission.*

■ WHY TEAMS?

One of the Six Sigma seminars I teach is called *Facilitative Leadership.* The desired outcome of this course is for participants to develop and hone their abilities to lead teams and run meetings more effectively. Years ago, I purchased a business simulation video that I use to begin the facilitative leadership training with teams. Created by Human Synergistics, the business simulation is a survival exercise. I show a brief video of a pontoon plane that has just crashed in a subarctic, uninhabitable region of Canada. After a brief review of the situation logistics, I review a list of 15 items available to assist those who were on the plane in their survival efforts. The participants in the class become the survivors of the plane crash. Without group discussion, I ask each individual to rank order and record in the booklet provided the 15 items he believes would help him survive, beginning with the most important item. These items include among other things, razor blades, sleeping bags, snowshoes, and a bottle of rum.

Once the participants have completed this first assignment, I then tell them that they will have 90 minutes to obtain agreement as a team with regard to how the 15 items should be ranked in order of importance to their survival. Once completed, the answers are compared to an expert's rating. In the nearly 10 years I have been using this simulation, the same two things generally happen. First, the team's ranking, as compared with the expert's ranking, is almost always significantly better than any individual's ranking, even in those cases where a participant has had camping or survival experience. Second, even though the teams achieve superior results, they accomplish their results with unusually poor team dynamics. We have made the following observations:

- ➤ They do not identify a leader.
- ➤ They do not establish roles and responsibilities and they do not discuss what each participant "brings to the party."
- ➤ They do not establish a set of goals/objectives.
- ➤ They do not establish an agenda for managing the 90 minutes allotted to complete the assignment.
- ➤ They do not establish a method to determine how they will reach agreement.
- ➤ They do not establish a set of ground rules for running their meeting.
- ➤ They do not use quality tools.
- ➤ They exhibit maladaptive behaviors for which there are no consequences.
- ➤ They waste an extraordinary amount of time getting started.

Any good consultant knows that when using a business simulation, the debrief of the simulation is far more important than the simulation itself. This is especially true for the survival exercise. During the debrief, I first query the participants on what they learned from doing the exercise. Without prompting, the discussion quickly moves to the dramatic improvement of the team's performance as compared to the individual's performance. Thus, the exercise has achieved its first goal: To demonstrate the potential advantage of teamwork. Although we live in a society that was created on the basis of individualism, most great achievements in our nation's history have come about through teamwork. Can you imagine what our country would be like without the teamwork shown in the Manhattan Project? Or the accomplishments of NASA over nine years in its successful effort to place a man on the moon and return him safely to earth? Even the most jaded participants are somewhat startled when they see such a dramatic difference between their individual performance and the team's performance in the simulation.

Even more dramatic is what I do at the end of the simulation debrief. Once we have established the success of teams versus individual performance, I then provide feedback on the team's performance by reviewing the observations from the previous page. My feedback has not always been well received over the years. Even when the feedback was not challenged, the participants would inevitably pride themselves on the fact that the results of their team's efforts were greater than any individual performance. To make my point, I started videotaping the team's performance (with their permission, of course). I then would roll to the spot on the videotape where my feedback applied. Team members were often aghast at some of their behaviors. Let's now examine some insights that explain the need for future chapters of *Six Sigma Team Dynamics: The Elusive Key to Project Success.*

➤ They Do Not Identify a Leader

A common mistake teams make is the failure to recognize that in any team endeavor a leader must either be identified or emerge. In our survival exercise, a leader is usually not immediately identified, but generally comes forward within the first 10 minutes or so. In this particular simulation, the person with the most outdoor survival-type experiences usually emerges as the leader.

Six Sigma teams *must* have leadership. In fact, *two* key leaders are required for the project team. One leader is the *strategic leader,* known as the Project or Team Champion. In Six Sigma parlance, the *tactical team leader* is called either the Black Belt or Green Belt. The Black Belt is a full-time Six Sigma expert who leads three to four project improvement teams a year, while a Green Belt is usually a mid-level manager whose Six Sigma leadership is a part-time position in addition to his or her other managerial duties. Although the Project Champion is not a full-time team member, nevertheless he or she plays a crucial role in the success of the team. The Champion is involved in all stages of the team's work: *before* the team is formally created, *during* the team's four- to eight-month project, and even *after* the team disbands. Chapter 2 of *Six Sigma Team Dynamics: The Elusive Key to Project Success* addresses the various responsibilities of the Champion before the team starts its work. Additionally, Chapter 2 also addresses how the Champion and Black Belt/Green Belt must work cohesively to achieve team success.

➤ They Do Not Establish Roles and Responsibilities, and They Do Not Discuss What Each Participant "Brings to the Party"

I have loved baseball since I was a small boy. Since becoming an adult, I love it even more—and on different levels. Baseball is made up of teams. Many general managers anxious to make their next season a success, actively pursue big name players and end up paying them vast amounts of money. In the past several years, the Los Angeles Dodgers have pursued players like Kevin Brown, Gary Sheffield, and Shawn Green. These stars haven't done badly, but the Dodgers have not even flirted with the playoffs in the past few seasons.

Compare the Dodgers with the 2001 Seattle Mariners. In the past three years, the Mariners have lost three superstars. First, flame-throwing southpaw Randy Johnson left the Mariners, then Ken Griffey Jr. went back "home" to the Cincinnati Reds, and during the off season Alex Rodriguez, arguably the best young shortstop in baseball, signed a $250 million contract with the Texas Rangers (wow, and you thought Six Sigma consultants were paid a lot).

Yet, in 2001 the Seattle Mariners had the best regular season in baseball. As their manager, Lou Pinella, indicated in an interview, the players on his team know "what they bring to the party" and each knows his roles and responsibilities.

Whether the topic is the survival exercise or project team building, understanding the various roles and responsibilities of the team is critical to its success. We cover the roles and responsibilities of the team members beginning in Chapter 2 and continue throughout the remainder of the book.

➤ They Do Not Establish a Set of Goals/Objectives

In Six Sigma teams, recognition of the goals of a project team is important. While Six Sigma is a long-term objective of an organization, project teams must set technical and process goals as part of their work. In Chapter 3, we discuss the need for teams to establish goals and objectives around how their work is done. We introduce the concept of the "what" (the content) and "how" (the method) of Six Sigma project work.

Many Six Sigma teams make a common mistake early and often. The mistake is focusing totally on the "what" of their work. This is understandable. Project teams are chartered to achieve process improvement in a four- to six-month period. They also recognize that Six Sigma is receiving considerable attention within their organization and are anxious to get results. Thus, the understandable focus on the "what" of their work. However, Six Sigma project teams must understand that they cannot achieve these results using the same methods they have historically used to conduct business. The kind of project results many Six Sigma teams hope to achieve require understanding and mastering "how" the work gets done. Chapter 3 explains the necessity of gaining greater appreciation for this topic.

➤ They Do Not Establish an Agenda for Managing the 90 Minutes Allotted to Complete the Assignment

In our survival business simulation, most of the work of rank-ordering the items that would aid in survival occurs in the last 15 minutes of the exercise. In similar fashion, most of the work to be completed in a Six Sigma project is done in the last few weeks of the four- to six-month endeavor. True, that final push undoubtedly and overwhelmingly helps them achieve a successful result. However, the teams that do a better job at managing their time invariably achieve even better results. The concept of agendas is critical to better time management, whether the application of the concept is focused on Six Sigma project teamwork or meetings in general. Chapter 3 addresses how to create vibrant, useful agendas that help teams to be both effective and efficient.

➤ They Do Not Establish a Method to Determine How They Will Reach Agreement

Everyday individuals make decisions quickly. Whether deciding what to wear or what to have for breakfast, individuals use some rational (or sometimes irrational) method to make a decision. However, when two or more people attempt to make even the simplest decision, chaos can result.

How are decisions made in a group of two or more? Without a formal method agreed on before decision making occurs, informal methods are commonly used. In some groups, the person who has the loudest voice has the final say. In other cases, it is the person who feels the strongest about the issue. In other cases, it is the person who holds the largest position of authority. Think of how you make decisions about driving directions or when and where to stop when you are traveling. Generally, decisions are deferred to the driver. In our business simulation, typically there was deference to the person who had the most camping experience.

There are a multitude of problems with these informal decision-making methods. First, they tend to take time away from actual decision making. In the case of the "loudest voice approach" to decision making, often there have been previous unsuccessful attempts at trying to persuade other parties. Have you ever attended a meeting where someone feels strongly about a position, but in the early stages of the "discussion," the individual tries to sweet talk the others into his or her position? "That's a great thought, Mary, but have you given consideration to how this would affect the others in Department B?" We see my favorite word, "but," in this remark. "But" is purely and simply an eraser for any comment that comes before it. Thus, in this comment, the person talking to Mary doesn't *really* think her idea is great. Rather, his focus is on how Mary's idea (an idea that the speaker doesn't highly regard), affects Department B.

All of these wasted discussions are the result of the team's failure to agree beforehand on a decision-making method. In Chapter 3, we discuss five major ways that decisions are made, recognizing that each of these five methods has applicability to Six Sigma teams. We also address the different methods of decision making and when and where they may be applied throughout the duration of a Six Sigma project.

► They Do Not Establish a Set of Ground Rules for Running Their Meeting

As referenced by Sandra Derickson in the Foreword, "An ounce of prevention is worth a pound of cure." As it relates to Six Sigma teams, no truer words can be spoken. When teams meet, there should be a set of standards that establish how the team members will behave toward one another. This is not just a way to ensure courtesy to one another, but also a way to ensure that the team's time together ends up being used effectively and efficiently. Ground rules permit Six Sigma teams to work cohesively so that work time is spent on Defining, Measuring, Analyzing, Improving, and Controlling the process to which they have been assigned, rather than being detoured into personal agendas and petty arguments.

In our survival business simulation, we see how the failure to set ground rules affects performance. In some cases, we see several people talking at the same time, individuals trying to "pull rank," people leaving the simulation, and a host of other behaviors that could be prevented if the team establishes ground rules for behavior at the outset of the meeting. Thus, in Chapter 3, we discuss typical ground rules that can expedite the work of the Six Sigma team.

► They Do Not Use Quality Tools

In the survival business simulation, the team is expected to generate the preferred order of a series of items that can ensure survival in the wilds of subarctic Canada. Often these teams lack knowledge of the quality tools that drive Six Sigma improvement. In Chapter 4, we review the more common quality tools that can expedite team dynamics. While we do not review the entire list of quality tools available to a Six Sigma team, we concentrate on the type of quality tools that will help a Six Sigma team become more effective in reaching decisions.

➤ They Exhibit Maladaptive Behavior for Which There Are No Consequences

No matter how well a team prepares for maladaptive behavior and attempts to prevent it, such behavior will eventually occur. While this is true for all teams, it is especially true for Six Sigma teams. Embracing Six Sigma is a daunting task for even the most sophisticated organizations. For organizations that are not as sophisticated in their management of facts and data, the move to data-driven management will result in Six Sigma teams having individuals who manifest their resistance in maladaptive behavior. Ironically, this type of behavior will be even more evident at the tactical level when executive management has committed to Six Sigma.

When these maladaptive behaviors are left to fester, they are like a dead elk left to rot in the living room. It is not a pretty sight nor does it smell very pleasant either. Teams must learn to recognize maladaptive behaviors and how to intervene in such a way that the team quickly returns to its intended goal of improving effectiveness and efficiency in its assigned project.

Later chapters reveal common maladaptive behaviors and the more successful strategies used not only to stop the maladaptive behaviors, but also to motivate the individuals exhibiting these behaviors to begin being more productive.

➤ They Waste an Extraordinary Amount of Time Getting Started

Teams waste a lot of time before actual work begins in our survival business simulation. This is true to an even greater extent with Six Sigma teams. We address the root cause of these delays and offer general guidelines to remedy this problem.

In recent years, my organization has observed a higher success rate in first-wave Six Sigma project teams when they have expertise in project management skills. At Eckes and Associates, we have continued learning even more about project management from our client base. One of the better project management groups now engaged in Six Sigma execution is Wells Fargo Financial in Des Moines,

Iowa. We highlight some of the more important project management tools in Chapter 5.

Good facilitative leadership is important in any venue. All organizations can profit from any improvement in their team meeting skills, whether they are tactical team meetings, basic staff meetings, or the myriad of meetings that are so prevalent in twenty-first century organizations.

However, Six Sigma teams are unique in their need for this vibrant methodology. There are several reasons pointing to their uniqueness. First, Six Sigma teams are faced with learning new quality tools, how to collect data, do data analysis, and develop statistics, which initially will seem complicated to many team members. Learning a new methodology with old skills is like putting a Porsche engine in an old Chevrolet Impala. It is important for teams to augment the simple tools by learning a new and potent management system that can better tap into their inherent skills.

The second reason that Six Sigma teams are unique in their need for improved facilitative leadership skills is that during the course of learning this new methodology they are applying what they learn to actual improvement projects. As such, they are in natural work groups. These natural work groups are expected not only to learn the new Six Sigma methodology but also to apply it to their real work and achieve successful improvement. Without good team dynamics, this is next to impossible. The success of a Six Sigma "team" is often the result of just one or two individuals (often the Black or Green Belt) who end up making major changes to the process in an attempt to achieve short-term results. These efforts, although often well intentioned, ultimately thwart what Six Sigma is attempting to do: Change the entire culture of the organization from that of the "firefighter" to a culture based on everyone being an "arsonist catcher." Without a cultural change at the facilitative skills level, Six Sigma results are often short-lived and ultimately frustrating for everyone involved.

Six Sigma has been the predominant management philosophy of the late 1990s and continues into the early twenty-first century. Cynics claim that Six Sigma is nothing more than a fad, soon to fall out of favor on the business scene like so many quality initiatives before it. Those who think this way are wrong. However, without Six Sigma team dynamics, the cynics may justifiably point to failed project teams as evidence that this vibrant management approach doesn't apply to their business. In reality, failure cannot be blamed on Six Sigma. The failure undoubtedly occurred as a result of not following the techniques found in this book.

■ HOW THIS BOOK IS WRITTEN

This book is written in a slightly different manner than our two previous books on Six Sigma. While we address the issues of how to create vibrant Six Sigma teams, we do not use actual case studies from my 20 years of consulting experience. In both *The Six Sigma Revolution* and *Making Six Sigma Last,* we shared examples with you of actual people and organizations who had utilized Six Sigma as a management philosophy as a result of their work with Eckes and Associates. These clients were General Electric, Household Retail Services, Wells Fargo, and Lithonia Lighting, to name a few.

In this book, we provide you with plenty of detailed information to help make your Six Sigma teams successful. However, since we address many of the pitfalls that lead to Six Sigma failure, we have created a fictitious organization to assist us in highlighting both positive and negative team behaviors. While our fictitious organization, Alpha Omega, is purported to be a Denver-based credit card company, it actually is a composite of the many organizations we at Eckes and Associates have encountered throughout our years of consulting. We share both our successful and less-than-successful efforts we have observed, painting our story on the canvas of Alpha Omega. As we have done with our previous books, we end each chapter with a list of Key Learnings.

In Chapter 2, we introduce you to Alpha Omega's key players and spend much of the chapter discussing the importance of the various roles and responsibilities associated with a Six Sigma team. These roles include executive management (even though they will not be part of a tactical Six Sigma team), and the pivotal role of the project sponsor, otherwise known in Six Sigma parlance as the Project Champion. You will be introduced to the various responsibilities of a Champion that must be completed prior to the formation of the Six Sigma project team. We then introduce you to the Alpha Omega Call Center project team, including its team leader, Joy Schulenberg, and the Call Center's potential resistors, Robert Wallace and Jeff Seimonson.

In Chapter 3, we introduce you to the mechanics of good facilitative leadership. First, we discuss the difference between the content (the "what") of a Six Sigma team's work and the methods used to achieve the content (the "how"). The method of achieving the Six Sigma team's content is called *facilitative leadership.* We address good facilitative preventions, including the components of a useful agenda and making sure each Six Sigma meeting has a list of specific desired outcomes. Also addressed in Chapter 3 is the formation of the team's operating agreements, from the ground rules the Six Sigma team should set to reviewing the various decision-making methods available to Six Sigma project teams, looking at both the advantages and the disadvantages of each method.

We discuss *authoritarian* decision making, which is decision making vested in one person. We also discuss *consensus* decision making where each team member is involved in the decision and everyone agrees not to sabotage the result. Consensus is the preferred method of decision making that ensures all Six Sigma team members participate. However, sometimes consensus will not be reached. For this reason, a back-up decision-making method needs to be established if Six Sigma teams are expected to move forward. Therefore, we discuss additional decision-making methods for Six Sigma teams to use.

Also included is the concept of the *parking lot*, which is a method used to capture items that are beyond the scope of the team's current Six Sigma responsibilities, along with the roles and responsibilities of a Six Sigma team. The chapter ends with a discussion of pluses/deltas, the method used to evaluate Six Sigma meetings.

No matter how well a Six Sigma team attempts to prevent maladaptive behaviors, they will still occur. In Chapter 4, we address how to handle maladaptive behavior when the best of the preventions have failed. We cover a full spectrum of various maladaptive behaviors, along with an equally full spectrum of interventions. Chapter 4 also discusses criteria that are useful in giving and receiving feedback.

Chapter 5 begins the journey of our fictitious Six Sigma team through the process improvement methodology of Six Sigma, known as DMAIC (Define, Measure, Analysis, Improve, Control). Each step in this methodology has a set of tollgates for the team to formally review with their Project Champion. In addition, this chapter revisits the role of Champion and describes the multiple responsibilities he or she has during the team's existence. Finally, Chapter 5 introduces key project management tools such as *Work Breakdown charts, Linear Responsibility charts,* and *Activity Reports.* Each of these tools help Six Sigma teams keep to the task and accomplish improved sigma performance within the time frame of their project.

Chapter 6 reviews the various methods used to assist Six Sigma teams become more productive. First, we review Tuckman's four stages of team behavior, beginning with *forming,* then *storming,* followed by *norming,* and ultimately *performing.* We then provide specific guidelines a team can use to move through each of these four stages more expeditiously. We introduce the concept of resistance to the Six Sigma team and methods to overcome resistance. These methods include *creating the need* and *shaping a vision* for the Six Sigma project. We review typical sources of resistance among our fictitious team members and reveal interventions that are generally used in the early stages of the Six Sigma project team.

In Chapter 7, we complete the Six Sigma team project and show how the level of interventions may have to escalate as maladaptive behaviors escalate. We also describe the responsibilities of the Champion once the team has completed its Six Sigma work.

As we do in all our Six Sigma books, we devote the last chapter (Chapter 8) to a discussion of the pitfalls to avoid in creating Six Sigma team dynamics.

KEY LEARNINGS

➤ Data shows that a predominant reason for failure of Six Sigma teams is due to poor *team dynamics.*

➤ A team is defined as *two or more individuals associated in some joint action.*

➤ Team dynamics are defined as *the motivating and driving forces that propel a team toward its goal or mission.*

➤ Poor team dynamics include:

—Failure to identify a leader.

—Failure to establish roles and responsibilities, and failure to discuss what each participant "brings to the party."

—Failure to establish a set of goals/objectives.

—Failure to establish agendas.

—Failure to establish a method to determine how the team will make decisions.

—Failure to establish a set of ground rules for running the Six Sigma meetings.

—Failure to use quality tools.

—Allowing maladaptive behaviors to exist without consequences.

—Wasting time getting started.

Chapter 2

The Roles and Responsibilities of a Six Sigma Team

"Read their hips, not their lips."

Maternal advice from Lucy Eckes

In the last several years, Six Sigma has become a predominant management philosophy among organizations large and small. One noticeable difference in a Six Sigma management philosophy is the amount of true management involvement as opposed to previous quality efforts that emphasized methodology or tactics.

Our discussion of roles and responsibilities of teams begins with the role of executive management and what they must do to ensure project team success. In later pages of this chapter, we discuss the various roles and responsibilities of a successful Six Sigma team, from the project sponsor (called the Project Team Champion), through to the team leader (called either the Black Belt or Green Belt), to the last and most important elements of a team, the team members.

". . . to realize the projected $2.5 billion in cost savings will require a large number of lay-offs."

September 5, 2001, page 1, *New York Times* article on the merger of Hewlett Packard and Compaq computer

■ EXECUTIVE MANAGEMENT ROLE AND RESPONSIBILITIES IN SIX SIGMA TEAMS

Consider the following executives for a moment:

➤ James McNerney
➤ Robert Nardelli
➤ Gary Wendt
➤ Jeffrey Immelt

These executives have several things in common. First, they all were business leaders within General Electric in 1995 when Jack Welch proclaimed that Six Sigma was to be the most important initiative he was to undertake as the chief executive officer (CEO). James McNerney, Robert Nardelli, and Jeffery Immelt eventually became the three finalists on the succession plan to take over the reins of General Electric—the greatest conglomerate of the twentieth century.

Having been a consultant to General Electric for over 10 years, I had watched the careers of these three men over that period. While I did not work with either McNerney or Nardelli, I was fortunate to have spent some time with Immelt at a quality retreat in 1991. At the time, Immelt was working with General Electric Plastics and I was part of a consulting group working with them on process improvement. One evening I was working with an executive group that included Immelt. During a discussion on process capability, I was instructing the team on Cpk, which is a method to calculate process performance. After the tutorial, Immelt commented to me that while using Cpk was fine, using *sigma calculations* could provide a universal language for an organization similar to what Motorola was doing. I was highly impressed with his sigma knowledge. In 1995, when General Electric committed to a Six Sigma management philosophy, my hunch was that Immelt was on a path to succeed Jack Welch.

What I didn't know at that time was the level of commitment both McNerney and Nardelli also had to Six Sigma. In fact, their commitment to Six Sigma may have been stronger than Immelt's. As it became common knowledge that these three men were finalists to become GE's next CEO, adherence to what Jack Welch called the most important initiative in the history of his leadership became their management mantra. McNerney at General Electric Aircraft Engines, Nardelli at General Electric Power Systems, and Immelt at General Electric Medical Systems dutifully and effectively implemented Six Sigma, generating literally billions of dollars in cost savings.

On Thanksgiving weekend 2000, the successor to Jack Welch was announced. Imagine what it would have been like being either McNerney or Nardelli upon hearing Welch's announcement that he had chosen Immelt as his successor. (To his credit, Welch flew to Cincinnati and Albany to present the bad news to each of the men personally.) After being lifelong General Electric employees, they had come up short to take over the most prominent conglomerate in the world. Their first feelings had to be of vast disappointment. Quickly, however, their natural competitiveness took over. Within hours of the Immelt announcement, every major recruitment firm was calling them with offers. Within a week, McNerney was picked to be the new CEO of 3M, while Nardelli became the CEO of Home Depot.

What happened next chronicles perhaps one of the most dramatic endorsements of Six Sigma as a management philosophy. In their first weeks on the job, both McNerney and Nardelli announced to their new organizations that they were committed to the Six Sigma management philosophy. In fact, McNerney even spent his first few months at 3M *teaching* Six Sigma to the employees. Clearly, both men wanted to create their own management style in their new organizations. Yet their commitment to Six Sigma was so tangible that they made it the first order of business in their new roles.

Gary Wendt did the same thing after leaving General Electric Capital. The "wunderkind" who transformed General Electric into a financial power through expanding the traditional manufacturer into mortgages, banking, and leasing, left General Electric in 1998. Wooed by a number of powerhouse financial institutions, he settled into the CEO position at Conseco Insurance in 2000. One of his first hires was Ruth Fattori, the former Quality Leader at General Electric Capital, who was chartered to create a Six Sigma culture at Conseco.

Then there is Jeffrey Immelt himself. Taking on the CEO position after Jack Welch's retirement, he must have felt a bit like Harry Truman after the death of FDR. While he has indicated his plans to place his personal stamp on General Electric, in his first formal comments as the CEO, he echoed his firm belief in Six Sigma as the management philosophy that would continue. In a September 2001 interview with the *Wall Street Journal,* he referenced Six Sigma a total of four times. Committed to the management philosophy of Six Sigma, Immelt even indicated his desire to extend the concept further into General Electric's customer base and expand the effort into sales and marketing.

What do these stories have to do with Six Sigma team dynamics? While a CEO may not be a part of a Six Sigma team, Six Sigma team dynamics are greatly affected by the attitudes and behaviors of the

CEO. Both top leadership and project teams must understand that Six Sigma is more than a tactical improvement methodology—it is a way of life. When a Six Sigma team co-exists with active, lively management support and involvement, many of the issues and concerns typically facing teams in terms of poor team dynamics are either mild or nonexistent.

Consider the Hewlett-Packard quote that we used at the beginning of this chapter, ". . . to realize the projected $2.5 billion in cost savings will require a large number of lay-offs." As evidenced by this quote, Hewlett-Packard has opted to derive cost savings the traditional management way, through economies of scale by buying out the competition and slashing jobs. The problem, of course, is that this barbaric method of cost cutting leaves the survivors with bad attitudes and the difficult challenge of trying to merge two battle-weary organizations into one corporate culture. In the short term, the balance sheet looks good, but the long-term value of this approach to management as a way to make an organization more effective and efficient continues to diminish over time.

For the tactics of Six Sigma to work, executive management must set the right tone for the organization. This tone must stress Six Sigma as a method of management where everything an organization does is *customer focused, process focused,* and *employee focused.* An organization cannot be employee focused when it treats employees as expendable commodities, always at risk of being laid off or fired to help the organization meet cost savings goals. The benefits of improving processes, and ultimately the bottom line, through Six Sigma project teams are felt not only by the organization but also by the people who work within the organization.

Executive management has a pivotal role in Six Sigma team dynamics: To create the Business Process Management (BPM) system that is the foundation for the Six Sigma teams to work (see Chapters 2 and 9 of *The Six Sigma Revolution*). In addition, executive management must create a Six Sigma culture where participation on Six Sigma teams is considered a part of the work to be done by employees. Further, they must create support for Six Sigma at the midmanagement level, mobilizing commitment to both the concept and activities of Six Sigma. These concepts were covered in our second book, *Making Six Sigma Last.*

Management 's involvement in the strategic and cultural elements of Six Sigma is critical to the success of Six Sigma team dynamics. Pure and simple, the top executive level of management must support Six Sigma in the same way as Immelt, McNerney, and Nardelli have done, making Six Sigma a way of life within the organization.

■ THE DIRECT ROLES AND RESPONSIBILITIES OF A SIX SIGMA TEAM

While executive management plays a critical role in setting the stage for a Six Sigma culture, they play an indirect role in the tactical piece of Six Sigma. The *direct* roles and responsibilities of the Six Sigma project team are discussed in the following pages. The roles are:

➤ The project sponsor (called the Champion).

➤ The project team leader (called either the Black Belt or Green Belt).

➤ The project team members.

Initially, I had decided to highlight multiple teams who had progressed through a Define, Measure, Analyze, Improve, and Control (DMAIC) project. Instead, I decided to develop a representative composite of the teams I have encountered. I take you through the six months it typically takes for a project team to complete a DMAIC project using a fictional story that highlights both the good and the bad of typical Six Sigma teams.

■ THE CASE OF THE ALPHA OMEGA CORPORATION

The Alpha Omega Corporation employs 1,200 people in two states. The company is a multimillion-dollar business focused on financial services, predominately in the mortgage and credit card arenas. Profitable through the late 1990s, in large part due to the thriving economy, times have become tough for Alpha Omega. A part of their problem now is the result of decisions by organizations like General Electric Capital, Wells Fargo Financial, and Household Finance to implement a Six Sigma management philosophy. By the end of the first two years of the new millennium, Alpha Omega had quickly become an "also ran" in the financial services arena.

Their CEO, Brenda Sexson, had hired a new CFO from General Electric who was telling her about the benefits of Six Sigma as a management philosophy. Whether due to business performance or her own curiosity, she began to do her own research into reputable consulting firms and settled on Temojoe Consulting, a Colorado-based firm that had been General Electric Capital's highest rated consulting group.

Sexson realized the power of Six Sigma within the first three months of Alpha Omega's Six Sigma rollout. Temojoe Consulting had coached them through the strategic component of Six Sigma, Business Process Management. Sexson had learned that being process focused was a critical first step toward being a Six Sigma company. She and her staff soon had identified the processes that most directly impacted Alpha Omega's Strategic Business Objectives (SBOs) and soon thereafter targeted eleven Six Sigma projects to begin the work of improving both the effectiveness and efficiency of Alpha Omega.

Sexson had been coached that for Six Sigma project teams to be successful, the best and brightest had to be involved. Temojoe Consulting had made that apparent in the identification of process ownership, a key element of Business Process Management. Process Owners must be subject matter experts, and they have to experience the most pain or gain from the process, as well as having an aptitude for process thinking. Perhaps most importantly, they needed to have the respect of those around them since they would eventually be trying to create influence through the strength of their argument rather than through the clout of the organizational chart.

Temojoe Consulting argued that Sexson needed to identify the best and brightest for this endeavor for a multitude of reasons. First, success would come more quickly and more dramatically by having the best and brightest assigned to Six Sigma activity. Second, Temojoe Consulting had encouraged her to assign the best and brightest to send a message to all of Alpha Omega—a message that she was serious about Six Sigma. If Sexson was going to task her top managers to the quality initiative, then Alpha Omega as an organization had to be serious about this cutting-edge management approach.

At the strategic level, Sexson had done an outstanding job of assigning process ownership to the best and brightest of the organization. In some cases, this meant that current management would be given a new, though uncompensated title of Process Owner. In other cases, nonmanagement personnel took on the role of Process Owner. By the end of the first few months of Six Sigma implementation, Alpha Omega had selected 11 high-impact, low-performing subprocesses for tactical Six Sigma improvement. Among the processes targeted for improvement was an underwriting project, along with the customer maintenance process, which included the function known as the Call Center.

The Process Owner for customer maintenance was Charles Zukor, an 11-year veteran of Alpha Omega who had been the Call Center director for a little more than a year. Being the Call Center director was a thankless job, but Sexson had asked Zukor to use his management skills to see what he could do to improve the ailing level of customer satisfaction experienced in this critical area. Of particular concern were problems with *first call resolution, timeliness of response time to customer issues,* and *courtesy of the Call Center staff.* The first two issues had become a concern during the past year.

During the Business Process Management consulting, Zukor had learned that first call resolution, timeliness of response time, and courtesy constituted what is called the Critical to Quality (CTQ) customer requirements. Together these three quality characteristics represented the totality of the customer maintenance subprocess "dashboard."

Zukor's attitude toward Six Sigma was cautious at best. He had been part of a Total Quality Management (TQM) program in a previous position in the late 1980s. His experience with TQM was negative. He had seen some T and Q but not much M. While not yet a convert to Six Sigma, he had already observed that Six Sigma seemed different. Temojoe Consulting had taken on the assignment with Alpha Omega with the assurance that the first months of consulting would be focused exclusively on management issues. First on the agenda was Zukor attending a workshop aimed at understanding Alpha Omega's Strategic Business Objectives, along with gaining management's agreement to the SBOs. Next, Zukor participated in the creation of the seven high-level core processes that impacted Alpha Omega's SBOs.

The Temojoe consultants then had the Alpha Omega executive team drill each core process down to the sublevel where five to seven subprocesses that constituted each core process were identified. It was at this point that the customer maintenance subprocess was created. The Call Center function was a significant part of that process. When each Process Owner reported on process performance based on measures of effectiveness and efficiency, it soon became apparent that customer maintenance (and the function of the Call Center) would be a target for improvement.

When a Process Owner has a process targeted for Six Sigma tactical improvement, it is customary for the Process Owner to become the project sponsor or, in Six Sigma vernacular, the Project Champion.

Shortly after the creation of Alpha Omega's Business Process Management system, 11 subprocess project improvement teams were formed. Eleven Process Owners were then anointed as Project Champions—charged with the strategic responsibility of guiding their teams to success through the tactical elements of Six Sigma.

Temojoe Consulting informed the Champions that they themselves must be trained in both the tools and techniques of DMAIC *before* they form the project improvement teams. Only then would the teams be selected and trained to understand and apply the DMAIC methodology. In addition, the Champions were told that they must also learn more about the specific role of the Champion.

This meant that each of the 11 Champions would be required to go through a business simulation made popular by the Rath and Strong consulting firm. This consulting group created an ingenious business simulation called *Move It* that creates the need for Six Sigma, while at the same time teaching the Champions about their roles.

The first day of the business simulation, Zukor felt a little uncomfortable as Temojoe's lead consultant, Joe Hawke, reviewed the business simulation. The business simulation used a courier service as the backdrop for the exercise. The service delivered packages to various customer sites, similar to Federal Express or UPS. Hawke asked each of the Champions to pull a name card from a bowl that would define the role each would play over the course of the next two days. Zukor felt a little better when he saw Hawke's assistant, Kylie Madrid, a quiet but altogether attractive 40-something consultant who was dressed stylishly yet professionally in a black business suit.

When Kylie passed the large bowl filled with name cards around the room, Zukor randomly selected the role of Courier. Madrid uttered her first words to Zukor with a chuckle as she asked him if he had any health conditions that would prevent him from working hard in the business simulation. Confidently, he responded that he was in great shape (all the while, consciously tightening his stomach muscles in order to appear in better shape than his 51 years actually made him look).

After all of the name cards had been selected, Hawke had each participant sit at an assigned location where a tent card indicated their role for the simulation. He then instructed the participants to silently read the job description that was placed just below the tent card. While each of the participants was doing this assignment, Zukor noticed Kylie walk off with four Alpha Omega employees who had chosen the Customer name cards.

Zukor settled in to read his job description. His job was to pick up packages at each of the four customer locations in the far corners of the room. He then was to take the packages to the center of the room and place them in the in-box of the Mail Room Clerk. As subsequent packages were ready for pick-up at the customer locations, he was to repeat the pattern, and at the same time watch the out-box of the Mail Room Clerk for customer deliveries.

Zukor read his assignment in less than two of the five minutes assigned to the task. With the remaining time, he surveyed the room. The customer locations were in the four corners of the room, and in the center of the room were the other Alpha Omega Champions reading their job descriptions. At the end of the five minutes, Hawke and Madrid returned with the four Customers who had been tutored privately in another room.

Hawke first asked if everyone had a general understanding of his or her role. The question was rhetorical since he quickly indicated he planned to go through a brief run-through of Round 1 of the *Move It* business simulation.

"Okay, when I begin the first round," said Hawke, "I will instruct the four customers to place two packages in their out-box. That will trigger something to happen." As his eyes turned in the direction of Zukor, Hawke asked, "What might that be?"

Zukor was only passively listening for a couple of reasons. One, his assignment seemed benign, and two, his eyes were wandering in the direction of Madrid, whose attention was focused on Hawke's instructions. After about 10 seconds or so, Zukor responded with a tone of pride in his voice, "Oh, that would mean I would pick up the packages at each of the four customer locations and return them to the in-box of the Mail Room Clerk."

"Those short naps are nice aren't they, Zukor," Hawke quickly quipped. His comment was followed by a burst of laughter. "Okay, gang," Hawke sharply continued as if he had done this literally hundred of times before, "What happens next?"

Hawke then had the Mail Room Clerk walk a package through the current process, from first delivering the package to the in-box of the In-Sort Clerk. The Mail Room Clerk was to wait for packages to be placed in the In-Sort Clerk's out-box which would trigger the Mail Room Clerk to pick up the packages and deliver them to the in-box of the In-Sort Supervisor. From the In-Sort Supervisor's out-box, the Mail Room Clerk was to deliver the packages to the Out-Sort Clerk, on to the Out-Sort Supervisor, then to the Weight Fee Clerk, on to the Distance Fee Clerk, and then to Mail Room Clerk's out-box. This would trigger Zukor, the Courier, to pick up and deliver the packages to the four customers.

Hawke then said that Round #1 was about to begin. He indicated that the Round would take approximately 30 minutes, but it could take less time if the Alpha Omega Champions worked really hard. In a taunting voice, he notified them that a General Electric group finished the first round in 23 minutes once. This "challenge" noticeably charged the competitive juices of the Alpha Omega troops.

Both Hawke and Madrid had stopwatches in hand. Madrid kicked off Round #1 with, "Ready, 3—2—1, Customers, put two packages in your out-box labeled zero minutes—now." The stopwatches were started. For a split second, Zukor was distracted by Madrid, but then snapped back as he realized that his job as the Courier had begun. He quickly traversed the room, picking up two packages from each of the four Customers and quickly put them in the Mail Room Clerk's in-box.

It soon became apparent that this process was broken. After one minute, Madrid instructed the four Customers to place two additional packages in their out-boxes, while the first eight packages were still in the queue. After 10 minutes, Charles Zukor had picked up 88 packages and had delivered not one. Meanwhile, a backlog of packages had accumulated in the in-box of Bam Kellogg, Alpha Omega's information technology director who had randomly been selected the In-Sort Clerk.

"Kellogg, work a little harder, will you?" prompted Brenda Sexson who had picked the role General Manager.

"Hey, Bam, what about doing your job," said Jeremy Wainright, Distance Fee Clerk. Wainright began casually reading the newspaper that he found on a vacant table.

Kellogg was too busy to pay much attention to Wainright. He was trying to match the outgoing and ingoing customer directory so that packages were properly delivered to the right location. He had processed only four packages in the first 10 minutes. While his workstation was clearly a bottleneck, things weren't much better at the Weight Fee Clerk position, where another bottleneck was forming. The Weight Fee Clerk was J. D. Snow, the director of underwriting for Alpha Omega. Soon both Kellogg and Snow were hearing catcalls from others who had less to do in the simulation.

At the 28-minute mark of the first round, Madrid signaled that there were two minutes left in Round #1. The in-box of the In-Sort Clerk looked like a ski lift in Vail, as did the in-box of the Weight Fee Clerk. Both Kellogg and Snow were still receiving barbs from the others for their "poor performance."

Meanwhile, Zukor looked to Kylie Madrid for her approval of the 40 or so packages he had delivered to customers. Madrid, however, was already busy helping Customers with their calculations for Round #1. Hawke had called for a 20-minute break before he would do the all-important debrief of the first round.

After the break, Zukor couldn't help but notice Madrid's absence as Hawke began his debrief. Among the questions asked were:

➤ What were the subjective impressions of Round #1?

➤ Who knew the most about what was going on for the entire process?

➤ Most importantly, how did Round #1 remind you of how work is done at Alpha Omega?

The discussion that ensued was lively. Of particular importance was the discussion of how Round #1 of the *Move It* business simulation was very reminiscent of how work was conducted at Alpha Omega, where each function attempted to get its work done and sometimes succeeded but often did not. If the work was not completed, the team agreed, it was obviously the fault of some other department or function, or possibly both.

Without Madrid present to distract him, Zukor became deeply engaged in the debrief discussion. Zukor recognized Hawke's animated talent as he made the point that Round #1 of the business simulation often represented how businesses typically conduct their work.

Thirty minutes into the debrief, Madrid, along with the four Customers, returned to the room. She was holding a sheaf of overheads in her hand. Hawke soon concluded his comments and rhetorically asked if the group would like to see the objective picture of how well the Alpha Omega group had done in Round #1. With reluctance, they agreed, and Kylie took center stage.

Kylie began going over the slides that documented Alpha Omega's first round performance. In her first overhead, Madrid showed that the group had delivered a total of 41 packages to the customers. Then she shared the bad news about those 41 packages. As it turned out, the average delivery time was 12 minutes and 23 seconds. Madrid then asked the group if the Courier or Customer Service Representative (another of the roles assigned in the first round) had ever thought to inquire about the Customer's requirements for the package they were delivering. Nary a sound was uttered. She informed them that if either the Customer Service Rep or Courier had simply asked the Customer, they would have been told that their requirement for a package delivery was 10 minutes or less.

Madrid next showed that of the 41 packages delivered, virtually half (19) of the packages had been sent to the wrong location. "That was the fault of the Courier," said Tom Lacross, Alpha Omega's human resource director, who had been the Customer Service Rep. "I think he was paying more attention to you than he was to his deliveries."

Before Zukor had a chance to defend himself, Kylie interjected, "Tom, that is the comment of a manager unaware of the concept of *common cause variation*, a key concept of Six Sigma. What all of you experienced was a broken process. Processes are made up of Machines, Materials, Methods, Measurement, Mother Nature (the environment), and the People in the process. These factors are called the '5 Ms and 1 P.' The vast majority of the time, particularly in service businesses, the *methods* are the predominant source of the problem. By the time you have completed your role as a Six Sigma Champion, you will have learned that focusing on the people in the process usually just makes things worse."

With that, Madrid looked at Kellogg, the In-Sort Clerk, and asked how he felt about his performance. "Well, I felt bad that I was the backlog for the team. Then I got angry when everyone was criticizing me," Kellogg said. "You shouldn't feel bad," assured Madrid. "Every time we do this simulation the back-log is greatest in the In-Sort position. Remember, the problem is the process, not the people in the process."

Madrid returned to her report-out, becoming quantitative in her remarks. In the next 20 minutes, she pointed out two opportunities the executive team had missed. Not only did the business simulation group not uncover the two obvious requirements of the Customers, *timeliness of delivery* and *accuracy of package delivery,* but there was yet another requirement that the Alpha Omega group failed to identify *courtesy.* At that moment, Zukor had his first Six Sigma epiphany. Two of the requirements in the business simulation—timeliness and courtesy—were the same as the requirements in his Call Center operation, though he had never spent much time thinking about or, more importantly, measuring those requirements.

The report-out from Madrid continued as she showed the group their sigma performance. Combining the inaccuracies of deliveries, the lateness of deliveries, and poor marks for courtesy, Alpha Omega had registered a 1.1 sigma performance based on a Defects per Million Opportunities (DPMO) calculation. This means that if the Alpha Omega team had delivered one million packages, as many as 650,000 deliveries could have had something wrong with them.

Madrid finished her presentation with statistical pictures of the variation in the first round of performance. They included statistical pictures of where the greatest backlogs occurred, a statistical picture called the histogram of delivery performance, and ratings of courtesy on a Likert scale, a 1 to 5 rating where 5 = *great courtesy* and 1 = *poor courtesy.*

In the first round of the simulation, Hawke and Madrid had created the need for Alpha Omega to learn the Six Sigma process improvement methodology to improve their broken process. Of particular importance was the team's discussion detailing how the first round of the business simulation paralleled how work was typically done in their organization. The people at Alpha Omega worked in their individual "silos" (or more politely, functions), often without any thought about the customer, whether that customer was internal or external. During the next two days, the Alpha Omega management group went on to improve their sigma performance on the *Move It* simulation utilizing the DMAIC methodology. They had experienced the power of the tactical Six Sigma methodology that the Alpha Omega project teams would begin utilizing in the coming months.

Clearly, the Alpha Omega managers had dramatically increased their support for the need of Six Sigma in their organization. Now, it was time for Hawke and Madrid to help the Alpha Omega managers better understand their role as Champions.

With 11 first-wave projects, and a corresponding number of Champions, Hawke and Madrid split the Champions into two groups. The Temojoe consultants scheduled one-on-one meetings with the Champions, Hawke with one group and Madrid with the other. The meetings were to take place at Alpha Omega's headquarters the next day. Zukor waited curiously to see which group he would be in—Hawke's or Madrid's. As Hawke revealed the flip chart, Zukor saw the following:

Group 1 (Hawke)
- Andrew Rends
- Bam Kellogg
- Colt Kanin
- Jeremy Wainwright
- Justin Waverly
- J. D. Snow

Group 2 (Madrid)
- Aaron Gregson
- Sid Milstone
- Tom Lacross
- Brenda Sexson
- Charles Zukor

Zukor would be the last to be coached on his role as Champion at 4:30 P.M. He looked forward to the meeting with schoolboy anticipation. He even reviewed the recommended reading material on being a Champion, suggested by Hawke.

➤ The Champion's Role before the Project Team Is Formed

The appointed time for Charles Zukor's meeting couldn't come fast enough. At 4:30 P.M. sharp, Kylie entered his office. Zukor ushered her to a seat at the conference table. He asked her if she wanted something to drink and was surprised when she asked for a Coke Classic. He had expected someone so thin to drink Diet Coke. Ah, he thought, the beauty of metabolism.

Kylie quickly sat down and brought out a sheaf of materials, swiftly moving into a business mode. "There are three major areas that a Champion's work centers around during the DMAIC phase of a project. First, there is work done *before* the project team is formed. That work will be completed during the next month. Second, there is the work you will do *during* the six months the team will officially be working on the project. And finally, your work as a Champion will continue *after* the team disbands."

Madrid brought out a sheet of paper with the following bulleted list under the heading:

Before the Team Is Formed:

➤ Select the team members.

➤ Create the business case for the project.

➤ Formulate the preliminary problem statement.

➤ Identify the preliminary scope of the project.

➤ Identify the preliminary goals of the project.

➤ Allocate the resources for the team to complete its work.

➤ Identify the team leader (either a Black Belt or Green Belt).

➤ Communicate the business case to each team member.

➤ Establish the timeline for the project team to complete its work.

➤ Establish the milestones along the way for input from the Champion.

➤ Distinguish decisions requiring Champion input from independent team decisions.

Kylie waited for some reaction from Zukor, who at least initially was focused on Madrid's muted freckles that framed her face, as well as looking at her sinewy arms. The only question Zukor asked was centered on team membership and his team leader:

"What I am not sure about is who I will pick for the team members and the team leader. What you may not know, Kylie, is that our Call Center is a very hectic place and my best people are working on our most difficult customer issues. I can spare some people, but it's going to be tough to get them focused on this project."

"That would be the biggest mistake you could make, Mr. Zukor," Madrid said abruptly. "Six Sigma projects must be populated with the best and brightest from your organization. When you select the best and the brightest, two things happen: First, the odds of success for your project improve dramatically, and second, you and the rest of the Champions send the cultural message to employees of Alpha Omega that you are serious about Six Sigma as a management philosophy. You are serious about Six Sigma aren't you, Mr. Zukor? I know Brenda Sexson, your superior, is serious about it. After all, she assigned you as Project Champion after we told her to assign her best and brightest. And you are Alpha Omega's best and brightest aren't you, Charles?" Madrid flirted rhetorically.

Zukor was not prone to blushing, but apparently did so as Madrid's words sank in. She informed him that she would be back in four weeks to begin DMAIC training, and she wanted to see most of the *Before* list completed by that time. She asked Charles if he anticipated any problems with the list. He resisted the temptation to ask her to review his *Before* list over dinner the next time she was in town. Instead, he insisted he would do his best. After a brief exchange of goodbyes and best wishes, Kylie was out the door, and Charles was left staring at a blank sheet of paper.

He eventually took out the sheet that Kylie had given him—the list of things that needed to be done *before* his yet-to-be-chosen team would begin DMAIC training. First and foremost, he carefully considered Kylie's "best and brightest" comments. With those thoughts in mind, he went to work on the first action item.

Select the Team Members

Zukor began writing the following list:

1. Aaron Gregson—a three-year Call Center veteran, who had argued long and hard to improve the way Alpha Omega did its business.

2. Maria Carballo—a two-year Call Center veteran who had increased her performance ratings more than any employee during the same two-year period.

3. Leroy Barney—a three-year veteran who believed others within Alpha Omega didn't do their jobs, resulting in the Call Center being overwhelmed.

4. Robert Wallace—an eight-year Alpha Omega veteran, who had been passed over in favor of Charles Zukor for the Call Center leadership.

5. Suzanne Jackson—a General Electric Capital Mortgage transfer who knew improvement was important, but felt neutral

toward any formal approach. While she had excellent performance reviews, she was not popular among Alpha Omega personnel.

6. Joy Schulenberg—well respected, although idealistic, was recommended as a future Alpha Omega leader.

7. Aaron Brown—a three-year veteran of Alpha Omega. Aaron had excelled in every assignment he was given, but seemed subdued and had the reputation of not being a future leader.

8. Jeff Seimonson—a bright 12-year veteran of Alpha Omega, Jeff knew virtually every facet of the business. Certain to be a naysayer about Six Sigma, he also was not only knowledgeable about the Call Center, but Jeff also knew a lot about the processes that affected the Call Center. Certainly Jeff would be a handful, but his input was necessary if this project was to be successful.

As Zukor looked over his newly formed list, he had one nagging thought. Obediently, he had bravely assembled his best and brightest, but how would the Call Center function if these "best and brightest" employees devoted 20 percent of their time to Six Sigma? What would happen to the urgencies of running the Call Center? He engaged in temporary denial as he thought of how Kylie Madrid would be proud of his assemblage of the best and brightest for the Six Sigma team. His second thoughts were to wonder how such a disparate group of highly skilled people could work together as a team.

Create the Business Case for the Project

During the Champions' training, Joe Hawke and Kylie Madrid had discussed the importance of the business case. The business case was the statement created by the Project Champion that did three things:

1. It established the focus of the Six Sigma team. That meant the statement needed to create the reason this project team was needed, why it was needed now, and why this project was of higher priority than any other work.

2. It was a statement of purpose to create motivation of emotion.

3. It was a statement of purpose to create motivation of behavior.

Zukor had been coached by the Temojoe consultants that the business case should be one or two sentences, and it needn't be quantitative. A quick glance at his watch showed that it was just past

5:45 P.M., but he was motivated to construct his business case. Less than 30 minutes later, he had created the following:

> *Alpha Omega has experienced a significant decline in its operating profits and customer satisfaction, both of which are Strategic Business Objectives (SBOs). To positively influence both of these SBOs, improvement must occur across all business processes. Currently, the Call Center could positively impact both operating profits and customer satisfaction through improvement of first-time call resolution, timeliness of response, and improvement in courtesy to the customer.*

While Charles knew this statement could be improved, he was reminded of Joe Hawke's words not to worry about word-smithing since the project team would provide input to the statement.

Over the next week, Zukor would take each of the remaining items from Kylie's *before* list and spend no more than 30 minutes a day on the action items. By the end of the week, he was justifiably proud of his work in a number of areas.

Formulate the Preliminary Problem Statement

The materials from Champions' training said the following about problem statements:

The Problem Statement Should:

➤ Describe how long the problem has existed.

➤ Describe the problem in specific and measurable terms.

➤ Describe the impact of the problem.

➤ Describe the gap between the current and desired state of performance.

➤ Describe the problem in neutral terms, meaning there is no mention of cause, solutions, or blame.

Zukor had been coached in Champion's training that he should create a preliminary problem statement that would be modified by the team and then finalized when the project team is in the measure phase of their project work. The Champion's job was to create a preliminary problem statement that should have blanks in it which would indicate work to be done by the team. Zukor created the following preliminary problem statement:

Since _____, Alpha Omega's Call Center has experienced a _____ decrease in first call resolution that has resulted in _____ customer satisfaction ratings. In addition, courtesy ratings of Alpha Omega's Call Center have declined from a high of _____ in 1999 to _____ in 2002. This resulted in a reduction of Alpha Omega's revenue.

While Zukor knew that it was acceptable to have blanks in the preliminary problem statement, he was curious about what the numbers were in reality. Creating this preliminary problem statement inspired him to motivate his team to collect the actual data that would show the severity of the problem. After completing this work, Zukor began to realize more fully the importance of this project. His awareness motivated him to continue with the Champion work that needed to be completed before the project team would begin its training.

Identify the Preliminary Scope of the Project

Scope had been described to Zukor as the boundaries for the project team. In Champion's training, he had been told by both Hawke and Madrid that it was important for him as the Champion to indicate to the team his perceptions of what was inside the boundaries of this project team, and more importantly, what was outside the boundaries of the project team. Two stories told by Madrid had had a significant influence on Zukor's appreciation for the importance of project Scope. One was a positive story relative to management of Scope in the United States. The other story was an example of "Scope creep," which Madrid had described as one of the top three technical reasons for Six Sigma project failure.

Kylie's first story brought a smile to Charles' face. She told the story of NASA in the 1960s, perhaps one of the best examples of proper Scope management. From President John Kennedy's proclamation of putting a man on the moon and returning him safely to earth, to Neil Armstrong's immortalized lunar quote, "That's one small step for a man; one giant leap for mankind," the Scope of work completed by the NASA team was managed to near perfection. Madrid used several examples of what was *inside* the Scope of NASA (e.g., orbiting the earth and lunar module creation), and more importantly, what was *outside* the Scope of putting a man on the moon (e.g., space station creation and exploration outside of the lunar path).

Madrid then asked the participants for a national example of Scope creep—an example in which we as a nation had good intentions but did not clearly identify what was inside, and more importantly, what was outside the project scope. Nearly half the Champions raised their hands, and references to Vietnam were uttered. Of course, they were right. While our original intent was to *advise* the South Vietnamese, over time the scope had crept to include incursions into Laos and Thailand, and eventually to taking over the combat responsibilities for the South Vietnamese. Madrid had made her point. Failure to properly manage Scope usually spells frustration and failure for the project team.

With this in mind, Zukor made his list of what was *inside the Scope* of his Call Center project, and what was, at least initially, *outside the Scope* of the project:

Inside	Outside
External customer calls.	Internal issues with other departments.
Issues related to first call resolution.	Policy issues with customers.
Improved courtesy within the Call Center.	Organizational structure.
Process structure.	
Job description.	

Even though he thought his initial list was skeletal, he decided to move on. He had been coached by Temojoe Consulting that one of his first responsibilities as the Project Champion would be reconciling the project team's input to the project Scope. Therefore, he proceeded with his list of preliminary action items.

Identify the Preliminary Goals of the Project

Zukor was initially stumped as he examined this item. He wondered how he could identify the preliminary goals for the project if he didn't know the current extent of the problem. Taking Madrid's business card from his desk, he realized this was an appropriate reason to call her. As the phone rang, Charles was excited with anticipation.

"Temojoe Consulting, this is Hannah Holly."

While the voice at the other end of the line was pleasant and professional, Zukor's dejection was palpable. He thought he had Kylie Madrid's direct line. "Is Ms. Madrid available?" Zukor inquired hopefully.

"I am sorry, Ms. Madrid is out of town with a client. May I help you," the cheery Ms. Holly responded.

"I had a technical question about my project team here at Alpha Omega. Is Joe Hawke available?"

"No, Mr. Hawke is also out of town. I am the assistant to the president. I would be happy to help you if I can," Hannah said with professional determination.

"I have a question about my prework with my team. How can I tell the team what their goals and objectives are when they haven't met and collected data? Ms. Madrid indicated I should come up with this as a *before* action item and I don't see how I can." Hannah could hear the frustration in Charles' voice.

"Oh, I can answer that one for you," Ms. Holly commented confidently. "First projects typically should have a 50 percent improvement over the baseline sigma measure. If your baseline measure of sigma is greater than 4, you have either picked the wrong project, or the improvement should be in increments of 10. Most of the projects in a Wave 1 launch like yours should strive for 50 percent."

Zukor felt confident that Ms. Holly knew her stuff. He thanked her and proceeded to the next item on his prework check sheet.

Allocate the Resources for the Team to Complete Its Work

Zukor thought about resource allocation that would be necessary before the team started its journey through improvement. Temojoe Consulting had recommended that Zukor consider a "War Room" for the team to have as its own. Not only would this room be used for team meetings, it was suggested that the wall space be large enough to accommodate the documentation of work done by the team. Quickly, he called Brenda Sexson's secretary to check the availability of Alpha Omega's boardroom.

"Nancy, this is Charles Zukor. Any chance I can schedule the boardroom starting next month a minimum of once a week for the next six months?

"Sorry, Charles, Ms. Sexson scheduled that room for the same amount of time two days ago. However, I can get you the auxiliary boardroom right next to it. It's about the same size with the same amount of wall space. Really the only difference is the quality of the carpeting."

"Sign me up, Nancy, just put down the Call Center Six Sigma team."

Zukor went back to work. Among the other resource considerations was secretarial support and IT support. After quickly talking to his assistant and obtaining her support for the team, he called his friend, Bam Kellogg, and obtained support from IT for up to four hours of support per week for IT assistance. Kellogg's only request was that to balance the needs of other teams Zukor would provide a team member to assist IT from the Call Center so that help would be only for the most critical elements associated with the Call Center project. Zukor had no problem with that request.

Finally, he remembered from Champion's training that if any of his team reported to another manager, he needed to create the need for their participation on the team. He again reviewed his proposed list of team members, all of them reported to him. No problem there.

Identify the Team Leader (Either a Black Belt or Green Belt)

It was time for him to designate his team leader. He had been instructed that a Black Belt was the full-time team leader who led three or four Six Sigma project teams over the course of the year. A Green Belt typically was a mid-level manager who retained his or her daily job functions but would lead one project if the project affected his or her work area. There were pros and cons to both the Black Belt and the Green Belt approach. Organizations like General Electric and AlliedSignal had committed to the Black Belt approach. The major advantage with Black Belts was quicker, sometimes more dramatic results. The big disadvantage was placing a layer of potential bureaucracy into the organization that many times could be inaccurately perceived as having the responsibility of implementing Six Sigma, as opposed to creating a culture of having everyone recognize his or her responsibility toward Six Sigma.

The Green Belt approach helps to embody Six Sigma throughout the organization. However, two problems exist with this approach. First, results from first projects usually take longer. Green Belts have their *regular* work to manage in addition to working on improving the process targeted in their Six Sigma project. Typically, the Green Belt and his or her team will have Six Sigma training spread out over a longer period of time (close to six months) and will need additional time to implement the solutions generated in the Improve phase of DMAIC. Second, Green Belts are learning the concepts, tools, and techniques of Six Sigma while simultaneously attempting to improve the processes they live in. This can result in greater levels of frustration for the Green Belt.

Zukor didn't have to make the decision of Black Belt versus Green Belt because Brenda Sexson had already committed Alpha Omega to the Green Belt approach. That meant he would have to identify one of his team members to be the team leader. He had been instructed that the Green Belt must have the respect and admiration of the team. In addition, they must be a skilled communicator, an expert in project management, and experienced in facilitation leadership. (Each of these characteristics is covered in future chapters of this book.)

While Zukor had only cursory knowledge with regard to most of the requirements of a good Green Belt, he immediately thought of Joy Schulenberg. While young and idealistic, Schulenberg had impressed virtually all management with whom she had come in contact. During her first year at Alpha Omega, she had played a major part in the roll out of the new IT system implemented by the Call Center—receiving widespread praise for her efforts. She also had garnered high performance ratings in her first two years. This was particularly impressive since Alpha Omega had adopted performance reviews that included the concept of the "internal customer." This meant that she had been highly rated by both *internal* and *external* customers.

Since most of Schulenberg's contacts with external customers were with those who had unresolved issues, questions, or complaints about Alpha Omega, her high rating was especially significant. Knowing how difficult unhappy customers can be, Schulenberg obviously had demonstrated her professional skills as evidenced by the high marks she had received from these customers.

Based on the internal customer concept, everyone within Alpha Omega to whom Schulenberg provided a product or service was considered to be a customer. These internal customers, located in other departments and functions, sometimes were superior in rank to Schulenberg, and, in other cases, they were peers. Regardless of whether the customer was internal or external, and regardless of the internal customer's rank, Joy was universally rated high on these customer evaluations.

Even with this knowledge, Zukor still wondered how others within the proposed Six Sigma team would receive Schulenberg as the team leader. She had a pleasant, upbeat personality, and she had clearly been identified as a future Alpha Omega leader. Sexson had made special note of her contributions. Zukor's primary concern was the reception she might receive from some of the other team members, most notably Robert Wallace and Jeff Seimonson. Thoughts of both men raised concerns. Wallace had been passed over for the Call Center management position. Seimonson, Zukor predicted, would certainly be negative toward Six Sigma. However, the concern didn't stop him from making the decision—Schulenberg would be his Green Belt team leader for the Call Center project. After all, he reasoned, if Schulenberg was on the fast track to being a business leader within

Alpha Omega, what better way to enhance those skills than leading this project.

Communicate the Business Case to Each Team Member

His first call was to Joy Schulenberg to inform her that she was about to take over as the Green Belt for one of the first Six Sigma projects at Alpha Omega. Her reaction made him feel confident in his choice. After a brief discussion on the phone, Schulenberg came quickly to Zukor's office. Zukor greeted her with his appreciation, "First, I want to thank you for enthusiastically taking on this assignment, Joy."

"Chuck," Schulenberg responded with an informality that Zukor wished she did not possess, "I had heard we were embarking on a Six Sigma initiative. I was thrilled! Although I've only been around here for a relatively short time, I knew we needed to improve Alpha Omega's effectiveness and efficiency. In addition, in our Process Management course at Notre Dame, we studied Six Sigma. We even did a field trip to General Electric Capital. I was quite impressed with their effort. In fact, you need to know I desperately wanted to work for General Electric because I was so impressed with their Six Sigma initiative. That and Jack Welch."

"I am thrilled with your support, Joy. And even happier you didn't take the job at General Electric Capital. We have our work cut out for us." Zukor cautioned, "There will be those on the team that don't possess your level of commitment."

"I am fully aware of how Robert and Jeff may be resistant to our efforts," Schulenberg said with determination. "It will be our job to bring them on board. Let's not forget I work with both of these gentlemen and I seem to have their begrudging respect."

After the brief meeting, Zukor was convinced that he had made the right choice for his Green Belt. Now was the time to notify the team members of their assignments. He called a meeting with Aaron Gregson, Maria Carballo, Leroy Barney, Robert Wallace, Suzanne Jackson, Aaron Brown, and Jeff Seimonson. Zukor began the meeting by asking the group if they had heard anything about Six Sigma. "It's Greek to me," Carballo confessed, prompting the laughter of her peers. "I know Brenda has been listening to Jeff Carpenter since he came over from General Electric Capital," Barney offered. Then he continued, "I know what I read in *The Wall Street Journal*. Six Sigma seems to be taking most organizations by storm, where businesses are driving cost reductions through Six Sigma. I have heard that General Electric has saved literally billions since they instituted it in the mid-1990s."

"Very well said, Leroy." Barney had provided Zukor with a platform for his opening comments. "Six Sigma is a management philosophy that drives improved effectiveness and efficiency in everything we do. Moreover, anyone who has been a part of the Call Center certainly knows that we need to improve in both areas. We've been working with a highly respected Six Sigma consulting firm that has guided us in our selection of high-impact, low-performing processes. That includes the Call Center, which has been selected as one of the first 11 Six Sigma projects here at Alpha Omega." Zukor continued, "We have an opportunity to dramatically improve our performance and be at the cutting edge of what will be our long-term management philosophy. This philosophy includes focus on our customers, and improvement of the process of customer service delivery. This initiative is sure to dramatically lower the current stress level all of us experience in the Call Center. If we are successful, we will encounter less difficulty in the work we do, have greater work life balance, and ultimately improve our quality of life in the Call Center."

As Zukor talked, his eyes migrated in the direction of Wallace and Seimonson. Both men were nonverbally exhibiting the kind of resistance that both Hawke and Madrid had indicated would likely happen. "Jeff, what are your thoughts?" All eyes focused on Seimonson. While a known naysayer, he was widely respected for his process knowledge, his years of experience, and his ability to get the job done. Exhibiting a sardonic, jaded humor, always at the expense of others, was typical "Seimonson" style. "Well, Chuck, the Call Center problems are in large part a result of failures found elsewhere in the company—from order fulfillment to market launch to our failure to have a true forecasting and marketing strategy. I also know for a fact that many of the customer calls to our center are caused by difficulties in understanding the billing statement." Wallace then chimed in, "Besides, we did a Total Quality Management effort my first year at Alpha Omega and it went nowhere. Motorola started Six Sigma in the 1980s and look at all the problems they're having."

Before Zukor had a chance to respond, Schulenberg intervened, "Total Quality Management or TQM as it was known, had a lot of T and Q, but not much M, Robert. I'll bet you couldn't cite a single business leader who has quoted TQM. On the other hand, many top-notch business leaders are actively engaged in Six Sigma as a management philosophy. Have you seen Jack Welch's autobiography yet?" She continued without giving Wallace a chance to answer, "He said that over the 20 years he was at the helm of General Electric, he sponsored only three initiatives, and Six Sigma was one of them. His successor, Jeffrey Immelt, indicated his plans to expand Six Sigma at GE in his first official interview with the *Wall Street Journal*. In fact, he referred to Six Sigma four times in the interview. You don't find executives quoting TQM with the same fervor as they do Six Sigma."

Wallace looked as though he was at a loss for words, and then sheepishly fell back on his trump card. "Okay, maybe I need to look into this a bit more. But what about Motorola?" "I'm glad you mentioned Motorola, Robert," Schulenberg responded as Zukor looked on in wonder at his newfound Green Belt. "Motorola has made several mistakes relative to what customers want from them. Six Sigma isn't going to solve every problem at Alpha Omega. Maybe an example would help. Six Sigma could be used to help manufacturers of horse buggies or eight-track tapes make better buggies and tapes, *but if the customer doesn't want their product,* Six Sigma is not going to help them. Or think of it this way. Even if you lead a healthy lifestyle, you don't smoke or drink excessively, you still might get sick. I'm not saying that we'll never get sick again if we embrace Six Sigma. What I *am* saying is that with Six Sigma, Alpha Omega will get sick less often and less violently. I like the idea of being a healthier company with Six Sigma than being an unhealthy company without it."

Zukor looked on in astonishment. While Wallace and Seimonson's silence didn't suggest they were converts yet, he noticed that the other team members showed clear signs of admiration for Joy, along with a growing motivation to being a part of the Six Sigma team. "So, what are the next steps?" Carballo asked. "We begin with five days of scheduled training, starting in three weeks," Zukor responded. "Then, over the next six months we will have two- to three-day training sessions, followed by four to six weeks of what is called "intersession" work. That's where we actually work on our Call Center project to improve effectiveness and efficiency.

Realizing that actual work was going to be involved, Wallace asked his next question. "Who is going to do our regular work while we are off doing Six Sigma?" Deciding to take the onus off Schulenberg, Zukor provided the rejoinder, "Six Sigma is not something else we do *in addition* to our jobs. It *is* our job. Improving how we do things in the Call Center should be considered a part of every job description. Ultimately, improving the Call Center is the responsibility of the key members of the Call Center, and I am looking at that group now."

No one responded. Zukor wasn't sure if the silence was due to the persuasiveness of his comments, or simply a sign that no one wanted to challenge him. Regardless, the silence was welcomed.

After some basic logistics, the meeting concluded. Later in the day, Zukor went back to complete the last items on his checklist.

Establish the Timeline for the Project Team to Complete Its Work

Temojoe Consulting had advised Alpha Omega on what the first wave of project work would be like. They indicated that all training would be in conjunction with what is called "action learning." This concept meant each of the 11 project teams would be taught the elements of Define, Measure, Analyze, Improve, and Control over the course of the next five months. The actual training would be taught in hotel conference rooms in blocks of two, three, or four days. Then the teams would disperse and work on their projects during the time allotted between formal education sessions. The *intersession* was considered vital to the success of the projects. Temojoe Consulting laid out the schedule as follows:

February 4 and 5	Facilitative Leadership Training
February 6, 7, and 8	Define and Measure Training
February 8–April 7	Intersession 1—Teams Work on Define and Measure
April 8, 9, 10, 11, and 12	Analyze Training, including Design of Experiments
April 13–May 20	Intersession 2—Teams Work on Analyze
May 21, 22, and 23	Improve Training
May 24–June 24	Intersession 3—Teams Work on Improve
June 25 and 26	Control Training
June 27–September 30	Postsession project work where solutions are implemented and cost savings are actualized

According to this schedule, the project teams would spend up to 15 days in classroom training. However, work in the classroom was only the tip of the iceberg. Most of the work would occur in intersession and postsession work. As mentioned earlier, about 20 percent of their time would be spent on Six Sigma tactics. Zukor promptly wrote a memo containing the training dates and circulated it to his entire team.

Establish the Milestones along the Way for Input from the Champion

Zukor needed guidance with regard to the establishment of milestones. He decided to ask for Kylie's input later about what his input was to be relative to the team. He took out his Champion's training manual from Temojoe Consulting and found the following passage:

> *Champions should allow the team to do its work. The Champion should provide guidance and remove roadblocks yet not be a full-time member of the team. In addition, the Champion should work out a schedule to meet with his or her team leader once a week at a minimum.*

With this input, he proceeded to call Schulenberg to schedule a weekly Friday morning breakfast with his impressive team leader. During this call, he also informed Schulenberg that during the Define, Measure, Analyze, Improve, and Control elements of process improvement there were self-described tollgates that were natural points for review and approval from the Champion. Schulenberg understood that she was not yet expert in these tollgates but with Zukor's help she mapped out natural review periods based on these tollgates.

They included: (italicized elements are the tollgates)

Define

➤ Reconciling the *Project Charter* completed by the team.

➤ Review the *Customers, their Needs and Requirements* completed by the team.

➤ Review the *High-Level Process Map* completed by the team.

Measure

➤ Review the *Creation of the Data Collection Plan* completed by team.

➤ Review the *Implementation of the Data Collection Plan* completed by team.

Analyze

➤ Review the *Data Analysis* completed by the team.

➤ Review the *Process Analysis* completed by the team.

➤ Review the *Root Cause Analysis* completed by the team.

➤ Review the *Financial Opportunities* captured by the team.

Improve

➤ Review the *Solutions Generated* by the team.

➤ Review the *Solutions Selected* by the team.

➤ Review the *Solution Implementation Plan* created by the team.

Control

➤ Review the *Control Method* selected by the team.

➤ Review the *Response Plan* created by the team.

Distinguish Decisions Requiring Champion Input from Independent Team Decisions

In accordance with the project team training, Zukor and Schulenberg agreed on the schedule for the formal review for each tollgate. These tollgate meetings would be above and beyond the weekly meetings they had scheduled for Friday morning breakfasts. Zukor had made the decision to be an active Champion and review all decisions made by the team.

One final time, Zukor reviewed the *before* list of what a Champion should do before a team begins its work. He was pleased that he had completed the list with over a week to spare before Temojoe Consulting returned for project training. His participation had started to move him toward greater acceptance of Six Sigma. He started to imagine what the Call Center would look like if this project was successful, and began to get excited about the possibilities. He was also excited about seeing Kylie Madrid again.

■ SUMMARY

Chapter 2 introduces you to our project team who will attempt to improve their Sigma performance. We highlighted the importance of executive management's support for Six Sigma that is required for team dynamics to thrive. We concentrated on the key role of the Project Champion. The Project Champion is the responsible party for the ultimate success of the project team, including team dynamics. We also addressed the key steps a good Champion must employ before the team's formation so that the team can get a good start on their work once their training commences.

KEY LEARNINGS

➤ Among the roles important for Six Sigma teams to thrive are executive management, the Project Champion, the team leader, which is either a Black Belt or Green Belt, and the team members.

➤ Executive Management will not be a member of the project team. However, their responsibilities to create vibrant Six Sigma teams include, first and foremost, utilizing Six Sigma as a management strategy. This sends the message to the Six Sigma team members that management is serious about their commitment to the project team's work.

➤ The strategic leader of a Six Sigma team is the team sponsor, commonly called the *Champion*. The Champion has the responsibility of creating the strategic direction for the team to accomplish its work.

➤ A Champion has multiple responsibilities *before* the Six Sigma team begins its work. The first thing the Champion does is select the team members. Each of them should be a subject matter expert within the process selected for improvement. They should also be the best and brightest. Choosing the best and brightest has two positive impacts. First, the odds of attaining success in projects increases dramatically. Whether you are talking about baseball teams or Six Sigma teams, if you don't have the right players, it is unlikely you will achieve your goals. Second, when management chooses the best and brightest, it sends a message throughout the entire employee base that the organization is serious about using Six Sigma as a management philosophy.

➤ Champions are also responsible for the creation of the *business case* for the project before the team begins its work. The business case usually is a nonquantitative statement that explains how the project impacts the Strategic Business Objectives of the organization. Further, the Champion must explain why this project has priority over other project work within the organization.

➤ Champions are also responsible for the formation of the *preliminary problem statement* before the team is formed. This statement must be specific and measurable, include a time

(Continued)

frame, describe the gap between the current and desired performance state, and describe the impact of the problem. In addition, it should be stated in neutral terms (which means it should not suggest root causation or solutions, and it should not assign blame for the problem). It is important to note that the problem statement is considered *preliminary* in the beginning stages of the project. The project team may complete and quantify any of the elements in the statement as they gather more data.

➤ A common problem for project teams is *unmanaged project scope.* Scope refers to the boundaries surrounding what the project team *will* work on, and more importantly, what the project team *will not* work on. Although the final decision regarding the Scope of the project is made exclusively by the Champion, even the best Champions will need the input and guidance from the project team. Just as he or she did with the preliminary problem statement, the Champion should generate ideas about what is inside and what is outside the Scope of work for the team. Champions are encouraged to keep an open mind to the ideas that will be generated by the project teams in the first days of DMAIC training before they make the final decision about the project Scope.

➤ *Preliminary goals* for the project team should be established and communicated to the project team by the Champion. In first wave projects, the goal is usually a 50 percent improvement over the baseline sigma performance. As performance improves, some teams set a 10 percent improvement goal. This is particularly true in later waves of training as sigma performance improves.

➤ Since the Champion sets the strategic tone for the ultimate success of the project team, it is imperative for the Champion to arrange for and assist in the acquisition of the *resources* necessary for his or her team to be successful. This includes everything from office space for team meetings to supplies for the project team's work. Of a more substantial nature is ensuring proper Information Technology support.

(continued)

(Continued)

➤ One of the most important personnel decisions a Champion must make is choosing the *team leader*. When an organization devotes full-time team leaders to guide three to four projects throughout a calendar year, these team leaders are called Black Belts. When a mid-level manager is selected to lead a team, possibly one a year, and maintains his or her "regular job," they are called Green Belts. Whether the team leaders are Black Belts or Green Belts, they have the tactical responsibility of leading the team to achieve its goals. Their responsibilities include scheduling agendas, facilitating meetings, and coordinating the tactics of the team's work. A final key responsibility is being the liaison to the Champion—keeping him or her apprised of the progress (or lack thereof) of the project team.

➤ The Champion must *communicate* the importance of the project to the team members before they begin training. In most cases, the team will ask key questions. These questions provide the Champion with his or her first opportunity to gain acceptance and reduce resistance by providing the correct answers.

➤ The *timeline* for completion of the team's work should be created before the team begins training. Typically the timeline will be determined by the external consultant chosen to assist you in your efforts. Usually the DMAIC training is conducted in three- to five-day sessions for each element of the methodology. This is followed by four to eight weeks of intersession work where the teams apply the Six Sigma tools, techniques, and concepts. This means that after approximately five months of training and intersession work, solutions are implemented. Cost savings are generated typically over the next 30 to 90 days following the implementation of the solutions. With these tentative dates in mind, the Champion should carve out the timeline for the team and clearly communicate this schedule to the project team.

➤ A good Champion should also address the *milestones* of achievement with the above schedule in mind.

➤ Finally, the Champion and team leader should agree on the types of decisions that require the Champion's input, and which decisions can be handled independently by the team.

Chapter

Team Effectiveness

How the Lack of Facilitative Leadership Results in Six Sigma Failures

"Don't mistake motion for action."

Ernest Hemingway

Six Sigma is noted for its rigor and discipline. Traditionally, this rigor and discipline refers to precision and accuracy centered around a set of statistical tools and techniques. This perception is partially inaccurate. Rigor and discipline also refer to the degree to which facts and data are used in the decision-making process, moving away from management based on anecdotes and gut feel.

In this chapter, we address another major component of rigor and discipline in the use and application of Six Sigma as a management philosophy. This additional component deals with why so many well-intentioned and talented teams fail in their goal of improved sigma performance. It focuses on facilitative leadership.

Facilitative leadership is the compilation of simple but effective tools that must be established and enforced for Six Sigma teams to complete their work. These tools and techniques include understanding the difference between Content versus Method, also known as the *what of a project* and the *how the what is accomplished*. It also includes simple but effective tools such as obtaining agreement before a team begins its work on what type of decision-making method they will

45

employ to reach agreement on diverse ideas that are generated by the Six Sigma process improvement methodology.

In addition, facilitative leadership deals with the creation of meaningful agendas, both for individual meetings and for the entirety of the work done by the team. Finally, good facilitative leadership establishes a set of vibrant and effective steps that can prevent problems from occurring in a Six Sigma team as well as examining appropriate interventions when problems surface.

We now return to the Alpha Omega team as they embark on their Six Sigma work.

■ UNDERSTANDING THE IMPORTANCE OF FACILITATIVE LEADERSHIP

Eleven Six Sigma teams assembled at the Omni Interlocken Hotel in Broomfield, Colorado. Joe Hawke and Kylie Madrid were busy at flip charts writing agendas for the day and arranging the front area of the large main room for training. Eleven round tables were arranged throughout the room with a poster card on each indicating the project. They included the Call Center project team, Merchant Launch, Order Fulfillment, and others. In the back of the room was a large rectangular table where additional Temojoe consultants were located as well as the internal resource personnel that Brenda Sexson had designated to help with the Six Sigma launch. On the overhead was a digital counter that read 14:09, and it was counting down as Charles Zukor entered the room. He looked down at his watch and saw it was 8:16 A.M. The punctuality appealed to his former Marine background.

Promptly at 8:30 A.M., the digital counter beeped. Time was up and Hawke began speaking. He reviewed the overall agenda for the full week of training indicating that the first two days were devoted to the concept of facilitative leadership with the Define and Measure elements of the Six Sigma project not beginning until Wednesday. After a brief introduction of his staff and a review of the history of Temojoe Consulting, he reviewed the desired outcomes of the first day of training. The flip chart he reviewed indicated the following:

- Understand the difference between Content and Method.
- Recognize the importance of gaining agreement on a decision-making method.
- Learn how to create detailed, useful agendas.

- Know how to create and enforce good team preventions.
- Know how and when to use proper interventions.

Joe Hawke then went to another flip chart and indicated that while he and Kylie were teaching, there would be a set of agreed-upon ground rules. He reviewed the suggested ground rules, asking if anyone disagreed with them.

Ground Rule #1 Start on time and finish on time.

Charles appreciated this ground rule being a former military man. Joe Hawke indicated they would teach in 90-minute increments, followed by 15-minute breaks, with a one-hour lunch. When he indicated that if the participants were punctual returning from breaks and lunch they would not go past 4:30 P.M., there was noticeable agreement.

Ground Rule #2 One person speaks at a time.

Hawke said that with close to 60 people in the room, respect for one person speaking would be showing courtesy to others in the room and would allow everyone to hear what the person was saying. Again, he asked if anyone disagreed and when no one did, this became the "law of the land."

Ground Rule #3 Limit sidebar conversations.

Indicating that this was an extension of the previous ground rule, Hawke indicated that talking to a neighbor for a sentence or two might help clarify some item but such "sidebars" should be held to a minimum. Hawke elicited some laughter when he went on to say that if one person said to his neighbor he could understand why Temojoe Consulting was rated the highest Six Sigma consultant group by General Electric, that was okay but other comments had to be limited.

Ground Rule #4 No stripes in the room.

This rule had to be explained. Hawke indicated that many organizations make decisions based on who is ranked highest on the organization chart. Thus, when someone in higher levels of management talks, their words are held in higher esteem than others. Hawke said that this would hamper work done by the teams. He went on to further state that a decision-making method should be agreed to before any significant decisions were made on the team.

Ground Rule #5 Everyone participates.

Hawke indicated that to learn, everyone must participate. He said that participation could take many paths, from paying attention to everything that was said by both consultants and participants, to note taking, to asking questions. Once again, he asked if anyone disagreed and when no one did, he went on to the next ground rule.

Ground Rule #6 Cell phones on vibrate.

Little had to be said about this ground rule that was universally accepted.

At this point, Hawke went to yet another flip chart where the following was written:

Be prepared after 10 minutes at your table to:

- Introduce your team.
- Add one desired outcome, if necessary.
- Add one ground rule, if necessary.

By the time this exercise was over, the list of desired outcomes had not been considerably altered but the following ground rules were added.

Ground Rule #7 No acronyms without first defining them.

At first, one team had indicated that the ground rule should be no acronyms. Hawke amended it to if there was an acronym, it should be properly defined and all parties agreed to this.

Ground Rule #8 Manage your biological needs.

Although breaks were going to occur regularly, this ground rule was added without reservation.

Charles was impressed with Joe Hawke's professionalism and knowledge. His attention heightened, however, when Kylie Madrid took center stage to begin the first facilitative leadership lecture.

Instead of using overheads or a PowerPoint presentation, Kylie began by saying she would show the group a video. She turned on the videotape player as Hawke turned off the lights.

The video began with the drone of an airplane clearly in trouble. The participants heard the pilot radioing for help as the plane crashed into the tundra in Canada along the Quebec/Newfoundland border.

With eerie sounding music in the background, a narrator reviews the facts of the crash: The pilot has died and the plane has sunk in a marsh with the radio on board. Each team represents the remaining survivors of the plane crash.

The narrator indicates that the crash occurred 30 miles from the intended destination. Further, the flight plan filed by the pilot indicated they would not return for at least two weeks. The narrator says that there is agreement that all the participants will stay together. Last, the narrator indicates that the survivors were able to salvage 15 items before the plane sunk. Those 15 items are:

1. A magnetic compass.
2. A gallon can of corn syrup.
3. One sleeping bag per survivor (dry and in good shape).
4. Water purification tablets.
5. A tent.
6. 15 matches.
7. 200 feet of rope.
8. A flashlight.
9. A set of snowshoes for each survivor.
10. A fifth of vodka.
11. A make-up kit with compact mirror.
12. An old-fashioned wind-up alarm clock.
13. A Swiss Army knife.
14. A 10-speed bike.
15. A book on astronomy.

Kylie turned off the video as Joe turned the lights back on. In near military precision, the two other Temojoe consultants passed out a scoring sheet for each team member. The scoring sheet had five columns as shown in Figure 3.1.

Kylie tells each individual to fill out the list of items in order of importance from 1 (most important for survival) to 15 (least important

Items	1	2	3	Difference between Steps	
	Individual	Team	Expert	1 & 3	2 & 3

Figure 3.1 Survival exercise template.

for survival). Kylie tells each individual to fill out the form silently and that they will have 10 minutes to complete this first step in the process.

Immediately the group takes out pencils and goes to work. Kylie has to chasten some sidebar conversation that goes against both the ground rules and the instructions for this first exercise. After 10 minutes, Kylie reads a flip chart that instructs each team to go to its breakout room and return in 90 minutes with the second column filled out using whatever skills exist in each breakout room. She also reviews the item on the flip chart that indicates she will begin teaching in 90 minutes and when all teams return to the main teaching room. With virtually no discussion, the various groups begin to rise and move to their breakout room after replenishing their coffee cups.

➤ The Call Center Survivor Exercise

Little was provided by way of instruction as to how each of the 11 Alpha Omega teams were expected to manage their 90-minute breakout. This was done purposely. Temojoe Consulting wanted to establish a baseline as to how each team currently practiced facilitative leadership. The Call Center team was typical of most teams that had no formal training in facilitation skills.

In the first minutes of the meeting, Joy Schulenberg attempted to take control of the meeting. "All right team, who has camping experience?"

Charles had been asked to observe his group in action without formally participating. He quickly observed Joy trying to get the team first to share information that would determine expertise around possible survivor experiences.

The query was met with muted, disorganized response.

"I spend summers in Alpena, Michigan, camping. But that's far away from Canada," Aaron Gregson said.

"I once was homeless," Robert Wallace said jokingly.

"I have watched all the episodes of *Survivor*," Suzanne Jackson said innocently but that too was met with team laughter.

"Okay, we have to get serious here." Joy was visibly anxious about trying to get the team focused. "All right, what about getting everyone's opinion on what's the most important item. We could maybe take one of the items and everyone rank it and I will calculate the average."

This suggestion was met with derision as were several others that Joy came up with in the next 10 minutes. Clearly, she was becoming emotionally exhausted. Finally, frustrated and embarrassed, she became silent and introspective, freely giving up the reins of leadership she never had.

Over the next 45 minutes, various team members took the "stage," sometimes giving anecdotes about camping experiences and sometimes arguing about whether to stay together or separate and get help. Later, a team member suggested evaluating why an item could either help or hurt the chances for survival. All of these discussions went undocumented, with many good ideas generated but just as quickly thrown away.

The Call Center team had 20 minutes left and had decided nothing. One final time, Joy attempted to guide the team while simultaneously showing her leadership skills:

"Could we at least separate the 15 items into three groups, the five most important, the five least important, and the five in the middle?"

"Great idea, Joy, why don't I take notes on the flip chart." Leroy offered.

With that in mind, over the next 15 minutes, the group completed a preliminary ranking as shown in Figure 3.2.

5 Most Important	Middle 5	5 Least Important
➤ Compass	➤ Alarm clock	➤ Vodka
➤ Sleeping bag	➤ Rope	➤ Bike
➤ Mirror	➤ Corn syrup	➤ Tablets
➤ Tent	➤ Flashlight	➤ Astronomy book
➤ Matches	➤ Knife	➤ Snow shoes

Figure 3.2 Survival exercise preliminary ranking.

In the last five minutes, the team quickly ordered each of the three columns with little consensus but with little disagreement since they had to return to the main training room.

The Call Center team was neither the first nor the last to return to the main training room. When the Call Center team returned, Temojoe's digital counter had already gone off. Within five minutes of the Call Center team's return, all but two project teams had returned with Madrid still in front silently waiting for the remaining two teams.

"Hey, come on, let's get this show on the road," said one team member who had come back punctually.

Kylie remained stoic during the criticism and referenced the flip chart for the restart time (after 90 minutes *and* when everyone returns from the exercise).

After nearly 10 minutes, the last two teams came into the room to the hoots and hollers of the other nine teams. Madrid began her next teaching points.

"The good news is that you are about to find out that your team efforts far surpassed your individual performance. Let's review what the experts from the Canadian Para Rescue Transport and Rescue Squadron think are the most important items that would maximize your chances of survival."

Kylie returned to running the videotape. A Canadian rescue expert goes through the items indicating that items such as the compact mirror should be rated high (to attract rescuers) to the magnetic compass that would be rated low since it wouldn't work in that part of the world. Dutifully, the teams filled out the forms to calculate which score was better: the work of each individual or the work of the 11 teams during the breakout. In each case, the 11 team efforts were better than any individual performance.

Kylie was quick to point out that Six Sigma teams succeed more than individual efforts within an organization. Next, she asked each team to brainstorm some of their experiences in the 90-minute breakout. She also requested Champions to share their thoughts with their team during this exercise.

During the report outs, the following pattern of responses occurred:

➤ The teams wasted time getting started.
➤ Most of the decisions occurred in the last 15 to 20 minutes.
➤ They didn't establish a method to reach agreement.
➤ They didn't identify a leader.

While these were the most common comments from teams during the reports, there were other isolated comments:

➤ They didn't establish any roles and responsibilities.

➤ They didn't establish an agenda or ground rules.

➤ Certain nonproductive behaviors existed with no consequences for those maladaptive behaviors.

At this point, Hawke returned to the front of the room and began his lecture on the facilitative skills that need to be practiced by Alpha Omega's Six Sigma teams if they were to be successful.

➤ Content versus Method

What teams often fail to recognize is that there are two components to any kind of work. First, there is the content of the work to be accomplished. Think of this as the "what" of the work. In a Six Sigma context, a team that progresses through Define-Measure-Analyze-Improve-Control (DMAIC) has a project for which they will be attempting to improve sigma performance. DMAIC is the "what" of the team's work. In addition to the "what" of work, there is also "how" the work gets done. This is called the method. Think of the content and method constituting two halves of a sphere (Figure 3.3).

As was evidenced in the survivor business simulation, the effort to rank items (the content or "what") received the exclusive attention of the teams. Because their focus was on the content, little or no

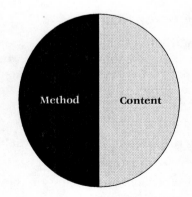

Figure 3.3 Content versus method.

attention was spent on the method of how the team got their work done. The temptation to focus exclusively on the content when these Six Sigma teams begin work on DMAIC will increase exponentially.

Thus, without consciously focusing on method (the "how") when the teams begin work on their projects, many of the aforementioned observations with the survivor exercise become even worse. For example, is it any wonder that so many Six Sigma teams end up failing to meet their goals and objectives in four to six months when they had difficulty in ranking 15 items in 90 minutes? When Six Sigma project teams begin trying to improve the effectiveness and efficiency of processes they "live" in, emotions run very high. Without the skills we reference later in this chapter, Six Sigma teams become inefficient or, even worse, derail entirely when they don't develop a methodology to handle the content of their work.

■ FACILITATIVE PREVENTIONS AND FACILITATIVE INTERVENTIONS

When we talk about the "how" of work (method) we are talking the language of facilitative leadership which has two major components:

1. Facilitative preventions.
2. Facilitative interventions.

We address facilitative *preventions* in this chapter. In Chapter 4, we address facilitative *interventions*.

➤ Facilitative Preventions

When we think of facilitative leadership, we should think of the totality of actions anyone can take to make project work run smoothly. To put it yet another way, everyone on the team practices facilitative leadership. Facilitative preventions include the following:

➤ Creating and utilizing vibrant agendas.

➤ Determining the desired outcomes for each Six Sigma meeting.

➤ Agreement on team ground rules for each Six Sigma meeting.

➤ Agreement on a decision-making method for the Six Sigma team.

➤ Use of a "parking lot" for Six Sigma team meetings.

➤ Obtaining agreement on specific Six Sigma team roles and responsibilities.

➤ Agreement on an evaluation method for each meeting.

Creating and Utilizing Vibrant Agendas

An agenda is a work plan for each time the Six Sigma team meets. On average, a Six Sigma team may meet 20 to 30 times over the course of several months. Each time the Six Sigma team meets, an agenda should highlight what is to be accomplished, the method as to how the action item is to be accomplished, who is the responsible party, and the amount of time designated for the action item to be completed. Figure 3.4 shows an example of an agenda for a Six Sigma team.

In Figure 3.4, the Six Sigma team wants to work on their Project Charter (the Element). The specific desired outcome is clarification of the project scope. As we saw in Chapter 2, project Scope refers to what is inside the boundaries and what is outside the boundaries of the project team. While the Project Champion makes the ultimate decision regarding project Scope, Champions are encouraged to get the input of the project team before making their final decision on Scope. Therefore, the project team is to provide the Project Champion their input for his or her consideration.

The method to be used is a form of a popular quality tool called the Affinity Diagram. Figure 3.5 shows how the Affinity Diagram can be used for this task.

The responsible party is the Black Belt. This does not mean that it is the responsibility of the Black Belt to do the scheduled item on the agenda. Instead, it means the Black Belt is the responsible party to see that the item is completed and in most cases to act as the facilitator for the item. Later, we discuss the various roles and responsibilities associated with facilitative leadership of which the facilitator is obviously the most important.

The last item on the agenda is the allocated time for the activity in question. For this exercise, the team has allocated 45 minutes.

Element	Desired Outcome	Method	Responsible Party	Time Allotted
Project Charter	Clarify project Scope	Affinity Diagram	Black belt	45 minutes

Figure 3.4   Example Six Sigma team agenda.

EXERCISE TO CLEAR THE SCOPE ISSUE

First, the team leader should create three columns on a wall of the meeting room. At the top of the first column should be a 5 by 7 card that says "In." At the top of the second column should be a 5 by 7 card that says "Out." In the third and final column should be a 5 by 7 card that is labeled with a question mark. The team leader should then describe the business case and present the preliminary problem statement using the guidelines described earlier in this chapter. The team leader should then hand out a series of blank 5 by 7 cards. He or she should then instruct each team member to write down on each card what is inside the Scope of the project team's activities, what is outside the Scope, and what he or she is not certain about.

The team members can then post their cards to the appropriate column. The team leader should review the cards in each column clarifying what is written while at the same time looking for duplicate ideas that the team has generated. Most importantly during this process, the team leader should be looking for ideas that appear in more than one column. These cards should be put in the question mark column, along with ideas team members are uncertain about.

It is the responsibility for the team leader to take this work created by the team and immediately report back to the Champion. It is then the responsibility of the Champion to take this input and create only two columns; what will be inside the Scope for the team and what is outside.

Figure 3.5 Scope exercise.

Determining the Desired Outcomes for Each Six Sigma Meeting

Each meeting of the project team should list the desired outcomes of the team meeting. For example, Joe Hawke showed a list of the desired outcomes for the class in the first minutes of the session:

➤ Understand the difference between content and method.

➤ Recognize the importance of gaining agreement on a decision-making method.

➤ Learn how to create detailed, useful agendas.

➤ Know how to create and enforce good team preventions.

➤ Know how and when to use proper interventions.

A Six Sigma team should also list the desired outcomes for each meeting. For example, when the team begins its journey through DMAIC, they will be introduced to a series of *tollgates*. These tollgates are formal sub-elements of Define, Measure, and so on. For example, the first tollgate under Define relates to finalizing and validating the Project Charter. The charter is made up of:

➤ The business case.

➤ The preliminary problem statement.

➤ The project scope.

➤ The project's goals and objectives.

➤ The roles and responsibilities of the team.

One project team meeting would not address all of the above items. However, for a given meeting, the desired outcomes might look as shown in Figure 3.6.

Agreement on Team Ground Rules for Each Six Sigma Meeting

As mentioned earlier, ground rules are among the most potent prevention tools a team can use to keep on track and be effective and efficient in their work.

Recall the ground rules that Joe Hawke created at the beginning of the class. First, notice that Hawke had a predetermined list of ground rules he wanted the class to abide by. In addition, he didn't force these rules on the group but used what is called a "negative poll" to reach agreement on them. For example, a common ground rule for any meeting or class is limiting sidebar conversations. If a series of sidebar conversations begin, they tend to spread like wildfire in a meeting or classroom situation. Therefore, preventing this type of behavior is the best recipe for them not happening. Of

---

➤ Explain why this project is worth doing.
➤ Explain why the project is worth doing now.
➤ Identify what strategic objective(s) are affected by the project.
➤ Explain why this project has priority over other projects.
➤ Create an agreed-upon statement around the above.

Figure 3.6   Desired outcomes—business case.

course, demanding that sidebars not occur does not lead to the buy-in necessary to ensure that sidebars will not occur. Therefore, recognize how Hawke created the buy-in for that ground rule. He asked, "Is there anyone who disagrees with the ground rule of limiting sidebars?" This negative poll (asking for agreement among those affected by inquiring if anyone disagrees) allows the opportunity for anyone who feels strongly to object but doesn't require each and every person on the team to provide feedback to the proposed ground rule.

Ground rules can help a team in many ways. First, they can improve efficiency in the group by identifying a code of conduct necessary for the team to do its work. Second, they allow for certain behaviors either not to occur or to occur less often because there has been agreement up front that these potentially maladaptive behaviors will not occur.

Third, ground rules can be established to either prevent or deal with someone who has shown maladaptive behaviors in the past. For example, let's say that a Six Sigma team has a participant who is anticipated to dominate the discussions of the team. A ground rule of "Balanced participation" or "No stripes in the room" (or both) establishes a group norm that can go a long way toward preventing this person from being a potential problem for either the team or the team leader.

Agreement on a Decision-Making Method for the Six Sigma Team

While Six Sigma teams ultimately make decisions based on fact and data, it also is true that teams must agree on a decision-making method.

While there are many decision-making styles, there needs to be two decision-making methods for a Six Sigma team to use with facts and data. First, a primary decision-making method must be agreed to by the Six Sigma team, then a back-up decision-making method must also be chosen.

Before agreeing on a decision-making method, a Six Sigma team needs to understand the decision-making spectrum (Figure 3.7). We now examine each of these decision-making methods and review their advantages and disadvantages.

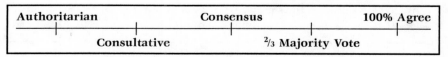

Figure 3.7 Decision-making spectrum.

Authoritarian. Authoritarian decision making is a decision vested in the hands of one person who makes decisions quickly and without regard for input from others. Typically, authoritarian decision making is necessitated when either there is a crisis calling for an immediate decision or when the decision is mundane in nature, not needing the kind of buy-in that other decision making entails.

For example, on the battlefield, a general may order his men into battle (or retreat) because he may possess more information than those affected. When the authority figure has the respect of those who are affected by the decision, a "life-or-death" decision would call for an authoritarian decision. An example of a mundane decision that would require authoritarian decision making would be deciding what doughnuts to bring to the Six Sigma meeting (although we strongly encourage the choice to be Krispy Kremes). Like all decision-making methods we will discuss, there are advantages and disadvantages. The first advantage to authoritarian decision making is the speed that one person can make a decision. In addition, authoritarian decision making has the advantage of having the decision not watered down with compromise. Thus, when in the hands of the right person with the right judgment and facts, authoritarian decision making can have the advantage of the right decision being made swiftly and with certainty.

However, authoritarian decision making also has many disadvantages. First, authoritarian decision making lacks involvement of those affected by the decision. Thus, the chances of lack of buy-in from these stakeholders are high. It's one thing to make quick decisions; it's another thing entirely to ensure that the solutions are implemented. Second, if an advantage of authoritarian decision making is quick, correct decisions, then obviously a disadvantage would be incorrect decisions made with poor judgment or the incorrect facts.

In the context of a Six Sigma team, it is rare when authoritarian decision making is the decision-making method of choice. The exceptions include the business leader making the decision to embrace a Six Sigma management methodology. Of course, this is a decision that is enlightened with many facts to support it. The other authoritarian decision that is the correct one with regard to Six Sigma teams is bringing Krispy Kreme doughnuts to the meetings.

Consultative. In October 1962, one of the best examples of consultative decision making occurred in our nation's history. During his morning National Security Briefing, President John F. Kennedy was informed that his U2 spy planes had detected offensive nuclear weapons on the island of Cuba, 90 nautical miles off the shore of the United States.

Over the next 13 days, the United States was on the precipice of World War III. In those 13 days, the President of the United States was vested with ultimate decision-making authority as the Commander-in-Chief.

President Kennedy was empowered to use authoritarian decision making if he chose to. He immediately and unilaterally could have started bombing Cuba (and later notified Congress). Instead, Kennedy carefully and deliberately sought out varied opinions concerning his options. These included not only trusted advisors like his brother, Attorney General Robert Kennedy and Secretary of Defense Robert McNamara, but those of dissimilar minds like General Curtis Lemay and former Secretary of State John Foster Dulles.

Ultimately, it was Kennedy's decision to create a blockade around Cuba and later to accept a compromise of withdrawal of U.S. weapons and munitions from Turkey (albeit quietly) in exchange for the withdrawal of Soviet missiles from Cuba.

The type of decision making where decision-making power is in the hands of one person but the person actively solicits the ideas, suggestions, and opinion of others is the hallmark of consultative decision making.

One advantage of consultative decision making is that those who are affected by the decision are sought out for their input. This allows for greater buy-in to the ultimate decision that is made by the decision maker. Another advantage is that by seeking input from varied sources, a better decision can be made. For example, in Kennedy's situation, solicitation of input from varied sources resulted in a blockade rather than an embargo of Cuba (which would have required Congressional approval).

There are several disadvantages to consultative decision making. First, it takes longer. The blockade of Cuba could have occurred quicker but it took Kennedy time to solicit opinions. Second, buy-in of the ultimate decision with consultative decision making only occurs if *your* input is finally decided on by the decision maker. Finally, if the person in the role of decision maker is just "going through the motions" and has a predetermined decision already made but is using the process of seeking input as a ruse, this type of decision making can backfire badly.

Consensus. There are many misconceptions about consensus. Some mistakenly believe consensus is total agreement among the team. Others believe it is a type of voting. Neither is the case. Consensus is a decision-making method where all parties involved have input to the decision to be made and whatever agreement is reached (i.e., compromise) will not be sabotaged by the team.

The first and obvious advantage of consensus is the full participation of the entire team. The first element in our definition of consensus involves *total* involvement of the team. In later discussions, we address quality tools that allow for total participation. Total participation of the team in the decision-making process creates buy-in from the team. This is another major advantage of consensus decision making. Since everyone is involved and the final decision is not made until there is agreement, by definition there is buy-in from the entire team.

Since an agreement through consensus is not made until there is agreement not to sabotage the final decision, consensus takes longer than other methods. For example, Hawke's review of the Alpha Omega ground rules at the beginning of the class was a way to gain agreement using consensus. His use of the phrase, "Is there anyone who can't live with . . ." is an example of gaining everyone's input to the final decision. While gaining consensus to ground rules is one thing, other decisions on a Six Sigma team may be far more emotional and thus take significant time to reach agreement.

In addition to taking longer, many times a final decision that is reached by the team is a "watered-down" decision that is not as vibrant a decision that could have been reached by another method. Of course, a "better" decision that has little buy-in accomplishes little.

Majority Vote. Often consensus will not be a viable option in decision making. Therefore, a back-up decision-making method must be decided on by the Six Sigma team. Usually this decision-making method is some type of majority voting. This voting is usually two-thirds of the team present. Majority voting is rarely used as the primary decision-making method. The advantage of majority voting is that a decision on a less watered-down solution can be made rather quickly.

The major problem with voting of any kind is that it creates winners and losers. While the winners feel great that their decision has been agreed to, those who lose become potential saboteurs to the decision, thus creating the possibility that whatever decision reached will not be properly implemented.

100 Percent Agreement. Another type of decision-making method is the attempt to reach 100 percent agreement. It is a rarity when any diverse group such as a Six Sigma team can have 100 percent agreement on what to have for lunch let alone the more dramatic type of decisions that are required as a team traverses through the DMAIC process. Thus, it is strongly recommended that this not be a method of reaching agreement on a Six Sigma team, not even as a back-up method.

Use of a "Parking Lot" for Six Sigma Team Meetings

A common problem with Six Sigma teams is meeting deadlines. While commitment to a formal DMAIC project calls for a significant investment in time, teams often get sidetracked.

While all of the discussion around facilitative preventions can help make a Six Sigma team more efficient, teams may still digress during a meeting. First, there are the digressions from well-intentioned team members who have a genuine belief that what they are discussing relates to the meeting at hand when in reality their input is varying from the agenda topic.

A less benign situation exists when a team member has a hidden agenda. Hidden agendas are strongly held beliefs by a team member that they wish to have embraced by the team but do so in an indirect manner. For example, say a team member believes that the DMAIC project could be used to enlarge his power or control within the organization. He may then attempt to covertly keep bringing this issue up during the DMAIC process hoping to have his hidden agenda implemented through the DMAIC process. These attempts can sidetrack a team, sometimes permanently.

The third and most egregious type of digression is a form of resistance to either the Six Sigma team or Six Sigma in general. Similar to a filibuster, where a congressional representative or senator may go on speaking without closure to avoid reaching a vote on a bill he or she doesn't want passed, this can happen in a Six Sigma team. In the previous paragraph, we referenced a Six Sigma team member who attempted to digress to enact a hidden agenda. Just the opposite type of situation is going on with the Six Sigma team member who is attempting to digress to avoid something he or she perceives as a negative. For example, a Six Sigma team member may believe that a successful project will diminish his control or power within the organization. That individual may filibuster and subtly attempt to derail the progress of the team.

There are many strategies to combat these digressions. One simple tool used during a meeting when the team leader perceives digressions is the *parking lot*. As the name implies, a parking lot is used to hold those items that do not directly relate to the topic to be addressed on that day's agenda. One or more pages of a flip chart can be designated as the parking lot.

Some mistakenly use this parking lot as a landfill—a place to dump items that will never be seen again. This is not the correct use of a parking lot. At the close of each meeting, the team leader should spend five minutes or so addressing how parking lot items should be dispatched. In some cases, the parked item should be dealt with in a meeting solely devoted to that topic. In other cases, the parked item needs to be transmitted to the Champion for an executive decision. Finally, in other situations, the parked item may result in a separate project or an action item for someone outside the Six Sigma team.

When parking lot items are dispatched properly, two things begin to happen. Those who are more obstinate in their digressions soon learn that their efforts to implement a hidden agenda or derail the group are futile. Thus, their digressions lessen. For those whose items end up in the parking lot due to less sinister reasons, they too learn the importance of staying on track, because they soon see that their ideas are not forgotten and are dispatched to more appropriate channels.

The failure to properly manage Six Sigma team meeting digressions often leads to longer meetings, increased number of meetings, and more work outside of the meeting itself. Because the average DMAIC project team takes four to eight months to complete and implement their work, it is imperative that they limit diversions to an absolute minimum. The parking lot is one way to do this. Just remember: Any good parking lot must have a parking lot attendant.

Obtaining Agreement on Specific Six Sigma Team Roles and Responsibilities

In Chapter 2, we discussed the various roles and responsibilities of Six Sigma teams. They included the responsibilities of executive management with regard to Six Sigma teams, the Project Champion, the Black or Green Belt, and the various other team members.

We are not addressing those roles and responsibilities. Instead, we are talking about the more specific tactical roles and responsibilities associated with on-going Six Sigma team meetings. They include:

➤ The team meeting facilitator (usually the Black or Green Belt).
➤ The scribe.
➤ The timekeeper.
➤ Ground rule enforcer (usually the Black or Green Belt).

The Team Meeting Facilitator. The team meeting facilitator is usually the Black or Green Belt. Traditionally, facilitators for meetings have major responsibilities for getting a meeting started and keeping the group focused. Since the vast majority of the time a Six Sigma team facilitator is also the team leader, their responsibilities are greater. The responsibilities of a good Six Sigma team facilitator include prework (responsibilities before a Six Sigma team meets), work done when the entire Six Sigma team meets formally (responsibilities during the Six Sigma team meeting), and postwork (responsibilities completed after a Six Sigma team meets).

Team Leader/Facilitator Prework. The Six Sigma team leader/facilitator has the overall responsibility of keeping his or her team on track toward completion of their appointed action items through DMAIC. It is typical for a Six Sigma team to have 20 to 30 meetings over the course of four to eight months. The Six Sigma team leader/facilitator is responsible for creating the agendas for each of these meetings ahead of time. Successful team leaders/facilitators are encouraged to meet weekly with their Six Sigma team Champion. The suggested agendas created by the team leader/facilitator should be reviewed with the Champion. This both allows approval of the agenda by the Champion if necessary and also allows the Champion to see where his team is relative to DMAIC.

Once these agendas are created and input has been provided by the Champion, the Six Sigma team leader/facilitator is responsible for circulation of these agendas to the entire team. As seen in Figure 3.8, the agenda should be specific, referencing desired outcomes, the agreed-on decision-making method and assigned roles and responsibilities, and a potential list of ground rules. In the example in Figure 3.8, the Six Sigma team is in the Analysis phase of DMAIC. In a scheduled two-hour meeting they plan to brainstorm root causation for either the data analysis or process analysis conducted previously and then narrow the larger list down to the most probable causes.

In addition to the creation, review, and circulation of the agenda prior to the meeting, there is also additional prework done by the team leader/facilitator. Verifying scheduling of the team's work area is an often overlooked element of good prework. Often, a Six Sigma team becomes inefficient when at the appointed meeting time someone else is using their regular meeting place. Good prevention by the team leader/facilitator occurs when at the onset of the creation of their team, a specified "War Room," exclusively devoted to the work of that specific team is established.

There will be times over the course of a Six Sigma team that ad hoc members may need to be included for a specific Six Sigma team meeting. For example, when the Six Sigma team is calculating cost opportunities for their project, it is helpful to invite a member of the financial organization to participate.

Finally, the last prework done by the team leader/facilitator is coordinating arrival of the morning doughnuts if the meeting is in

Desired Outcomes:

_____

_____

_____

Decision Method:

- Consensus

- $^2/_3$ Majority

Agenda:

Topic	Method	Person	Time
Determine root causation	Cause/effect diagram	Team	90 Minutes
Narrow potential causes	Clarification/ duplication	Team	30 Minutes

<u>Roles</u>

_____ Facilitator

_____ Timekeeper

_____ Scribe

_____ Participants

Ground Rules	Parking Lot
•	
•	
•	
•	

Figure 3.8 Sample agenda templates.

the morning. Bonus points are awarded the team leader/facilitator who brings Krispy Kremes.

Team Leader/Facilitator Work during the Meeting. To a large degree, it is normally the responsibility of the team leader/facilitator to coordinate the completion of the agenda. There are two types of facilitators. The first is the up-front facilitator who has the "power of the flip chart pen." The other type of facilitator is the armchair facilitator who resembles a team member and provides guidance while maintaining a role as a participator. Again, most facilitators will be the team leader. Therefore, the vast majority of the time in Six Sigma situations, the facilitative type of choice will be the up-front facilitator.

A good facilitator will get the session started by reviewing the agenda, asking for input to the ground rules, and reviewing with the group the specific roles and responsibilities of that specific meeting.

During the meeting, it is the responsibility of the facilitator to keep the team on track relative to the agenda. This includes role modeling and encouraging high energy levels (the Krispy Kremes will help in the short run here), attempting to building consensus around the agenda topics, and addressing dysfunctional behavior should it exhibit itself (dysfunctional behavior will be addressed in later chapters).

For Six Sigma teams, there are additional responsibilities for a facilitator. Six Sigma team leaders/facilitators must have a solid working knowledge of the DMAIC methodology and the various quality tools. For example, a common tool used throughout the DMAIC methodology is the Affinity Diagram. While this is not the only tool, it is important for the team leader/facilitator to be skillful in the use of this tool, as well as all of the other tools.

Finally, a good team leader/facilitator must be aware of his or her limitations and plan accordingly. For example, if the team leader/facilitator is not at a desired level of proficiency with regard to a specific tool or technique, it is the responsibility of the team leader/facilitator to call in someone to facilitate the meeting using that tool. The Master Black Belt is the internal consultant who can do this since they are skilled in all aspects of Six Sigma tools and techniques. In addition, Black Belts should have knowledge and experience in good facilitative management. Sometimes a team leader/facilitator may want to participate more as a team member for a given element of the DMAIC methodology. For example, since team members are chosen for their technical expertise, the team leader/facilitator may have special process expertise that would require the team leader/facilitator's deeper involvement. In these cases, it is better for the Master Black Belt to take the "power of the pen" while the team leader becomes a team member.

Team Leader/Facilitator Postwork. The team leader/facilitator's job doesn't end with the conclusion of the meeting. Good team leader/facilitators ensure that all decisions made at the conclusion of the meeting are circulated to all pertinent individuals. In addition, some Six Sigma meetings are decision making meetings while others are status meetings. The status meeting is where work is done in subgroups and the status of the work done between meetings by these subgroups is shared with the entire team. This necessitates the team leader/facilitator to either facilitate these smaller group meetings or ensure that the work gets done by other means that would include monitoring the responsible party for the work of the smaller group.

The Scribe. A common problem with Six Sigma teams is ensuring that all work done either between meetings or during meetings is "captured." Therefore, a key role of the Six Sigma team is the scribe who is responsible for taking detailed notes during the Six Sigma meeting. A good team leader/facilitator saves a few moments at the end of each meeting for the scribe to give a report on all key decisions made by the team during that meeting.

In addition, much work done by the Six Sigma team uses various quality tools like an Affinity Diagram or a Cause-Effect diagram where the Six Sigma team posts their work on the walls. It should be the responsibility of the scribe either to take notes on the final product on the wall or be responsible for saving the work on the wall.

The Timekeeper. Many misconceptions center around the work of the timekeeper. As referenced in our discussions of agendas, any good meeting will identify the allowed amount of time to address each element on the agenda. It is the responsibility of the timekeeper to provide the Six Sigma team status on how much time remains for each element on the agenda. The problem with most timekeepers is their passivity. They wait until the time for an agenda item is completed and simply say "time's up." This is incorrect.

Good timekeepers are more proactive. This means giving periodic status on how much time exists for a given item on the agenda. The following example illustrates a Six Sigma team's timekeeper who provided good feedback to her team:

Team Leader/Facilitator: "All right team, now we are going to discuss the must and want criteria for project solutions."

Team Timekeeper: "We have 60 minutes devoted to this topic."

Later in the meeting, an emotional discussion ensues regarding criteria for solutions for this project team. Initially, the team leader/facilitator thought the activities associated with this topic would take 45 to 60 minutes.

Thirty minutes into the discussion, emotions were running high. The timekeeper then intervened:

Team Timekeeper: "We now have spent 30 minutes on this topic and have 30 minutes left."

The timekeeper has alerted the team that they are behind with regard to completion of the action item on the agenda. He or she will again remind the group in 15 minutes that they have 15 minutes left for this item on the agenda.

In this particular Six Sigma project team, the timekeeper indicates they have expired the amount of time on the agenda originally devoted to this item. It then becomes the decision of the team whether to continue this action item, with the conscious decision to "borrow" time from another item on the agenda, or to modify the agenda entirely to devote more time to the action item. Whatever decision the team makes is acceptable. The problem is making sure that the timekeeper is neither passive nor becomes too involved in dictating what happens relative to the agenda.

Sometimes, the timekeeper is seen as the "party-pooper," who can halt the momentum on a topic. However, a strong timekeeper needs to ensure that when a Six Sigma team goes beyond their allotted time, a conscious decision is made to borrow from other agenda items or defer the discussion to another meeting.

Ground Rule Enforcer. Most teams do not address how ground rules will be enforced. In recent years, team leaders/facilitators have done two things to ensure ground rules are enforced. First, they indicate to their Six Sigma team that ground rule enforcement should be a shared responsibility. This means that when a ground rule is being broken, it is the responsibility of the entire team to point out an infraction so that the norms of the team return to the task at hand.

While this egalitarian model sounds the best, team members are sometimes so involved in the agenda item in question that they do not "see" a ground rule being broken. Traditionally, it then becomes the team leader/facilitator's responsibility to identify a ground rule being broken. In normal meetings, the facilitator typically takes on the role of ground rule enforcement. However, this is an additional responsibility that adds unnecessarily to the Six Sigma team leader's workload. Given all the responsibilities of being a Black Belt or Green Belt, it is understandable that a new role in the Six Sigma team needs to be established. The *ground rule enforcer* is not a permanent position. It should be rotated from meeting to meeting, where a team member will have for a given meeting the responsibility of noting when a ground rule is being broken, whether it be a sidebar conversation or coming in late to the meeting. It is still the responsibility of the entire team to deal with maladaptive behavior, which in part is the focus of our next chapter.

Agreement on an Evaluation Method for Each Meeting

Each Six Sigma meeting should conclude with an assessment of how the meeting went with regard to the agenda. Saving the last few minutes of a Six Sigma meeting to discuss how things went in the meeting accomplishes two things. First, things done well can be recognized to increase their occurrence and things that need to be improved for the next Six Sigma meeting can be addressed.

Knowing that each meeting will address what went well and what didn't go well has an influence on attempting to make each meeting go well.

Evaluating meetings should focus on two items. First, what went well in the meeting should be identified. This should be done in part to celebrate success. In addition, many times teams don't know what they do well. Thus, identifying what a team does well in one meeting increases the likelihood of those positive things happening in the next meeting and beyond.

To avoid thinking in terms of positive and negative, each meeting should be evaluated in terms of *pluses* and *deltas.* Pluses refer to what went well in the meeting. Deltas need a little more explanation. Deltas are not those things in the meeting that are negatives. A delta is something that needs to be changed for the next meeting. Therefore, deltas should be phrased in terms of what needs to be different to improve the next meeting.

The concept of pluses/deltas should be focused in two areas. First, pluses and deltas should be brainstormed at the end of the meeting for the content of the team's work. The content of the meeting relates to the desired outcomes from the team's agenda. Pluses and deltas should be provided for both the quantity and quality of work done. Did the team successfully traverse through the entire agenda? The team should recognize this as a content plus. Did the team have a brainstorming session that produced a significant contribution to root causation? This should be captured as a content plus.

Similarly, did the team only get through half of the desired outcomes on the agenda? This would result in a content delta. Alternatively, what if the team went through the motions of the agenda and the quality of the content was perceived as a delta? This should also be captured.

The other area that a Six Sigma team should rate with pluses and deltas is with regard to the method of how they accomplished their work. Did the team abide by the established ground rules? Did the team members perform their assigned responsibilities, such as time-keeping, scribe, and facilitation? Was the parking lot used effectively? Were there ground rule infractions? Was there poor use of quality tools and techniques? Whether a plus or delta, methods need to be identified.

Why are pluses and deltas important? Teams need short-term reinforcement for progress toward their eventual goals. When a Six Sigma team exists for four to eight months, it is imperative that the

Content Pluses
➤ Completed entire agenda.
➤ Determined sample size criteria.
➤ Resolved how to calculate baseline sigma.
➤ Steve's (Master Black Belt) presentation.

Content Deltas
➤ Last item on agenda (interim meeting deliverables) rushed. Let's allow more time for last agenda item next time.

Method Pluses
➤ Use of parking lot for possible wave 2 project issue.
➤ Brainstorming.
➤ Everyone's participation.

Method Deltas
➤ Sidebar conversations still going on. Let's have everyone be enforcers next meeting.

Figure 3.9   Plus/Delta example.

team recognizes short-term progress. This will assist in keeping motivation for the team high, particularly when the team experiences the plateaus that inevitably occur during the process of project work. Second, most teams are new to the concept of facilitative leadership. It is important for Six Sigma team members to recognize when they are modeling positive new behaviors so that the likelihood of these behaviors increases in the future.

It is important to capture deltas for each meeting. Ignored behaviors that prevent the team from ultimately accomplishing their goals become habits over time. By formally recognizing what needs to be changed in the future, not only can corrective action occur but many times it prevents problems in future meetings.

Figure 3.9 provides an example of the pluses and deltas for one Six Sigma team. Note that both deltas mentioned in this meeting are phrased with ways to modify them at the next meeting. They are not phrased just as complaints or negative things about the meeting.

■ SUMMARY

Chapter 3 introduced the concept of facilitative management. We discussed the importance of Six Sigma teams recognizing that they must address both content and method in their work. Content refers to "what" is done while the method refers to "how" the work is done.

The method of how work is done is more properly called facilitative leadership. Facilitative leadership has two major components. The first component is the accumulation of various preventative elements that contribute to greater efficiency and effectiveness in Six Sigma meetings. The second component focuses on the various interventions needed to make meetings better (see Chapter 4).

The first key element of good prevention is a detailed agenda that includes specific detailed outcomes for each meeting. Other good preventions is the ability to establish ground rules for the Six Sigma team to abide by, gaining agreement on a decision-making method, the use of parking lots for unexpected diversions that may impact the team, gaining agreement on specific team meeting roles and responsibilities, and recognizing the importance of evaluating each Six Sigma meeting for what went well and what could be done better the next time.

KEY LEARNINGS

➤ Six Sigma teams must recognize the importance of both content and method associated with their work. Content is *what* needs to be accomplished through the DMAIC methodology. Method is *how* the work is to be done.

➤ The method of how work is to be done on a Six Sigma team is called facilitative leadership.

➤ Facilitative leadership is comprised of two components: preventions and interventions (interventions are addressed in Chapter 4).

➤ Preventions include detailed agendas, along with agreements on agreed upon desired outcomes, ground rules for Six Sigma team behaviors, agreement on a decision-making method, the use of a *parking lot,* understanding of team roles and responsibilities, and the evaluation of each Six Sigma meeting at its conclusion.

➤ Detailed agendas include a list of what should be accomplished in each meeting, who is the responsible party for the item to be addressed on the agenda, the method to be used to

(continued)

(Continued)

accomplish the item on the agenda, and how much time is to be allotted for the item on the agenda.

➤ Good Six Sigma meetings will always have a set of specific desired outcomes for each meeting.

➤ Ground rules are those operating agreements of the team relative to the norms or desired behaviors that should occur each time the team meets.

➤ Teams should agree on a predominant decision-making method. It is preferred that Six Sigma teams use consensus as their predominant decision-making method. Consensus is a decision-making method where all parties involved have input to the decision to be made and whatever agreement is reached (i.e., compromise) will not be sabotaged by the team.

➤ Even with consensus as a predominant decision-making method, teams should always have a back-up decision-making method because consensus sometimes cannot be reached and, in other cases, it may take longer than is allotted for a given item on an agenda. A typical back-up decision-making method is a two-thirds majority vote.

➤ Many times a team will diverge from the topic at hand. A parking lot is used to capture those items that need to be addressed in other forums.

➤ In each Six Sigma team meeting, there needs to be a set of specific roles and responsibilities. They include the team leader/facilitator, the scribe, the timekeeper, and the ground rule enforcer.

➤ Each Six Sigma meeting should conclude with an evaluation of the meeting. Pluses (what went well) and deltas (what could be changed for the next meeting) should be captured for both the content and the methods used in that meeting.

Chapter 4

When Six Sigma Meetings Go Bad

Facilitative Interventions and When to Use Them

"An ounce of prevention is worth a pound of intervention."

Meg Hartzler
Destra Consulting

In Chapter 3, we discussed a powerful variety of tools, techniques, and concepts that can help to make Six Sigma meetings more effective and efficient. Collectively, they are called *preventions*. Such tools as the detailed agenda and agreement on a decision-making method go a long way toward achieving better Six Sigma results.

In this chapter, we address the tools, techniques, and concepts that can be used when Six Sigma meetings go bad. Collectively, they are called *interventions*. Regardless of how well your preventions are laid out, Six Sigma meetings are gatherings of people. While the root cause of poor process performance is rarely due to the "people" factor, the same cannot be said of Six Sigma team meetings. As such, preventions cannot totally eliminate the problems that teams will exhibit. In this chapter, we discuss the more prevalent problems that may arise as a Six Sigma team progresses through the DMAIC methodology.

We discuss typical maladaptive behaviors that exhibit themselves in Six Sigma meetings. We talk about the spectrum of interventions, from lower level to higher level interventions. We also expand on the role of a good facilitator. We discuss 10 pitfalls that facilitators fall into that prevent progress toward Six Sigma implementation. We also discuss how to provide and receive feedback that is a vital element to a Six Sigma team progressing through their work. Finally, we discuss suggestions for good facilitation that all Six Sigma participants can practice—suggestions that will produce greater results in the Six Sigma DMAIC process.

■ ALPHA OMEGA PRACTICE SESSIONS

The first day of facilitative leadership had been completed, and the Temojoe consultants had asked for the pluses/deltas for the day. The majority of feedback was positive. It included the pace of the day and enjoyment of the new skills associated with running Six Sigma meetings. Joe Hawke and his team received deltas on the length of the breakouts. The Alpha Omega teams indicated to Temojoe that they didn't need all of the time allocated for these sessions.

The Call Center team lingered after the conclusion of training at the suggestion of Charles Zukor. He said he would buy a round of drinks for the team. In the Omni Interlocken bar, discussion surrounding the first day of training soon became spirited.

As the group settled into their seats, Aaron Gregson indicated his enthusiasm for the new skills developed during the first day. "I really liked the approach of stressing the importance of us being a team."

"Me, too, Aaron," replied Joy Schulenberg as she stirred her Ketel One and soda. "I am still nervous learning about statistics, but so far this is good stuff."

The team revelry continued while Charles observed the noticeable silence of both Robert Wallace and Jeff Seimonson. He decided to ask the two men about their reactions to the day.

"Oh, I've been through this before, Chuck," responded Jeff. "It's just 30 minutes of common sense spread out over a whole day so that a consultant can make a buck," Seimonson continued wryly.

Perhaps fueled by the alcohol or inspired by the day's events, Maria Carballo let go with her comments. "Jeff, you are so negative. We've been trying to work as a team at Alpha Omega for ages. Maybe if we use these tools some of your great ideas will be implemented in this project rather than just ignored like they've been in the past."

The silence in the room was deafening. Within moments, however, the team was buzzing again as the conversation moved on to the latest office gossip and the recent loss of the Colorado Avalanche hockey team. Jeff Seimonson had lost interest in the group and he and Robert Wallace were soon at another table talking between themselves.

One thing was certain, Zukor thought to himself. Since tomorrow's training would be focused on each of the Alpha Omega teams practicing the facilitation skills they had learned today, it promised to be interesting, to say the least.

■ FACILITATIVE SESSION 1—JOY SCHULENBERG

The second day of training began with Temojoe Consulting giving assignments to each of the 11 Alpha Omega teams. Hawke suggested that the team leaders go first in the facilitative leadership practice. Temojoe Consulting had created a series of generic facilitative situations that the teams could use as the topics with which they could practice the prevention skills they had learned the first day. The facilitative situations for the first round included the following scenarios that teams would have a chance to practice before beginning the actual work of facilitating their DMAIC projects:

➤ Brainstorming the steps in buying a new home.

➤ Selecting a restaurant where the team could dine, using the consensus method of decision making.

➤ Gaining agreement on the activities for a company picnic.

➤ Determining what went wrong with the previous quality effort at Alpha Omega.

➤ Brainstorming remedies to the poor security system at the airport.

Joy Schulenberg had chosen "brainstorming the steps in buying a new home." She had a hidden agenda (see page 62 for the definition of a hidden agenda) for selecting this topic for her facilitation effort. From her college education at the University of Notre Dame, she had learned about Process Mapping, which she knew would be a tool used in the Define phase of the DMAIC process. She reasoned that if she could preview this tool to the team, then when it was time to actually use it in the project, she would accomplish two things: First, she would gain greater creditability with her team, and second, it would give her team a head start on other teams because they would already have gained experience with the tool by practicing with a generic example.

As each team listened to Hawke give the final instructions, Joy anticipated her new role of facilitator with butterflies churning in her stomach. She remembered the adage told to her by her father when she was a child—"There is only one chance to make a first impression." In her mind, Hawke went on too long giving instructions for the breakout. Joy wanted to get started with her meeting.

"So in closing," Hawke seemed to drone, "remember that a consultant on the Temojoe staff will be assigned to each of your rooms, and will provide feedback to the up-front facilitator *after* the team has provided its feedback. Also, remember to provide pluses, then deltas, in that order. Providing feedback is going to be tougher than you think. Okay, for the facilitators going first, you have 10 minutes to set up your breakout room. The rest of you take a break and be in your breakout room in 10."

Schulenberg quickly moved to her breakout room and began furiously writing on flip charts. First, she drafted her agenda, allowing what she thought was sufficient time for each element that would lead to the creation of a process map. She moved quickly to create the parking lot, also. Then she taped the third flip chart on the wall and wrote the heading "Ground Rules." Finally, she wrote on a fourth flip chart the words "Desired Outcome," and beneath it wrote:

To create a Process Map that describes how a new home should be purchased.

She broke open a pad of Post-it notes and spread them out on the tables. She then opened a box of flip chart markers and carefully placed one next to each note pad. Joy's prework is shown in Figure 4.1.

The Call Center team soon began to filter into the breakout room. Within moments, everyone was seated. Joy initially felt what could best be described as exuberant confidence as she began her role as facilitator. She was pleased that Charles had decided to sit in on the session.

"All right, everyone, in this session we will create the steps for buying a home. We have a lot of expertise in the room and we want to tap into that. As you can see from our first flip chart, we want to create a Process Map that identifies the steps in purchasing a new home. Does anyone have anything to add to the list of desired outcomes?"

Without waiting for an answer, she proceeded to assign roles and responsibilities. She quickly got agreement from Leroy Barney to be her timekeeper, and Aaron Gregson agreed to be the scribe. Joy indicated she would be the up-front facilitator and Maria Carballo agreed to be the ground rule enforcer. Joy then proceeded to review the agenda.

Agenda Element	Outcome	Method	Person	Time (Minutes)
Review agenda	Agreement	Discussion	Facilitator	5
Buying a home exercise	Agreement on steps to buy home	Process Map	Team	30
Plus/Delta	Assessment of meeting	Plus Delta	Team	5

Desired Outcomes

To create a Process Map that describes how a new home should be purchased.

Parking Lot

Ground Rules:

_____
_____
_____
_____

Figure 4.1   Proposed agenda—Alpha Omega Breakout #1.

At this point in the meeting, Kylie Madrid came in and took a seat in the back. Joy noticed her presence as she finished her review of the agenda and began working with her group to set up ground rules for the meeting.

Quickly the team created the following list of ground rules:

➤ One person speaks at a time.
➤ Everyone participates.
➤ No cell phones.
➤ Talk to the ideas generated; not the person.
➤ No digressions.

The team was off to a good start. Five minutes had been scheduled for this part of the meeting and they were done in three.

"We want to brainstorm the steps in buying a home. We will use a tool known as a Process Map." Joy was now showing some authoritarian tendencies but no one was objecting. However, as she began to explain the use of the Post-its, Wallace and Seimonson began whispering to each other. Momentarily distracted by the sidebar, Joy went on to tell the team about the first step in the Process Mapping exercise. "Our first step is to name the process. It should have some action word associated with it."

"How about Home Buying?" A good suggestion, but one made by Joy herself. Again no disagreement from the team, so Joy moved on as the sidebar between Wallace and Seimonson continued.

Joy proceeded to explain to the team that the next step in Process Mapping is to indicate the start and stop points of the process. She asked the group for its input into what they thought the start and stop points of the process of buying a home would be. This time she waited for responses. Suzanne Jackson and Aaron Brown began a discussion of whether the start of this process would be when a wage earner gets a promotion, or when interest rates go down. Gregson then asked for more information. He wanted to know who was buying the home. Twenty minutes into the meeting, the team was still talking about who was buying the home. There had not yet been any real progress toward the desired outcomes of the meeting.

Joy valiantly tried to keep the meeting on track by giving examples of who might be buying the home—from a young couple to a new college graduate. However, these suggestions didn't stop the discussion. Throughout the discussion between Brown, Gregson, and Jackson, Wallace and Seimonson continued their sidebar conversation. They had escalated from their initial muted whispers to disruptive laughter about something that had nothing to do with buying a home.

Abruptly, Leroy Barney, the timekeeper, notified the group that there were 10 minutes left for this particular item on the agenda. He reminded them that they needed to do pluses/deltas at the end of the meeting, which was the last item on the agenda. Joy suddenly took a pen and Post-it notes in hand and instructed the group to move on to the steps of home buying. The group became silent as Joy single-handedly began to write six steps in buying a home on the Post-its. Some of the steps included determining the type of home, selecting the neighborhood, and ultimately ending up with financing the purchase.

Joy's initial confidence had ebbed. She finished the steps with a hollow sense of accomplishment. True, she had finished the task in terms of the desired outcome, but no one had to tell her that this was not the work of the team. Instead, it was the work *she* had done while the team looked on.

During the formal debrief of the exercise, Kylie Madrid first asked Joy how she felt. She shared feelings of frustration and exasperation. "I really don't feel there was much in the way of positives, so I would just as soon have you tell me how to improve."

Kylie asked the group to provide its plus feedback to Joy. There was very little in the way of substantive discussion. One member complimented Joy on her effort and attitude. Kylie then asked for delta feedback. Other than someone saying that the session seemed rushed, and that there wasn't much group consensus, there were very little details offered.

Kylie realized that she needed to intervene with a mini-tutorial on the session. She was very earnest as she began her tutorial.

"First of all, Joy, you did a lot of things well. Let me cite some examples. First, you created a detailed agenda that was specific with regard to the desired outcomes, roles, and responsibilities, and time allotment. Second, you solicited a set of ground rules and obtained agreement on them. Third, you attempted to use a quality tool you haven't even been trained on. That was risky, but overall it was positive. As you will experience going through DMAIC, you will need to take risks, and you set the tone for risk taking in this group by trying out a new tool. Fourth, you possess a natural style of enthusiasm and energy that is required of facilitators. With regard to the latter point, this is a people skill that a person either has or doesn't have. You possess a natural style for facilitation that will help you improve some of your deltas."

Joy's mood improved measurably as she listened to Kylie's feedback. She had focused so much on her negatives, she didn't realize she had done so many things well. Kylie's positive comments brightened Joy's mood for a couple of reasons. The first reason was the sincerity with which Kylie made her comments. The second reason was that Kylie cited specific examples of what Joy had done well. The focus on specific positives in her presentation made Joy anxious to hear how to improve.

"Now let's move to some suggestions to make your next facilitation better. Remember, we call them 'deltas,' not 'negatives.' To better help all of you with your facilitation, I came in earlier today and listed the 10 Mortal Sins of Facilitation on this flip chart." As Kylie said this, she was simultaneously moving toward her list (Figure 4.2).

The 10 Mortal Sins of Facilitation were being unfurled for the team to see. Kylie then solicited input from the group with regard to

The facilitator:

1. Chooses which comments made by the team are worthy of being documented. Interprets or modifies the words spoken and records their "spin" on the input rather than documenting what is actually said.
2. Showing a bias toward one tool or technique.
3. Permits digression without recognizing their role and the primary enforcer of keeping to task.
4. Permits ground rules to be broken without taking noticeable corrective action.
5. Creates the impression they have a bias toward one idea or one person in the group.
6. Speaks in nonneutral or emotionally charged language or allows a member of the team to do so.
7. Allows distrust or disrespect to occur between the facilitator and the team or between the team members.
8. Does not create a sense of purpose regarding the team's goals or objectives.
9. Ignores time keeping or underestimates the amount of time to get an agenda item accomplished.
10. Does the work for the team.

Figure 4.2 The 10 mortal sins of facilitation.

the "sins" that were committed by Joy that she could correct in her next facilitator opportunity. Before the team had a chance to address the deltas for Joy's performance, she offered her own comments on the "sins" list.

"Well, I can see that if these are the mortal sins of facilitation, I'm going to be spending a lot of time in 'Facilitator Purgatory.' I can see where I made a lot of mistakes. First, I clearly had a bias toward the Process Map. The next time I won't be so presumptuous. Second, I clearly permitted digression to occur when we were deciding on who the homebuyer was. I needed to somehow draw a line in the sand and keep the team focused on the task. Next, a number of ground rules were broken. I failed to note that I am the primary enforcer even though we assigned Maria to this task. I was hoping it would go away if I ignored it. Now I know that if I ignore a ground rule infraction, things will only get worse. And, if all that isn't bad enough, my worst sin was doing all the work for the team at the end of the session."

Kylie was noticeably pleased with Joy's assessment of her own facilitative performance. "Fantastic job, Joy. Your ability to recognize your own areas for improvement now allows you to take action on them since it's very difficult to ignore your own input. While all of your perceptions are accurate, I want you to pay special heed to the need to manage digressions. All teams encounter some of the disruptive behaviors you encountered in the exercise. Of significant concern for Six Sigma teams is recognizing the importance of sticking to the project schedule. Failure to abide by the schedule for the Define, Measure, Analyze, Improve, and Control phases of your project will often result in your team's failure to improve sigma performance. Finally, Joy, I can't stress enough that limiting digressions is a critical element of both your facilitation and leadership skills. Of course, you don't want to cut off valuable team participation, but allowing unproductive discussion to go too far will result in Six Sigma team failures."

Joy wondered out loud, "How do I know when I am allowing a digression and when I may be cutting off valuable team discussion?" "Facilitation is more art than science. First, you will gain a knack for this skill over time. Second, read your audience. Are they mentally 'checking out' of the meeting? That's a sign of digression. Third, conduct a perception check. A perception check is when the facilitator, or a team member for that matter, 'checks out' their perception that the meeting may be digressing. Inexperienced facilitators usually err on the side of too many perception checks early on. It takes time to get a feel for the team. Also, watch to see if there is an increase in ground rule infractions. That would be a sign that the team is digressing. Last, if you make a suggestion that the team move forward, always ask for feedback on the suggestion. For example, did anyone notice how Joe Hawke did that at the beginning of training yesterday?"

"I think I know," Aaron Brown offered. "Joe had a predetermined list of ground rules that he wanted to see in place. While he felt strongly about them, he offered an opportunity for objections as he addressed each one of them individually."

"Very good, Aaron. This type of agreement building is called a *negative poll.* Joe always asked if anyone disagreed with the ground rule and, as he made eye contact with each of the participants, he allowed time for anyone in the class to object if they chose to do so. The beauty of a negative poll is its efficiency. Since it doesn't require that every decision be agreed on by everyone, only those who are against the ground rule need to voice their objection."

"What about ground rule enforcement, Kylie? I can see it being a big issue for our team," noted Maria. (Remember, she was supposed to be the enforcer.) Kylie responded, "Joe is going to teach a tutorial on this topic when we get back to the main room, Maria. At this point, recognize that there are a series of interventions that could have been used, from lower level to higher level interventions. Also recognize that anyone can employ these methods, but the ultimate responsibility for enforcement falls on the shoulders of the facilitator, and remember, Maria, Joy gave that role to you. We will get into these interventions shortly. We all know now that doing nothing about the infractions and *hoping* that a team member points out that a ground rule is being broken is not the correct strategy."

The debrief was going well, with virtually everyone paying attention and demonstrating enthusiasm for what Kylie said. Kylie began to wrap up the debrief.

While the attention was on Kylie, Joy's thoughts drifted to last night's happy hour. She recalled seeing evidence of disrespect being shown to one of her team members. As she surveyed the list of the 10 Mortal Sins of Facilitation that Kylie had posted on the wall, Joy noted that disrespect was sin #7. In retrospect, she realized that she had missed a leadership opportunity. She had noticed that Maria was chastising Robert, and although Maria was "on the money" with her comments, Joy now realized that she had missed an opportunity to support Robert. She wanted to blame the "happy hour" alcohol for dulling her mind, but she couldn't help thinking it might have been an opportunity to help reduce Robert's resistance to Six Sigma.

At any rate, it was time to return to the main training room. As the 11 Alpha Omega teams gradually took their seats, the Temojoe consultants' digital timer beeped, and Hawke announced, "Time's up." Hawke began the session by asking for feedback on the breakout session. Most of the ensuing discussion was focused on facilitative performance similar to Joy's. Hawke echoed many of Kylie's comments during the large group debrief. He then asked the teams to brainstorm a list of the most notable maladaptive behaviors that were exhibited in their first exercise. During the report out, the following were the most common types of behaviors the teams displayed:

➤ *The Whisperer*—Engages in sidebar conversations with friends or neighbors.

➤ *The Storyteller*—Goes on with a story beyond the point of adding value.

➤ *The Dominant Personality*—Dominates the conversation with regard to experiences or opinions.

➤ *The Dropout*—Loses interest and either is a "no-show," works on nonrelated work, or seems to "pout" during the meeting.

➤ *The Naysayer* (also known as the "Yes, but" person)—Resists what is being discussed and is not honest about their resistance. Instead, they give reasons why the team's ideas will not work.

➤ *The Verbal Attacker*—Attacks other team members, either indirectly by attacking their ideas, or directly.

➤ *The Politician*—Plays one team member against another for personal gain by trumping other's ideas with their own ideas relative to the project.

➤ *The Team Clown*—Attempts to divert the group with humor.

Hawke indicated there are a host of other types of behaviors that team members may exhibit over the next several months, and that the list represents some common examples of what the Alpha Omega teams will encounter. When improperly managed, Hawke warns, these encounters can spell doom for the Alpha Omega teams. Which brings him to the second major component of good facilitative leadership—*interventions*.

■ FACILITATIVE INTERVENTIONS: WHEN, WHERE, AND HOW MUCH

In Chapter 3 we discussed the importance of facilitative preventions. As Meg Hartzler of Destra Consulting is noted for saying, "An ounce of prevention is worth a pound of intervention." Preventions will always be the priority for success in a Six Sigma team. However, even the most thorough applications of preventions will not ensure a team's success. Maladaptive behaviors will still crop up in Six Sigma meetings. Thus, a team must be prepared to deal with maladaptive behaviors through a series of interventions.

These interventions must be proportionate to both the *type* and *frequency* of the maladaptive behavior. Think of the levels of interventions as existing on a spectrum from low to high. It is always preferred to use the lowest level of intervention that will work.

As seen on the *intervention spectrum* in Figure 4.3, interventions can be both unobtrusive and nonverbal. In the early stages of intervening, it is always wise to assume that the person exhibiting the maladaptive behavior is not intentionally being disruptive. They should be given the benefit of the doubt in terms of their behavior. Facilitators and other ground rule enforcers that intervene at a higher level than what the situation calls for run the risk of making things worse in the long run. If a Six Sigma team member has engaged in some maladaptive behavior innocently, then the intervention by definition needs to be seen as mild, or low-level. Any

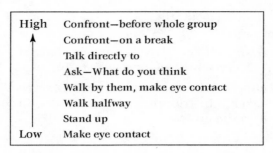

Figure 4.3   Levels of interventions.

intervention is an attempt to change someone's behavior, and people don't like to have their behaviors changed by someone else. Whenever there is an attempt to change behavior, it is always important to maintain their self-image within the group. Failure to do so may result in an escalation of undesired behavior.

Now let's examine specific types of interventions and their application to the maladaptive behaviors generated in the Alpha Omega facilitation exercise.

➤ Levels of Interventions

The importance of establishing levels of interventions is based on the fact that any type of intervention is a personal statement about the behavior of a Six Sigma team member. That is, an intervention is acknowledgment that at least one other person on the team wants another team member's behavior to change. Therefore, interventions must be done in such a way as to maintain the other party's dignity and self-respect.

With the dignity and self-respect of the other party in mind, it is suggested that interventions start at the lower level of the spectrum (Figure 4.3). The beauty of lower levels of interventions is that they will be known only to the person exhibiting the undesirable behavior and the ground rule enforcer.

Intervention with the Whisperer

The whisperer engages in sidebar conversations with friends and neighbors. This person is breaking the ground rule of "no sidebars." While it is possible that this infraction is more serious than it appears, the facilitator should assume the infraction is benign. It may be an innocent faux pas, or possibly the guilty party is simply asking his neighbor for clarification of some issue related to the discussion. In situations where the disruptive behavior is benign, an unobtrusive, nonverbal intervention will usually stop the undesired behavior. Thus, making simple eye contact in a casual, nonthreatening manner sends the message to the whisperer that his or her whispering has garnered the attention of the facilitator or ground rule enforcer. The message is sent, and hopefully received, that the whisperer is breaking a ground rule and that such behavior will not be tolerated.

What if the message of casual but sustained eye contact intervention does not deter subsequent whispering? Obviously, a higher level of intervention is required. Still, the facilitator must maintain the dignity and self-respect of the person exhibiting undesirable behavior. In most Six Sigma meetings, the facilitator will be standing, conducting any one of a variety of team exercises. Thus, an escalating intervention would be to move in the direction of the whisperer, possibly halfway to where the whisperer is seated while maintaining casual eye contact. At the same time, the facilitator should continue with the business going on in the meeting so as not to bring unnecessary attention to the whisperer.

Where a low-level intervention has failed, usually a slightly elevated intervention will cause the maladaptive behavior to stop. However, in certain instances it will not. If these lower to mid-level interventions prove to be ineffective in stopping the undesired behavior, then the interventions must continue to escalate to higher levels. Again, think of higher level interventions as existing on the upper end of the intervention continuum. The facilitator should move gradually up the continuum until the intervention effectively stops the undesired behavior.

As we continue up the continuum, the next item on the scale would be to approach the person exhibiting the undesirable behavior closer than just halfway. In addition, this physical proximity would be accompanied by more direct eye contact. As in previous interventions, the facilitator should allow sufficient time to see if the intervention has the desired effect of reducing or eliminating the undesired behavior. One mistake facilitators make is not allowing sufficient time to see if the intervention takes hold. Always allow sufficient time to see if the intervention has worked.

If the mid-level intervention has not worked, it's time to escalate the level of intervention to the point that others in the group might become aware of the intervention. Obviously, if the intervention becomes "public knowledge," there is always a risk of embarrassment to the person exhibiting the undesirable behavior. We recommend that if the behavior continues, the facilitator should redirect the member's behavior. For example, if the Six Sigma team is working with Post-it notes, the facilitator might ask the person exhibiting the undesirable behavior to be the "Post-it person." Or the intervention might be as simple as asking the person who is exhibiting the behavior what they think about the issue the Six Sigma team is working on at that moment.

This re-direction of a person's undesirable behavior is considered to be a significantly higher level of intervention. If the re-direction doesn't do the job, there are probably other issues underlying the person's actions. In other words, the behavior is simply a "veil" for some other issue going on with this individual.

If the series of interventions we have discussed fail to stop the disruption, we recommend two final interventions. The first strategy would be to talk to the person during a break and explore the underlying issues. This direct, yet nonthreatening (by being "off line") approach will likely uncover the real reason behind the undesirable behavior.

The second strategy is the highest level of intervention. This level of intervention should only be used after all other efforts have failed—confrontation of the undesired behavior in front of the entire group. Obviously, this highest level of intervention has equally high risks associated with it. Therefore, it should only be done with prior warning communicated to the person exhibiting the disruptive behavior that this will be the next step.

Confrontation in front of the group is said to be the highest level of intervention, yet there is one more—expulsion. If direct confrontation in front of the team does not work, then the Champion is required to be involved with the next and final step in facilitative intervention—expulsion from the group.

We have discussed an example of moving from lower to higher levels of interventions using the whisperer as the focus. Now let's look at other prevalent types of undesirable Six Sigma team member behaviors, along with proper intervention strategies for each of them.

Intervention with the Storyteller

The storyteller is someone that goes on with a story beyond the point of adding value. As is true with all undesirable behavior, an ounce of prevention is worth a pound of intervention. Whenever the facilitator anticipates the possibility of a storyteller being a member of their Six Sigma team, then the prevention is to ensure the inclusion of the ground rule "balanced participation and/or focus on agenda items."

Even when this type of behavior is anticipated, and the necessary preventions are in place, interventions will still sometimes be needed. A good facilitator will attempt to discern the underlying issue behind someone being the storyteller. Usually the storyteller is someone who is insecure and their stories are an attempt to embellish their participation. If this can be substantiated, it is wise to provide some validation for this person in the group around Six Sigma activities.

It is not unusual for employees to spin tales as a way to make themselves feel important. Through Six Sigma involvement, employees often feel more valuable to the organization. Thus, rather than just try to negate the storyteller, the facilitator may decide to re-direct the employee toward greater Six Sigma participation as a way to tap into his or her need to be a part of the organization.

Intervention with the Dominant Personality

This is the person who dominates the conversation with regard to their experiences or opinions. As is true with the storyteller, setting a ground rule for "balanced participation and/or focus on the agenda" is the best prevention. Again, a good facilitator will attempt to discern the underlying issue behind the dominant personality. Similar to the storyteller, this type of behavior may be the manifestation of an insecure person who needs to feel important. Therefore, validating this person and re-directing their need to feel important into the Six Sigma activities may help to prevent problems at a later time. Another strategy to use with the dominant personality is to ask the person to lead a meeting where their expertise can be tapped into in a way that is beneficial to the Six Sigma team.

Another ground rule that helps with the dominant personality is "start with the end point in mind." This means to give the "bottom line" comments *first* and then backtrack if needed for additional details that support the "end" thought.

Intervention with the Dropout

The dropout is the person who loses interest in the Six Sigma project. This team member may become a "no-show," or may work on non-Six Sigma-related work in the meetings, or may seem to "pout" during the meetings. First, the ground rule of "balanced participation" is helpful with mild cases of dropout behavior. In mild situations, the dropout has usually had an experience where their ideas have been ignored or, in worse cases, may have been ridiculed. Often, dropouts are the result of "plops" that occur in a meeting. A "plop" is when someone's idea is ignored. To avoid plops in a meeting, a good facilitator will use Post-it notes to capture everyone's ideas. Thus, by clarifying the ideas of all participants (a step in the "narrowing" phase of brainstorming sessions), the facilitator ensures that everyone providing input will have some time spent on their ideas.

The dropout may be exhibiting resistance to Six Sigma. In our second book, *Making Six Sigma Last,* we discuss four major types of resistance. When the dropout behavior is a form of resistance, it is indicative of a more serious issue. Six Sigma teams will often be populated with those who are not yet on board with the concept of Six Sigma. They are resistant to Six Sigma for a variety of reasons. One reason is that they may have been part of a previous quality effort and believe Six Sigma is nothing more than a way to drive increased performance from the employees, rather than the true goal of Six Sigma—improving the process that the employees live in. If a facilitator believes she has a dropout, we recommend using the strategies found in *Making Six Sigma Last* to assist in reducing or eliminating the resistance.

Intervention with the Naysayer

Also known as the "Yes, but . . ." person, this is an individual who is resistant to what is being discussed and is not honest about her resistance. Instead, she will explain and give reasons why whatever the team is working on will not work. Again, ground rules are a great way to help prevent this behavior. The ground rule we have seen work well with the naysayer is "no statement should begin with the word "but." "But" is an eraser. Those that begin their comments with "That's a great idea, BUT" are actually disagreeing with what was said, yet they are appearing to be polite. Knowing that a Six Sigma team must accomplish so much work in such a short period of time means that such manipulative attempts at digression must be stopped in their tracks.

While the above ground rule can be helpful, it is also important for the facilitator to deal with maladaptive behavior directly. Encouraging the naysayer to openly and honestly share his or her concerns with the topic at hand can save the team immeasurable time in the completion of its task. At the same time, issues around the naysayer may have to do with the individual's resistance to Six Sigma. Thus, the same strategies we recommend from *Making Six Sigma Last* are as applicable here as they are for the dropout.

Intervention with the Verbal Attacker

This is the person who verbally attacks another person in the group, either directly or indirectly. An indirect attack targets the person through veiled attacks on the person's ideas. The verbal attacker often uses "dark humor" or sarcastic humor as his vehicle of attack. As always, ground rules can be a beneficial prevention for this type of maladaptive behavior. We recommend the ground rule "talk to the idea, not to the person." However, more than any other type of maladaptive behavior, we find this type of behavior relatively immune to preventive techniques.

With the verbal attacker, it is usually necessary to move quickly to higher levels of intervention. In some cases, it may be necessary to initiate an "off-line" meeting to notify the attacker that personal attacks will not be tolerated. In many cases, the verbal attacks are reflective of the individual's basic personality. Thus, the facilitator can play a pivotal role in establishing the unwavering fact that verbal attacks will not be a normative behavior in the group.

Often, individuals who exhibit this behavior will stop the behavior when any of three things occur within the group. First, when the behavior is not rewarded with encouragement from the rest of the Six Sigma team. Thus, an initial strategy we encourage is having the facilitator work with *the rest of the team* to enlist their support by not responding to the verbal attacker. The second strategy involves establishing a clear understanding with the person exhibiting this behavior that the behavior will not be tolerated. Third, addressing this behavior early on with a high level of intervention is a critical success factor to stopping this from becoming a chronic problem.

Intervening with the Politician

The politician plays one team member against another for personal gain by trumping other's ideas with his or her own ideas relative to the project. Preventions typically do not work with this behavior. However, one key ground rule that allows for later intervention with the politician is "what is said in the room stays in the room," or, stated another way, "confidentiality prevails among the team."

While it is rare that ground rules will dissuade the political type of behavior, they provide the facilitator with the foundation for interventions whenever the behavior is exhibited. When the politician either breaks confidentiality or attempts to circumvent the work of the team behind other team members' backs, a reminder of the relevant ground rule is an appropriate intervention. Usually, the intervention should be high at the start. It is recommended that the intervention be a private meeting between the politician and the facilitator for the first infraction. If there is a second occurrence, a meeting should be scheduled with the Champion in attendance. A third infraction necessitates the expulsion of this team member from the Six Sigma project.

Intervening with the Team Clown

The team clown is the person who wants to divert the group with his or her humor, either in the form of jokes or sarcasm. First, it is important for the facilitator to recognize that this behavior is not necessarily always maladaptive. It only becomes maladaptive when the team clown is attempting to divert the work of the group.

Over the course of time that a Six Sigma team exists, tensions can run high. A team clown who knows when and where to interject appropriate humor can go a long way toward bringing the team together and helping the Six Sigma team achieve its goals of process improvement. Again, it is only when the team clown is attempting to divert the team's efforts that intervention becomes necessary.

It is important for the facilitator to be consistent with interventions. Often a team clown will be encouraged by laughter, which tends to increase this behavior. Thus, the facilitator must set norms for when levity is appropriate in the group and when it is not. If a facilitator knows ahead of time that they have a team clown in their group, they may be able to establish a working understanding with this person as a preventative measure. The facilitator could assure the team clown that humor has a place in the meetings, and agree on a "signal," in the form of a phrase or comment, that the facilitator can use to alert the clown if the humor is getting in the way of the team's work.

➤ Other Facilitative Interventions

In addition to understanding and practicing interventions that are appropriately linked with specific undesirable behaviors, facilitators also need to be aware of the other skills they need to possess for their Six Sigma meetings to be effective and efficient.

Facilitators, by virtue of the fact that they are in front of their team, have the ability to shape how the work is done in their team. Among the most important skills they can utilize to shape the way work gets accomplished are their verbal skills that will be discussed next. These verbal skills include:

The Direct Probe

A good facilitator will occasionally ask the team, or a team member, a direct question that helps to bring out or clarify an idea. For example, while the team is in the middle of a discussion the facilitator might ask questions such as:

➤ Why is that an important point?
➤ How does that point reflect on our discussion of . . . ?
➤ What is your rationale behind . . . ?
➤ What do you mean by . . . ?

The In-Direct Probe

While a direct probe's purpose is to bring out an idea or clarify an idea, an in-direct probe is best used when the facilitator thinks a team member has some ulterior motive for a comment or thought that has been shared with the team. For example, let's say a team member is trying to enforce a ground rule but is vague in his or her comments. The facilitator may indirectly probe as a way of testing what is really being said. Possibly a team member has not had his or her ideas recognized, and they appear to be on the verge of becoming a dropout. The facilitator might probe with something like, "How can we assure more balanced participation (a previously established ground rule)?" This is considered indirect because the purpose is to get the potential dropout back in the game rather than directly asking why this person isn't participating.

Re-Direction

A facilitator may sense that the team is digressing from the desired outcome for an issue on the agenda. Rather than always saying a ground rule is being broken, a more gentle way to get the team back on track is through comments that re-direct the group back to the task.

A chronic issue that a Six Sigma team facilitator will always have to deal with is the team members' tendency to think and talk about *solutions* (which are generated and selected in the Improve phase) when they are in the Define, Measure, or Analyze phase of the project. Many of these ideas will be valuable. However, if the team is jumping ahead to Improve when they should be in Define, Measure, or Analyze, they ultimately stand a good chance of failure. Thus, a good facilitator might say, "That's a good point, Susan. Why don't we capture that in our parking lot so we don't lose that thought? We can return to it when we are in Improve."

Confirmatory Statements or Questions

There will be times in Six Sigma team meetings that the facilitator will make a point to confirm what is being said by a team member. These confirmatory statements help to clarify what is being said and aid the team in concluding a discussion.

For example, let's say a facilitator thinks adequate time has been spent on clarifying the team's project Scope. Perhaps some team members think that implementing a solution is outside the Scope of the team's charter while others think it is inside the Scope. While discussion on this topic might be lively, the Champion must make the ultimate decision. A good facilitator would recognize that emotions are high within the group, and that further discussion is not likely to produce a viable decision. The facilitator might then say, "Most of you think this is inside the Scope of our work and others think it's outside. Neither side seems to be willing to change their opinion. Am I correct?" This simple question is a way to both confirm what seems to be obvious to the facilitator but also allows an opportunity to conclude the discussion and move on by suggesting that the Scope issue be passed along to the Champion.

Paraphrasing

Closely related to confirmatory statements is the concept of paraphrasing, sometimes called "reflective listening." When paraphrasing, the facilitator "reflects back" to the speaker what he or she just heard. Typically, the beginning of this statement begins with "What I just heard is . . ." and finishes with what they think the speaker said. For example, the facilitator might say, "It sounds like you want to move to the next item on the agenda. Is this correct?" Paraphrasing or reflective listening ensures that the team doesn't go off in a wrong direction and reassures the speaker they have been heard correctly.

Leading Questions

Another responsibility of the facilitator is to "jump start" the discussion when it appears that the team has reached a premature conclusion. In this situation, the facilitator will prompt further discussion by playing the role of devil's advocate.

For example, many times throughout the DMAIC process a team will use a tool that necessitates brainstorming. For instance, when the team gets to the Analyze phase, it will brainstorm a list of potential root causes for the poor sigma performance in the process they are trying to improve. If they only generate a short list (in the eyes of the facilitator), the facilitator might say, "What other root causes do we believe contribute to the current sigma performance?" Sometimes a facilitator who has good rapport with their team might say, "Wow, I thought this team would have a lot more ideas than this on possible root causes!"

If the facilitator uses a leading question or statement as a way of challenging the group, they need to recognize the importance of using this approach sparingly. If used too often, the team might resist the facilitator either verbally or by dropping out.

Behavioral Observations

One way to enforce ground rules and move the Six Sigma team forward in its work is for the facilitator to make a statement that states the obvious. This means to simply make a verbal observation about whatever the facilitator sees in terms of a certain behavior. For example, if the team begins to be tardy in starting meetings, the facilitator may simply state the observation, "I've noticed we're having trouble starting on time." The advantage of making behavioral observations, whether targeted toward an individual or the entire group, is that the statement is devoid of judgment. It points out a behavior that needs to be corrected but, also allows those affected to take their own corrective action rather than feeling the facilitator is in a policing role.

Idea Floating

Six Sigma facilitators often function purely as team facilitators rather than as participating team members. As such, they do not necessarily need to relinquish their own ideas relative to the work of the team. Thus, idea floating allows the facilitator to be an active part of the team.

Idea floating statements are made by the facilitator to continue a line of thinking between the group's thoughts and the facilitator's thoughts on the subject. Typical idea floating comments begin with:

➤ Does anyone have any thoughts on . . . ?
➤ Have we thought of the benefits of . . . ?

Unlike direct participation, idea floating allows the facilitator to give his or her opinion in a way that encourages the input of the entire team.

Boomerang

The boomerang is illustrated when the facilitator takes a question posed by one of the Six Sigma team members and "boomerangs" it back to the team to handle. For example, if a Six Sigma team member asks the facilitator, "How are we doing with our data collection?" and the facilitator responds with, "How do *you* think we are doing?" the facilitator has just used a boomerang.

The purpose of the boomerang is to get the group thinking and evaluating things for themselves, rather than the facilitator being responsible for all of the judgments and evaluations. While it is essential that the facilitator play a special role around leadership for the team, the boomerang can help the facilitator avoid playing this role in a way that usurps the team's responsibility.

The boomerang is best used for open-ended, evaluative type questions posed to the facilitator. It is also helpful when the facilitator wants to capitalize on the experience of the team members. For example, if the facilitator is asked, "What has been your experience in this situation?" he or she might ask the group if anyone else has been in this situation and, if so, ask them to comment. Here the facilitator uses the boomerang to broaden the involvement of the team members and to gain greater input to a problem or issue facing the team.

Finally, like any facilitative intervention, the boomerang can be overused and misused. In the latter case, the boomerang should never be used as a way for the facilitator to escape answering a technical question. For example, if the facilitator is asked the question, "How do we use the Cause-Effect Diagram?" this type of question should never be boomeranged back to the team. Facilitators should answer technical questions with direct answers. If they don't know the answer, they should seek the input of a Master Black Belt or the external consultant and report the answer back to the team.

Perception Checks and Process Checks

Facilitative Leadership is an art, not a science. As such, there will be times when the facilitator might use the exact tool in a meeting that she had used in a previous meeting, and get very different results. Facilitators must never be on automatic pilot. They must learn to "read" the situation so that the Six Sigma tools and techniques can be applied on a case-by-case basis. This means reading both the verbal and nonverbal behaviors of their teams.

For example, let's say the facilitator is using a brainstorming tool that was successful in a previous Six Sigma meeting, but this time the energy level of the team has dropped significantly. Maybe the team has been working hard for a long time and fatigue has set in. If the result of an exercise is not what the facilitator thinks it should be, they might do a perception check. They might say something like, "It seems that this approach isn't working. Do we need to use a different approach, or do we need a break?" This would constitute a perception check. That is, the facilitator's perception is that the energy level of the group is low and literally "checks it out" with the team.

A process check is similar to a perception check. Here, the facilitator may have the impression that a tool or approach that he had selected is not working. He may say, "I sense that the Affinity Diagram isn't working. Am I correct?" This is a check of a process tool. As the facilitator's Six Sigma toolbox grows through learning the DMAIC methodology, he or she will be able to quickly modify an approach using a variety of tools.

For example, Six Sigma teams will learn a variety of ways to validate root causation. They might do multiple regression or conduct a designed experiment, but rarely will they do both. If the facilitator suggests regression and it doesn't seem to be working, then a process check may result in conducting an experiment instead.

Lassoing

The concept of the lasso involves combining several thoughts from different Six Sigma team members into one idea. Suppose a Six Sigma team has been discussing a DMAIC concept called the "voice of the customer" over the course of 10 minutes, and the following statements have been repeatedly verbalized:

➤ "We have been having lots of delivery issues with our customers."

➤ "The warehouse has confirmed our excess inventory."

➤ "We have been dealing with transportation issues for a long time."

All of these comments deal with the issue of customer requirements and late delivery with those customers. Many times a Six Sigma team gets stuck by rehashing comments or restating the obvious. At this point, a good facilitator will "lasso" the comments and make a summary statement like:

➤ "It seems clear that we have a delivery issue with our customers that affects our inventory and may also involve our transportation issues."

By lassoing the similar comments made by the team members, the team is then able to respond to the facilitator's comment. At the same time, it is a method that allows the team to reach a conclusion and move on to another item on the agenda.

➤ Feedback—The Most Important Facilitative Intervention

Over the course of working together as a Six Sigma team, there will be multiple opportunities for feedback to be both given and received. Although feedback is not the sole domain of the facilitator, a good facilitator can set the right standard by role-modeling good feedback techniques. Good feedback techniques are a combination of knowing when and how to *provide* feedback and, equally important, how to *receive* feedback.

Providing Feedback

Feedback should be provided under two situations. As we have already mentioned, each Six Sigma team meeting should conclude with feedback about what went well and what could be done differently in the next Six Sigma meeting. We refer to these as the pluses/deltas.

The other situation in which feedback will need to be provided is when undesirable behaviors call for a higher level of intervention. Remember, there will be times when a team member may need to be provided with feedback off-line or, in the worse case scenario, in front of the entire team.

The most important element in providing feedback is talking to the behavior, not the person. An approach that can assist the feedback provider is to phrase feedback around the statement:

> *When you . . . I feel . . . (Note: Do not use "we." "We" might sound like a conspiracy, as if we've all talked about this behind your back.)*

When stated this way, the discussion focuses on the *behavior* of the person rather than on the *person* receiving the feedback. This is important for the same reason we stated earlier about the initial need for lower level interventions, specifically, the need to maintain the Six Sigma team member's dignity and self-respect. When feedback is directed toward the behavior, the recipient of the feedback is less likely to become defensive, resulting in a far greater likelihood that the message will be received, and the behavior will ultimately be changed.

In addition to being behaviorally focused, it is helpful to provide feedback with specific examples. In this regard, providing feedback is in keeping with what a Six Sigma culture is trying to achieve—management with fact and data. Saying to someone, "You have missed meetings on February 13 and on February 20, and been late for 50 percent of the other meetings" is far more descriptive and specific than simply saying, "I think we have a problem with your attendance."

Once the message is given in objective terms with specific examples, it is also important to suggest alternatives—called "corrective action." For example, if someone on the Six Sigma team is habitually late, the feedback given would be, "When you are late, I feel frustrated because I either have to start the meeting late and finish before all the agenda items are complete, or start without you. Is there anything we can do to ensure your prompt attendance?" During the ensuing discussion, the team may find that the meeting time is inconvenient for the latecomer. If that proved to be the case, an alternative would be to find a better time agreeable to the team to help reduce the latecomer's tardiness.

Receiving Delta Feedback

Everyone likes to hear good things about themselves. It is much more of a challenge to receive feedback that requires behavioral change—the "delta" feedback discussed previously. However, over the course of time that a Six Sigma team will exist, virtually everyone, including the facilitator, will be on the receiving end of delta feedback.

Receiving feedback can be more effective when the recipient of the feedback follows some simple rules. First, when receiving delta feedback it is important to reserve judgment on the message. This requires that the person who is receiving the feedback must *actively* listen to the message. People commonly, almost instinctively, move into a defensive posture, defending the behavior in question rather than actually hearing what the feedback provider is saying.

There are a number of things that the recipient of delta feedback can do to minimize the defensive posture. First, body language can help send the message that the feedback is being received. For example, the recipient should establish and maintain eye contact with the feedback provider. They should sit or stand in an open stance, rather than crossing their arms in a closed posture. The recipient should also be careful not to interrupt, allowing the feedback provider adequate time to finish a statement before responding.

It is understandably human to *feel* defensive about what is being said, regardless of how well the feedback is delivered. Thus, to allow time for the message to be digested, we suggest that the recipient first inquire about the feedback. This can be done by either asking for an example or asking the provider for more details.

Further, the recipient needs to acknowledge the feedback. This can be done without formally agreeing to change the behavior in question, and allows some time for the recipient to reflect on the feedback. Depending on the nature of the feedback, often the recipient can request time to reflect on the course of action he or she will take. A polite way to "buy" the time needed to consider the options is to confirm that the message has been received, and then suggest the possibility of scheduling an appointment to discuss the next steps at a future date. By doing this, the recipient of the feedback is not indicating there will be immediate change, nor are they ignoring the message.

Below are three feedback scenarios. In Scenario #1, we show feedback that is poorly given, and poorly received, as you would expect under these conditions. In Scenario #2, we show feedback that is properly provided, but poorly received by the recipient. Finally, in Scenario #3, we see feedback that is both provided and received properly.

Feedback Scenario #1 — Delta Feedback Poorly Given and Poorly Received

A Six Sigma team had experienced difficulty with Sharon, a member who was not following through with her assignments between meetings. Normally a solid performer, this team member had missed several assignments and had performed poorly on several others. It was time for the facilitator, Paul, to intervene. Unfortunately, this is what transpired:

Paul: "Sharon, I need to talk to you about your performance."

Sharon: "What do you mean, my 'performance?' I have been at every one of the Six Sigma meetings, even though they interfere with my normal work load."

Paul: "Well, Sharon, I've been wondering if you've had any bad team experiences in the past, because you are really letting the team down."

Sharon: "I have no idea what you mean. But now that you've brought it up, I would just as soon get off the team because my manager and I think Six Sigma is a waste of my valuable time."

Paul: "If that's the way you see it, fine. You haven't been contributing much anyway. This team can accomplish more without you. We'll call it 'addition through subtraction'."

This obviously was a poorly planned and executed intervention. Among his other faults, Paul didn't do his homework. If he had, he would have discovered that the issue with Sharon's performance might have had more to do with her manager's lack of support for Six Sigma than it did with Sharon. In addition to his not determining the root cause of Sharon's poor performance, his opening statement was neither specific nor aimed at her behavior. Stating specific behavioral comments about Sharon's attendance might have assisted her in sharing her apparent dilemma in serving two masters—her manager, who has some issue with her being on the Six Sigma team, as well as her colleagues on her team.

Note in this scenario that the feedback makes things far worse. As comments between Paul and Sharon escalate into personal attacks, both need to protect and defend their previous statements until ultimately they reach an impasse that will result in Sharon quitting the team.

This brings us to another key point in providing feedback—always allow the recipient an "exit strategy" if the initial response is defensive. Even when feedback is correctly provided, the recipient may not want to acknowledge what is obvious. Her reaction may be defensive even when she knows the feedback is accurate. A good facilitator will allow time for the feedback to be digested. Thus, delta feedback should not attempt to elicit an immediate change. Sometimes the willingness to make changes comes with time. This is yet another mistake Paul makes in the above scenario. He is caught off guard by Sharon's response. This surprise leads to Paul becoming defensive himself. Often the reason underlying a person's unwillingness to provide feedback is a fear of encountering results such as these.

Scenario #2—Delta Feedback Properly Given but Poorly Received

A Six Sigma team has experienced difficulty with Celeste, a team member who has been verbally abrasive toward others in the meeting. The situation is borderline since Celeste has an overall pleasant personality but seems to become excessive in teasing others. At first, the Six Sigma team leader/facilitator, Brian, simply observed the behavior without any intervention. It was not until Woody, another team member, complained to Brian about Celeste's behavior that he saw it as a problem. Brian initially felt compelled to personally provide the delta feedback to Celeste. After some reflection, however, he informed Woody that while he had originally considered handling the situation, he believed that Celeste would probably respond better if the feedback came from Woody. With some coaching from Brian on providing feedback, Woody agreed with Brian and decided to provide the feedback to Celeste himself.

> **Woody:** "Celeste, when you say I am insignificant and I don't add anything to the team, it hurts my feelings. It makes me feel I am an unworthy and unappreciated team member. In our last meeting, you called me a 'lightweight.' When you do that, I'm sure you are probably trying to be funny but it really doesn't have that effect on me."
>
> **Celeste:** "Oh, come on Woody. Don't you have a sense of humor?"
>
> **Woody:** "Your comments hurt me. I will try to get into the humor of this group, but I would be appreciative if you would be more sensitive to my feelings about your humor. I will do my best to laugh, even at myself, but if sometimes I don't, you may want to do a process check and see if my feelings are hurt."
>
> **Celeste:** "Oh, whatever."

In the above scenario, Woody has done several things very well. First, he was specific in his delta feedback, even referencing both the time and the specific comment that made him feel uncomfortable. Second, he did not go on the attack toward Celeste. Rather, he kept his comments directed toward her remarks (i.e., behavior) rather than calling her rude or insensitive. Third, he remained calm but insistent with his remarks when they were met by Celeste's resistance. Fourth, he provided an alternative for not only Celeste's behavior, but also his own (i.e., trying to get into her humor).

While Woody did a good job providing feedback, Celeste did not receive it well. She diminished Woody's feelings and failed to acknowledge either his feelings or her hurtful behavior.

While this does not appear to be a successful feedback session, only time will determine if further intervention is needed. First, it may take Celeste some time to reflect on this feedback. Upon reflection, she may see how serious Woody must have been to approach her about the impact her humor was having on him. Even if she does not change, the stage for a higher level intervention has been set by Woody. Now Brian can either intervene if Celeste's undesirable behavior continues, or establish a new ground rule that specifically addresses undesirable humor and enforce it with the concurrence of the team.

Scenario #3—Delta Feedback Properly Given and Properly Received

A Six Sigma team has experienced a problem with Nancy, a team member who is a naysayer. While not directly resistant to the team's work, Nancy is noted for her "Yes, but . . ." statements. John, the facilitator, has referenced ground rules about keeping an open mind, but to no avail. He now recognizes the need for an off-line intervention and plans to bring this up during a one-on-one meeting with Nancy between the scheduled Six Sigma meetings.

John: "Nancy, I first want to thank you for your hard work on this project. Your performance on collecting the customer survey data was exceptional. I have noticed that in our last two meetings when we have decided on our next set of customer surveys you *seem* to agree. However, I'm a bit puzzled but when you say 'Yes, but . . .' I am wondering if you're really on board."

Nancy: "Oh, I guess I support our approach but sometimes I am not sure. Apparently my ambivalence is showing, according to your comments."

John: "In your honest response to my thoughts, you provided a good example of a change that I believe would be helpful to the team's progress. You said, 'I guess I support our approach, *but* I'm not sure.' The word 'but' is an eraser for whatever comes before it. Your input is valuable to all of us. If you have issues with our approach, I suggest that you be more direct with regard to your concerns. And also become conscious about the *eraser effect* of saying 'Yes, but' . . ."

Nancy: "I wasn't even aware that I was doing that, John. I will work to be more conscious of that behavior. In addition, I'll also let you know when I have concerns. I appreciate your honesty with me."

This dialogue is positive from both perspectives—the giver *and* the receiver. John started by genuinely complimenting Nancy. The approach of beginning with a compliment before providing the delta feedback is fine as long as the compliment is sincere. If it is merely a ploy used to disarm the recipient, it will be seen as manipulative and it can backfire on the feedback provider. Here, it was both sincere and specific. From that point John was specific, highlighting his concern with Nancy's behavior. Nancy responded well by listening reflectively (e.g., "Your comments indicate that you are not always sure of my support") and then making a commitment to change her behavior by being more direct, and by becoming conscious about her use of "yes, but" in her comments.

Feedback can help make a Six Sigma team more effective and efficient. Following the example offered in our third scenario will help the Six Sigma team to be more comfortable in both providing and receiving delta feedback.

► Facilitative Session #2—Joy Schulenberg Tries Again

At the close of the tutorial on interventions and feedback, Joe Hawke tasked the Alpha Omega teams to return for one more practice facilitative session. He allowed the teams to select who will do the exercise—either the team leader or a team member.

As the Call Center team assembled in their breakout room, discussion was centered on their reactions to what they just had heard from Hawke. "That was great," Aaron Brown affirmed as he took his seat. "It really makes you realize that there's a whole lot of stuff that we need to manage other than just our project work."

Maria Carballo echoed Brown's statements, "I know we have lots of personality diversity in this room. Clearly, we're going to need good intervention skills."

Charles Zukor was again an observer in the second session. The next comment by Jeff Seimonson impressed him. "You're right, Maria. We have lots of interesting personalities here. I suggest we try to do our best to appreciate our differences as we move forward on this project."

As Seimonson concluded his comment, it was time for the second facilitative exercise to begin. Schulenberg asked the team members if they would mind if she gave it a second try. She told them she would like to have an opportunity to practice what she had just learned in the debrief with Kylie, along with the tutorial from Joe. Probably due to both her earnestness and the fact that no one else wanted to do the facilitation exercise, she got a "thumbs up" from the entire team.

Since Wednesday's schedule called for an evening session, Joy suggested they use "picking a local Denver restaurant for the Wednesday meeting" as the topic for the facilitative leadership exercise. She asked for five minutes of preparation time. In those five minutes, she prepared the flip charts. She started with the agenda, allowing what she thought was sufficient time for each element that would lead to choosing a specific restaurant for their Wednesday evening working session. Then she quickly created the parking lot. Following that, she taped a third flip chart sheet to the wall and titled it "Ground rules." Finally, she wrote on a fourth flip chart the words "Desired Outcomes" and beneath it wrote:

> To choose a restaurant in the Denver area for our Wednesday evening working session.

She broke open another pad of Post-it notes and spread them on the tables. She then opened a box of flip chart markers and again carefully placed one next to each Post-it note pad, just as she had done in her first session. Joy's prework is found in Figure 4.4.

Just as the five minutes of prep time were up, Joy was ready to begin. Once again, she began the session by reviewing the agenda, followed by assigning the roles and responsibilities for the timekeeper and scribe. Aaron Gregson was designated as the timekeeper,

Agenda Element	Outcome	Method	Person	Time (Minutes)
Review agenda	Agreement	Discussion	Facilitator	5
Select a place to eat	Agreement on where to eat	Affinity Diagram	Team	30
Plus/Delta	Assessment of meeting	Plus/Delta	Team	5

Desired Outcomes

To choose a restaurant in the Denver area for our Wednesday evening working session.

Parking Lot

$$\ggg\!\!\ggg$$

Ground Rules:

_____

_____

_____

_____

Figure 4.4 Proposed agenda—Alpha Omega Breakout.

and she asked Suzanne to be the scribe. Joy indicated that she wanted Aaron to give her 10 minute and 5 minute warnings for the selection section of the agenda.

Deciding on a different approach to the ground rule enforcer role, Joy said she would be the primary ground rule enforcer, and would appreciate everyone participating in the enforcement of the ground rules. At this point, Kylie informed Joy that while she was taking her 5 minutes to prep, Kylie had privately instructed the group to engage in several maladaptive behaviors during the session. Although Joy didn't know what the behaviors would be, her confidence was not swayed with the knowledge that "something was up."

She was more careful this time as she brainstormed ground rules with the group. Unlike her first time when it only took 3 minutes to get through the preliminary work, in this session it took the full 5 minutes that had been allocated. The additional time focused on a lengthier list of ground rules agreed upon by the team:

- ➤ No sidebar discussions.
- ➤ One person speaks at a time.
- ➤ Everyone participates.
- ➤ No cell phones.
- ➤ Talk to the ideas generated, not the person.
- ➤ No digressions.
- ➤ Stick to the agenda.
- ➤ Use the timekeeper.
- ➤ No "stripes" in the room.

To ensure everyone's participation, she thought it would be wise to use the Affinity Diagram, a simple tool in which the first step was for everyone to brainstorm their ideas about where to eat dinner on Wednesday, and write the ideas on Post-it notes. Wanting to avoid making the mistake she made the last time, she tried using a negative poll. "Does anyone have any objection to using a tool called the Affinity Diagram? The first step is to write possible restaurant locations on Post-it notes and put them here on the wall."

Zukor was again surprised when Wallace offered his input. "The first step seems easy enough, Joy. Let's give it a try."

Within a couple of minutes, there were 15 Post-it notes hanging on the wall. Next, Joy told the team she would review each Post-it note and, if everyone understood the restaurant location, she would go on to the next one. She would continue this procedure until she was sure that everyone on the team understood each of the brain-stormed locations. She stressed that no one should comment about whether they liked or disliked the location; only to comment if they needed clarification about the location. Joy quickly went through all 15 brainstormed locations with only one item questioned. It was a place called Bahama Breeze. Leroy inquired about the location, indicating that he had never heard of it. Joy asked the author of that location to explain. Maria said that it was a busy Westminster bar and restaurant that served Caribbean food. Leroy thanked Maria for the explanation, and that concluded this part of the exercise.

As Joy read each of the Post-it notes, she placed them in similar categories. Unbeknownst to the group, she was placing them in categories based on the type of food (i.e., Chinese, Caribbean, Italian, and so forth). By the time she had finished reading the notes to the team, she had created five categories.

Just as she was about to finish the clarification portion of the Affinity Diagram, Robert and Jeff began whispering. Whether it was the behavior assigned to them by Kylie or not, Joy was ready for her first intervention. Without interrupting her clarification activity, she made eye contact with both Robert and Jeff. Her eye contact was casual but sustained. As she turned around to read the last of the Post-it notes, she heard their continued whispers.

As she finished the last Post-it note, she turned and began walking in the direction of Robert and Jeff, again establishing eye contact with the two men. Even before Joy had a chance to see if this second, but still low-level intervention worked, she inquired, "Robert, do you or Jeff have any other suggestions before we categorize our locations?" "Uh, no, Joy. We don't."

Confidently, Joy then began the next stage of the Affinity Diagram—to name each of the categories in which she had placed the 15 Post-its. Just before she started, she turned to Aaron and asked for a status on time. Checking his watch, Aaron responded, "We have 20 minutes left."

Over the course of the next 10 minutes, Joy had the team generate names for each of the five restaurant location categories. Suzanne scribed the team's work (see Figure 4.5).

Joy then explained that the next step is to multi-vote. She gave out five sticky dots to each team member. When Leroy asked her why they got 5 dots, Joy told him that she arrived at that number by using a formula she had been taught in college. "The formula," she explained, "is $n/3$, where n is the number of items being voted on. Since we have 15 items that we'll be voting on, I divided that number by three and got five. So everyone gets 5 dots."

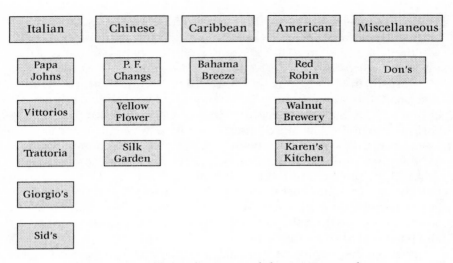

Figure 4.5 Affinity diagram—Alpha Omega Breakout.

Just as Joy finished giving out the dots to the last of the team members, she noticed Maria Carballo reading a newspaper. While the rest of the team members began to vote for their chosen locations, Maria stayed in her seat and continued to read.

Okay, thought Joy, this is yet another opportunity for a low-level intervention. She quietly sat down next to Maria, and in a soft voice said, "Maria, we really need everyone to participate. Could you make sure to vote before you go back to that article?" Message sent and received. Maria smiled as she went to the wall and voted.

"How much time left, Aaron?" Joy was told they had 10 minutes left before having to do the pluses/deltas for the meeting. Turning back to the Post-it note votes, she then reviewed the results of the voting aloud so that everyone could hear. As she did this, she stressed that multi-voting was not decision making. She informed them that it was simply a tool used to help prioritize the list of restaurant locations. Following is the prioritized list of finalists, along with the number of votes each received.

P.F. Chang's 8 votes

Giorgio's 4 votes

Walnut Brewery 3 votes

Once again, Joy used a negative poll in the restaurant selection exercise, "Is there anyone who would resist if we chose to go to P.F.

Pluses	Deltas
Completed task Used quality tools effectively Timely meeting Good intervention by facilitator Balanced participation	None

Figure 4.6 Pluses/Delta's—Alpha Omega Breakout.

Chang's?" With no negative responses, Joy indicated that P.F. Chang's had been chosen as the restaurant for tomorrow evening's meeting. Aaron glanced at his watch and announced, "We have five minutes left for this section of the agenda, Joy."

"Would anyone object if we finished up with pluses/deltas and took an early break?" Joy enjoyed yet another opportunity to use her new favorite facilitator technique—the negative poll.

The pluses/deltas list was reviewed with little discussion. The only delta, "none," prompted Joy to clarify the meaning of the feedback. The team members responded that this was the way they wanted *all* of their DMAIC meetings to run. Figure 4.6 shows the pluses/deltas for the meeting.

With that, the Call Center team finished the day and retired to the Omni bar for drinks and appetizers. (In Six Sigma parlance, this is called the "drinking process.") The content work of their team, along with the 10 other Alpha Omega Six Sigma project teams, was about to begin. They were upbeat and looking forward to tomorrow's session.

■ SUMMARY

Chapter 4 addressed the key components of the second key element of facilitative leadership—interventions. The *10 Mortal Sins of Facilitative Leadership* were introduced. They included such "sins" as *doing the work for the team* and *having a bias toward one person on the team* or a *bias toward a particular tool or idea*. We also introduced typical maladaptive behaviors that tend to exhibit themselves in Six Sigma meetings, from the whisperer to the team clown. We then covered the *intervention spectrum* and stressed why it is important to begin with lower level interventions to reduce or eliminate maladaptive behavior. Finally, we provided ways to both *provide* and *receive* feedback in a way that can sustain positive Six Sigma team dynamics.

KEY LEARNINGS

➤ There are two components to facilitative leadership—*prevention* and *intervention.* In this chapter, we discussed when and how to use interventions when Six Sigma meetings go bad.

➤ There are 10 "Mortal Sins" of facilitation. They include:

1. Choosing which comments made by the team are *worthy* of being documented.
2. Interpreting or modifying the words spoken and recording the "spin" on the input rather than documenting what is actually said.
3. Having a bias toward one tool or technique, or creating the impression of a bias toward an idea or a team member.
4. Permitting digressions without intervention.
5. Permitting ground rules to be broken without intervention.
6. Speaking emotionally charged words, or allowing another member of the team to do so.
7. Allowing distrust or disrespect to occur between the facilitator and the team, or between team members.
8. Failure to create a sense of purpose regarding the team's goals or objectives.
9. Ignoring timekeeping or underestimating the amount of time needed to get an agenda item accomplished.
10. Doing the work for the team.

➤ The most common types of maladaptive behaviors a facilitator will have to manage include the Whisperer, the Storyteller, the Dominant Personality, the Dropout, the Naysayer, the Verbal Attacker, the Politician, and the Team Clown.

➤ The levels of interventions run a spectrum from low to high. Lower level interventions include making eye contact with the person exhibiting maladaptive behavior as well as approaching the person while continuing the work of the team. Higher level interventions include re-directing the person, talking to the person off line, to the highest level intervention which is confronting the person in the meeting.

➤ With rare exceptions, interventions should start at a low level on the *intervention spectrum* as a means to maintain the recipient's dignity and self-respect.

(Continued)

➤ In addition to intervention skills, there are multiple facilitation skills necessary for effective facilitation:

- The *direct probe*—The facilitator directly asks the team or team member a question that helps the team bring out or clarify an idea.
- The *indirect probe*—The facilitator asks a question to test out a theory or perception.
- The *re-direct*—The facilitator may sense that the team is digressing from the desired outcome for an issue on the agenda, and rather than focusing exclusively on the enforcement of broken ground rules, uses re-directing comments to refocus the groups attention.
- *Confirmatory statement* or *paraphrase*—The facilitator confirms what a team member is saying. Confirmatory statements help to clarify what is being said and also aid the team in concluding a discussion.
- *Leading questions*—The facilitator "jump starts" the discussion if he or she thinks the team has reached a premature conclusion.
- *Behavioral observation*—The facilitator makes an observation that states the obvious as a means to keep the Six Sigma moving forward in its work.
- *Idea floating*—The facilitator participates indirectly in the discussion by asking questions that address the facilitator's thoughts or ideas.
- The *boomerang*—The facilitator throws, or "boomerangs," a question asked by a team member back to the team for a response.
- The *lasso*—The facilitator combines several thoughts from different Six Sigma team members into one combined thought.

➤ Feedback, both giving and receiving, is comprised of techniques that are crucial to a Six Sigma team's success.

➤ Feedback should be focused on the behavior of the recipient. A statement such as "When you . . . I feel . . . because . . ." is the best way to ensure the dignity and self-respect of those receiving feedback.

➤ When receiving feedback, it is important to keep an open mind, listen reflectively, and allow time for the message to be absorbed.

Chapter 5

Managing the
Six Sigma Project

"I don't skate to where the puck is, I skate to where it will be."

Wayne Gretzky

In our last two chapters, we discussed the importance of facilitative leadership in the Six Sigma team. Both facilitative preventions and interventions were discussed as important elements in achieving improved sigma performance. In Chapter 5, we move into management of the actual DMAIC content work using our Alpha Omega Call Center project. We will address the importance of project management skills as an important core competency to achieve the milestones in the DMAIC methodology. In Chapter 3, we discussed the role and responsibilities of the Project Champion *before* the project team was formed. In Chapter 5, we return to the role of the Champion, focusing on what the Champion needs to do during the four- to eight-month period their Six Sigma team exists as they apply the DMAIC methodology. Finally, we will take the Alpha Omega team through the first two elements of DMAIC (Define and Measure) and share some of the pitfalls they encounter that virtually every Six Sigma team goes through during this initial application of Six Sigma to their project work.

■ MANAGING DEFINE—TOLLGATE #1 (THE PROJECT TEAM'S CHARTER)

The Alpha Omega team settled into their seats for the important third day of training which would focus on the DMAIC education. Joe

Hawke began in earnest punctually at 8:30 A.M., reviewing the ground rules and agenda for the day. Figure 5.1 shows the agenda for the third day of training for the Alpha Omega teams.

Joe Hawke began with a tutorial on DMAIC, "How many people have children in the 4th, 5th, or 6th grade?"

A few hands rose casually as Joe Hawke continued. "Well, I have a son who came back from school on one of those rare days I was home being the father I should be. I asked as he came through the door what was the most interesting thing he learned that day at school."

"My son responded that in science class he learned the scientific method. My son went on to describe the steps in the scientific method. 'First, Dad, we learned to identify the problem. Second, we learned to quantify the problem to determine how bad it is. Third, we determined root causes for why the problem exists. Then we formed hypotheses that will impact root causation. We then tested and implemented the proven hypotheses and learned methods to control our new solutions.'

"When my son told me about his fifth-grade experience, I told him to study well. The scientific method is the foundation for the DMAIC improvement methodology. We will first learn how to define the problem associated with your current process. We then will measure current performance and determine the magnitude of the problem. In Analysis, we will determine the root causes of our current sigma performance. We will create solutions about how to change the process in a way to increase effectiveness and efficiency. This will happen in the Improve phase of the project. Finally, we will learn how to control our newly improved process.

"How many of you have ever been on a turnpike?" Several hands were raised as Joe Hawke continued. "If you have been on a turnpike you know periodically you have to stop at tollgates to pay the toll. In

---

➤ Review agenda, ground rules, and expectations.
➤ Tutorial—Overview of DMAIC.
➤ Tutorial—Overview of Define and the three tollgates of Define.
➤ Breakout 1—Define Tollgate #1—The team's Charter.
➤ Report-outs on the team's Charter.
➤ Tutorial on the second tollgate of Define—Customers, their needs, and requirements.
➤ Breakout 2—The project's customers, needs, and requirements.
➤ Wrap up day 3 of training.

Figure 5.1   Agenda—Alpha Omega day 3 training.

each element of Define, Measure, Analyze, Improve, and Control (DMAIC), there are similar tollgates. Each of these elements have two or three tollgates or subtasks for each project team to address before they move on to the next element of DMAIC."

Hawke then turned on the overhead projector and showed the overhead reflected in Figure 5.2. He proceeded to review the overhead describing the Define element and its associated tollgates. The three tollgates of Define include the Project Charter; Determining Customers, their Needs and Requirements; and Creating the High-Level Process Map.

"In our work with you today, we will focus on the Define tollgates. We will provide you with a tutorial on the elements of each tollgate one at a time. Then we will task you to begin work on that tollgate during a series of breakout sessions. It is important to recognize that you will not be done with the work of the tollgate during these breakout sessions. Instead, you will get some work done and recognize the work that remains to be done during *intersession work*. This intersession work refers to the time between the end of our training Friday and the day we return on April 8. On Friday, we will tell you the details of what your team needs to be working on relative to this important intersession work."

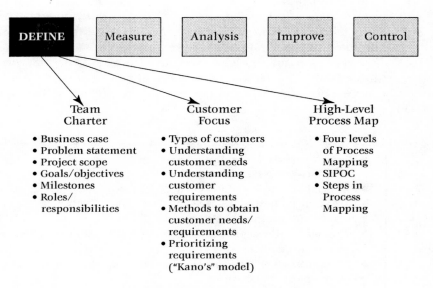

Figure 5.2 Define tollgates.

Joe Hawke spends the next 45 minutes on the Charter tollgate tutorial. He reviews that the Charter is made up of a business case, a preliminary problem statement, goals and objectives for the project, agreement on project Scope, establishment of the project milestones, and understanding the various roles and responsibilities of the project team.

As the tutorial concludes, Joe Hawke shows an overhead of a two-page template that he encourages each of the 11 project teams to use during their breakouts (Figure 5.3). For the team's first breakout he asks the team to work on their Charters. While the Project Champions had specifically been asked to not attend Wednesday's training, each had been requested to be available to answer questions or resolve issues that arise from the project team's work.

The 11 Alpha Omega teams proceed to their breakout rooms to begin actual Six Sigma work on their projects. The Call Center team went to the Cedar conference room that was to be their workroom during the training. They were tasked with getting through as much of their project Charter as possible with the full recognition that most of the work would be done during the intersession back at Alpha Omega headquarters.

Joy Schulenberg proceeded to set up the Cedar conference room while her other team members took their 20-minute morning break. Just as she had for her two generic facilitative exercises, she wrote out a detailed agenda for the 90-minute session on chartering. Figure 5.4 shows the Call Center's Charter, agenda, decision-making method, ground rules, and parking lot.

The 90-minute breakout for the Call Center project team went quickly and uneventfully for the most part. Thanks to the prework of Charles Zukor, most of the work was the review, discussion, and agreement of the work he had done before the team's formation. The Business Case was quickly approved as a thoughtful and motivating statement about the need to improve effectiveness and efficiency in the Call Center.

During the discussion of Charles Zukor's problem statement, Suzanne Jackson made note that the problem statement could be made more specific before the team collected data in the Measure phase of the project. She indicated that Alpha Omega and other businesses used a call index that reflects how often Call Centers are used. Various organizations like Alpha Omega had hired a market research firm that collected data on industry standards for the use of an organization's Call Centers. Suzanne had indicated that the industry standard for Call Center use from this market research group had shown

	Six Sigma Project Charter
Business Case (Connection to SBOs)	

Project Scope

IN	OUT

Goal and Objectives	Subject Matter Experts

APPROVAL

Champion:

Date:

Team Leader:

Date:

Six Sigma Director:

Date:

Figure 5.3 Charter template.

Problem Statement		

Expected Benefits	Target	Stretch
Total Savings	$ –	$ –

Milestones Start Date	Plan	Actual
Define		
Measure		
Analyze		
Improve		
Control		
Team:		
Champion		
Team Leader		
Master Black Belt		
Team Members	Role	Percent of Time

Figure 5.3 *(Continued)*

Element	Desired Outcome	Method	Responsible Party	Time Allotted
Review agenda and ground rules.	Agreement on agenda and ground rules.	Discussion and consensus	Joy and Team	5 min.
Review Business Case for Call Center project.	Provide champion input on Business Case.	Discussion and consensus	Joy and Team	15 min.
Review problem statement for Call Center project.	Provide Champion input on the problem statement.	Discussion and consensus	Joy and Team	15 min.
Review project Scope.	Determine additional items for what is inside and outside the project Scope.	Scope exercise (In/Out/? exercise)	Joy and Team	20 min.
Review roles and responsibilities.	Determine roles and responsibilities for Call Center team.	Discussion and consensus	Joy and Team	10 min.
Review the milestones for the project.	Gain agreement on timeline and determine amount of participation.	Discussion and consensus	Joy and Team	20 min.

Figure 5.4 Charter agenda—Alpha Omega Breakout.

Element	Desired Outcome	Method	Responsible Party	Time Allotted
Pluses/ Deltas	Determine what went well and what could be done different for the next meeting.	Plus/Delta exercise	Joy and Team	5 min.

Note: Decision-making method: Consensus with a back-up of two-third's majority vote.

Ground Rules:

➤ Everyone participates.
➤ No sidebar conversations.
➤ No "stripes" in the room.
➤ Cell phones and other electronic devices on vibrate.
➤ Keep an open mind.
➤ Stick to the agenda.
➤ Use the tools as they are supposed to be used.

Figure 5.4 *(Continued)*

that the industry norm was 30 percent whereas Alpha Omega's Call Center's index was 42 percent (where less is better). With this knowledge on already existing data, the Call Center modified Charles Zukor's problem statement from:

> *Since _____, Alpha Omega's Call Center has experienced _____ decrease in first call resolution, which has resulted in _____ customer satisfaction ratings. In addition, courtesy ratings of Alpha Omega's Call Center has reduced from a high of _____ in 1999 to _____ in 2001, which has resulted in a reduction of Alpha Omega's revenue.*

To:

> *Since _____, Alpha Omega's Call Center has experienced a call index of 42 percent versus the industry standard of 30 percent. This has negatively impacted customer satisfaction and*

operating expenses, placing Alpha Omega at a competitive disad-
vantage in meeting its Strategic Business Objectives for operating
profit and customer satisfaction.

The net effect of the two different problem statements meant that Joy had to meet with Charles and reconcile the two statements. This meeting between team leader and Champion should occur within the first week of the completion of the first training session. This meeting is meant to reconcile all outstanding issues coming out of the input provided by the team for the project Charter. As Kylie had indicated to Charles (in Chapter 2), even the best Champion will not be able to brainstorm every item associated with the project's Charter. Thus, the input of the team is vital to creating the final, validated Charter that ultimately is decided by the Champion. In this case, the two problem statements (one created by Charles, the Champion, and the other by the project team) need to be reconciled not just because of issues associated with wordsmithing. In the first problem statement, courtesy is on the "radar screen" of the project team. In the second problem statement, it isn't. In the first problem statement, the issue of the index being an ultimate issue to deal with isn't mentioned but if approved it will become a major focus for the project team. There isn't a right or wrong answer, necessarily. What is important is for the Champion to act quickly and reconcile the issue so the project team can proceed.

With regard to the project Scope, the team had little to add to Charles Zukor's list. They did the project Scope exercise where three Post-it notes were on the wall. The first Post-it note had the label "IN," while the second Post-it note had the label "OUT," and the last Post-it note was labeled with a question mark. Joy then instructed each team member to write out what they thought was inside the Scope of the Call Center project and what was outside the Scope of the project. Finally, if they were uncertain, they were to place that idea in the question mark column.

Silently, each member wrote their ideas, one per Post-it note, and posted them on the wall of the Cedar breakout room. When the team had finished posting their ideas, Joy approached the wall.

"All right, similar to our exercise using the Affinity Diagram, I will now read off each note in the In column. If you understand what it means, say nothing, even if you disagree with that idea being inside the Scope of our work. If you need clarification, speak up and we will get the clarification needed by the author of that note." Joy quickly reviewed the first three notes:

➤ External calls.

➤ Issues related to first call resolution.

➤ Issues related to the 42 percent index rate.

After reading the fourth note, "Other processes," Aaron Brown asked for clarification. The author, Jeff Seimonson, clarified his thoughts that if other processes meant that the data led the way into other processes, the Call Center should follow this information and consider it part of the Scope of the Call Center project.

At that moment Aaron began to disagree, saying he thought that should be outside the Scope of the project. Suddenly, Joy interjected, "Okay, we said we wouldn't be discussing opinion here, just seeking clarification. Aaron, if you understand what Jeff said, I will take Jeff's note and your input, and place them in the question mark column. This will be a decision for Charles to reconcile in my meeting with him next week."

The majority of the group looked on with nonverbal admiration at what Joy had just done. Rather than allow a hearty debate on whether this issue should or should not be inside the Scope of the Call Center team, she used the tool effectively, cut off debate, and promised the group an answer from the only person who had a vote on the matter, the Project Champion, Charles Zukor.

From there, the Scope exercise was completed with the three columns of work completed by the Call Center team found in Figure 5.5.

With plenty of time to spare, the Call Center team had completed what was expected of them by way of their first content breakout. They had over 10 minutes left in the meeting agenda time by the time they did their pluses/deltas list. The list was top heavy with pluses. Among that list was completing the task in a timely manner, the facilitation and interventions of Joy throughout the meeting, but particularly during the Scope exercise. There were only two deltas. One was that Joy had not been able to answer a question around understanding the role of the Champion during the time the project team was to exist. The other delta was a vague reference to the imbalance in participation among the Call Center team during the 90-minute breakout. With regard to the first delta, she made a mental note to ask either Joe Hawke or Kylie Madrid for their thoughts on the subject. Joy did not ask for clarification on the second delta. She had observed the less-than-total participation on the part of Robert Wallace and Jeff Seimonson. They had exhibited passive participation. There was no overt maladaptive behavior but clearly they were just going through the motions. Joy

Alpha Omega	Six Sigma Project Charter

Business Case (Connection to SBOs)

Alpha Omega has experienced significant decline in its operating profits and customer satisfaction, both of which are strategic business objectives. To positively influence both, improvement must occur across all business processes. Currently, the Call Center could positively impact customer satisfaction and operating profits through improvement of first call resolution, timeliness of response, and improvement in courtesy to the customer.

Project Scope

IN	OUT
External calls	*Policy issues with customers*
Issues related to first call resolution	*Organization structure*
Job descriptions	
Process redesign	
	?
	Other processes
	Customer index
	Customer courtesy

Goal and Objectives	Subject Matter Experts
Reduce the call index from 42% to 36%	

APPROVAL	
Champion:	
Date:	
Team Leader:	
Date:	
Six Sigma Director:	
Date:	

Figure 5.5 Completed charter template.

Problem Statement		
Since ___, Alpha Omega's Call Center has experienced a call index of 42% versus the industry standard of 30%. This has negatively impacted customer satisfaction and operating expenses placing Alpha Omega at a competitive disadvantage in meeting its strategic business objectives for operating profit and customer satisfaction.		
Expected Benefits	**Target**	**Stretch**
Total Savings	$ –	$ –
Milestones **Start Date**	**Plan**	**Actual**
Define	February 6, 7, & 8	
Measure	February 6, 7, & 8	
Analyze	April 8, 9, 10, 11, & 12	
Improve	May 21, 22, & 23	
Control	June 25, 26	
Team:		
Champion	Charles Zukor	
Team Leader	Joy Schulenberg	
Master Black Belt		
Team Members	**Role**	**Percent of Time**
Aaron Gregson		
Maria Carballo		
Leroy Barney		
Robert Wallace		
Susan Jackson		
Aaron Brown		
Jeff Seimonson		

Figure 5.5   *(Continued)*

didn't yet have a strategy for this issue. She thought she would reiterate compliance with the ground rules for balanced participation during the Call Center's next breakout, but she was less than optimistic that this would solve what she was sure to be a lingering issue with her potential resistors.

When the 11 project teams reassembled in large group, Joy took some pride in observing her team being one of the first back in the room. She did notice that most teams came back with several minutes to spare before Joe Hawke took center stage. Hawke began immediately after his timer went off with only one team (the Merchant Launch team) trailing in late from the assigned 90-minute breakout.

"I will start each large group session after a breakout by asking you two general questions," said the well-tanned, attractive, and articulate native of Palm Harbor, Florida. "First, what went well in your breakout? After we have discussed your pluses, we will move to our second question, what you struggled with during the breakout."

Most teams reported their work around the Business Case and problem statement went well. There was a degree of hesitancy about what went well overall, though each team stated they were off to a good start relative to the first tollgate of Define, the project Charter.

When it came time to discuss what the teams struggled with, there was greater enthusiasm. Most teams struggled with project Scope. Uncertain of what should be inside the Scope and what should be outside the Scope. Both Joe Hawke and Kylie Madrid emphasized that the team leader should simply take their ideas generated in the breakout, and within a week of the close of training on Friday, meet with their Project Champion. This meeting is when the project Charter should be validated and finalized. While the project team provides input to the Charter, the Champion sets the strategic direction for the team. One major way they do this is through determination of project Scope.

The discussion of the Champion validating the project Charter prompted Joy to ask Joe Hawke her question about the role of the Champion during the existence of the project team. Joe Hawke proceeded to inform the teams of the importance of an active, involved Project Champion. He also discussed the importance of "managing upward." This meant coaching the Champion into better Champion behaviors as the project teams begin to gain far greater knowledge through their training. Listed next are the key points Joe Hawke discussed relative to the Champion's role during the four to eight months a project team is in existence.

➤ The Champion's Responsibilities *during* the Project Team's Existence

Below, in order of importance, are the responsibilities of the Champion during the team's existence:

1. *Validate and finalize the Charter.* A pivotal role for the Champion is to validate and finalize the Charter. The largest responsibility relative to the Charter is to take the input regarding Scope generated by the team in their first meeting and determine whether their ideas result in an item being inside the Scope of the team or outside. Champions are encouraged to have limited Scope in first projects. In addition to learning the Six Sigma methodology, project teams are expected to produce actual results associated with the processes selected for improvement. Champions are always encouraged to limit the Scope of projects so that they maximize the opportunity for their teams to succeed. In addition to project Scope, the Champion must validate any additional input relative to team membership. Many times, when the teams review the team members, they will notice a subject matter expert who should have been a part of the team. The suggestions for additional team membership (even if only on an ad hoc basis) should be taken under advisement by the Champion and resolved quickly. To a lesser extent, Champions may be provided with input from the team relative to missing items on the Business Case or problem statement. As we see from the Call Center project, issues raised by the team will impact the problem statement as well as the project Scope. It is strongly recommended that this validation and finalization of the team Charter be done within one week of the conclusion of the project team's first week of training.

2. *Monitor and approve all project team tollgate work.* A good Project Champion will not overmanage their team. However, he or she should at a minimum review all work for each tollgate. Some tollgates are so significant that they are stand-alone reviews for the Project Champion. For example, as we have just stated, the project Charter is of such importance it should be a stand-alone tollgate review for the Champion. In other cases, several tollgates can be combined in a single review. As we shall see shortly, tollgates 2 and 3 of Define can be combined into a single review and approval session.

3. *Meet regularly with the team leader/facilitator.* One of the most important responsibilities a Project Champion has over the course of the four to eight months the project team exists is to meet with the team leader/facilitator a minimum of once a week. This meeting could last as little as 30 minutes. For more formal tollgate reviews, the meeting could be more extensive. However, this weekly meeting is imperative for the ultimate success of the project.

4. *Remove barriers or roadblocks to the team's success.* Over the course of a team's existence, barriers and roadblocks that call for management attention are inevitable. For example, what if a team member begins missing regularly scheduled Six Sigma meetings? If the team leader/facilitator determines that the team member's manager doesn't support his or her employees involvement in Six Sigma, the manager may directly or indirectly influence the participation of that team member's involvement with the team. This situation would necessitate the Champion approaching the team members' manager with the goal of gaining greater support for the participation of the team member in question. Another example of roadblock removal requiring Champion involvement is if their team is not receiving the necessary support from such functions as finance or information technology. If support from these groups is not sufficient, it is the responsibility of the Champion to assist the team in gaining support from these functions. There are a host of other barriers and roadblocks too numerous to mention here. A good Champion will actively solicit from his or her team leader/facilitator whether there are roadblocks getting in the way of the team rather than just be reactive to requests for help generated by the team leader/facilitator.

5. *Maintain momentum of the team and keep them on task.* Project teams working on DMAIC will normally exist four to eight months. Any team that exists for that period of time will reach plateaus or become discouraged with the course of their project. If this discouragement or frustration is allowed to grow, there is greater likelihood that deadlines will be missed or performed poorly. It is the responsibility of the Project Champion to maintain the momentum of the team. In some cases, this may call for the Champion to attend the beginning of a Six Sigma meeting and reiterate the importance of the project. Referencing the business case can be of value here. Reinforcing why the project is worth doing, why is it worth doing now, and why this project has priority over other work can help reinvigorate the team members. Many times, the focus of this encouragement will be aimed at the team leader/facilitator who will play a more day-to-day role in maintaining momentum. In addition, it is important for the Champion to maintain adherence to the milestones that are a part of every project team Charter.

6. *Deal with resistance among the team.* Team members are made up of subject matter experts. Many of these subject matter experts will be selected for their knowledge and involvement of the process targeted for improvement, not their support for Six Sigma. Exacerbating this dilemma are team members who have been a part of a previous quality initiative that has failed. Resistance must be dealt with in a timely, direct manner. A later chapter will review the many strategies available for a Champion to deal with resistance. As we shall discuss, worse case scenarios call for the removal of the team member if resistance cannot be overcome.

7. *Communicate progress to upper management.* Particularly in first projects, upper management is expecting quantitative results. Rather than waiting for the results of the project and reporting the outcome, a good Champion will communicate progress (or the lack thereof) to upper management periodically through the course of the DMAIC training and implementation.

8. *Continuing education.* Most Champions receive limited training before the launch of their Six Sigma teams. At the same time, Six Sigma project teams over the course of four to eight months will receive far more extensive training on the improvement methodology. While the Champion does not need to know as much detail associated with Six Sigma as the team leader/facilitator, the Champions who hone their technical skills on DMAIC manage their projects better than those who don't. Therefore, Champions should augment their training with both reading and coaching from others who are content experts. For example, the master Black Belt in an organization is the Six Sigma subject matter expert. Good Champions will seek out coaching on DMAIC so that they can ask the type of questions that make for better project work.

9. *Recognize efforts.* In typical first projects, cost savings is the measure that determines the ultimate success or failure of Six Sigma. In the best-managed projects, this may take months after the conclusion of the project team's work. Even when things are going well on a Six Sigma team, this long-term goal may not sustain enthusiasm for the team. Thus, it is the responsibility of the Champion to recognize efforts. This could be as simple as treating for pizza during a Six Sigma meeting or obtaining a free personal day for the team members. Recognition of the team's efforts is a critical success factor to maintain the enthusiasm for the project.

10. *Re-evaluate Scope during the project.* As data are collected and analyzed over the course of the project's existence, the Scope may need to be re-evaluated. This usually happens after baseline data collection is available or after the data and/or process has been analyzed. It is not unusual for the data to lead to a logical expansion of Scope. However, expanding Scope, even legitimately, has significant hazards for a Six Sigma team. It is recommended that Scope be expanded on an extremely limited basis. It is preferred to identify a second wave project and keep the original project as it was Scoped. Nonetheless, a formal review of the Scope should be the domain of the Champion during the course of the project's existence.

■ MANAGING DEFINE—TOLLGATE #2 (CUSTOMERS, NEEDS, AND REQUIREMENTS)

At its core, Six Sigma attempts to increase customer satisfaction. Customers are defined as the recipient of the product or service. This definition implies that a customer can be internal to the organization, not just the external entity that pays the bill or invoice. In any Six Sigma project, it is imperative for the team to identify the customers of the process targeted for improvement.

Once the various customers of the process targeted for improvement have been identified, it is important to note whether the customer base needs to be stratified or segmented. Stratification or segmentation refers to determining which are your most important customers. This can be done based on market segment, geography, revenue impact, or general business importance. For example, airlines cater to millions of passengers a year. To the airlines, the more frequent a flyer, the more important that passenger is to a given airline. Thus, there is not equality relative to customers. Some are more important than others.

The reason stratification or segmentation is necessary is because different customers may have different needs and requirements. A customer's need is equivalent to the product or service desired by the customer. A requirement is some characteristic that determines whether a customer is happy with the product or service.

The second tollgate of Define requires the project team to determine who are the customers of the process targeted for improvement. Once identified, the project teams must determine the customers' needs and requirements. The work to accomplish achievement of this tollgate is divided into two stages. The first stage is for the team to brainstorm the customers of the targeted process, their needs, and requirements. The second and more important stage is for the team to validate these needs and requirements with the actual customers of the process targeted for improvement.

For the Call Center team, this second tollgate was a relatively easy breakout. One challenge always facing teams is whether current data is available for the project team to use as they progress through DMAIC. For project teams that don't have currently available data, more time will be needed to go out and collect data relative to their

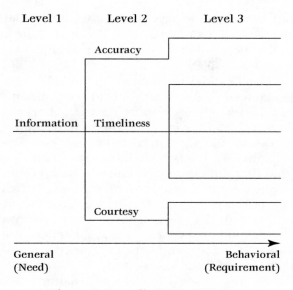

Level 1   Level 2   Level 3

Accuracy

Information   Timeliness

Courtesy

General   Behavioral
(Need)   (Requirement)

Figure 5.6   Call Center CTQ tree.

customers, their needs, and requirements. The market research group had done an admirable job in collecting data on Call Center needs and requirements. Joe Hawke had advised the use of the "Critical to Quality (CTQ) Tree." The CTQ tree takes the customer's need and breaks it out into more detailed, behavioral requirements. As Figure 5.6 indicates, this work was done through the information provided by the market research firm. It will be wise for the Call Center team to conduct some type of validation of the work that had been completed in the previous year. In Figure 5.6, the title clearly implies that the primary customer of the Call Center is the external customer. These external customers solicit the Call Center because of their need for information. This need for information has several key requirements including accuracy, timeliness, and courtesy.

■ MANAGING DEFINE—TOLLGATE #3 (CREATION OF THE HIGH-LEVEL "AS-IS" PROCESS MAP)

The first day of Define training was about to conclude with the last tutorial by Temojoe Consulting. This tutorial was focused on creation of the high-level "As-Is" Process Map. Sometimes called the "workhorse" tool of DMAIC, the process map is used during Define, Measure, Analyze, Improve, and Control. Thus, the work done by the project team on the first phase of Process Mapping is critical to the later success of the team.

Joe Hawke walks through an example of creating a Process Map using a generic example familiar to everyone in the training room. The example he chooses is buying a car. Hawke shares with his participants a model for creating the Process Map using a mnemonic device called SIPOC, which stands for Suppliers, Inputs, Process, Output, and Customers. This model states that suppliers provide inputs that through the steps in the process add value, which produces an output for the customer. SIPOC moves left to right. The final product reflects this movement. However, the steps in creating a SIPOC are slightly different. First, it is important to name the process. The name of the process should reflect some action word. It also provides the team a chance to impact the project Scope. Hawke shows that in the purchase of a car the name of the process could be the Car-Buying Process or the Car-Leasing Process. In the former, the Scope is more limited than in the latter. In the Car-Leasing Process, the process would last until the return of the car. Hawke cautions the teams to be careful of this dilemma occurring when they name their process. The second step in the process is establishing the boundaries (i.e., the start and stop points) of the process. Once again, Hawke cautions the teams that identifying the start and stop points of the process offers the teams a chance to impact project Scope. For the car-buying example, Hawke indicates the start point is the time he decides to buy the car (for him it was turning a certain age), and the stop point was driving the car off the lot.

Hawke goes on to use Post-it notes on the wall to indicate the next step in Process Mapping is to identify the output of the process that should be described as a noun. In the Car-Buying Process, the output is a car. Hawke stresses that many teams get into trouble by qualifying the noun with what later turns out to be requirements. He continues his tutorial by indicating the next step is to identify the customers of the process that in his car-buying example are his wife, children, and himself.

Hawke moves to the left side of the wall for next steps in Process Mapping. He stresses that processes can only be as good as the suppliers and the inputs they provide. In his example, he indicates two major suppliers, the car dealer (whose input is the car), and car magazines that Hawke researched to help him later negotiate the price of the car (thus, the magazine as a supplier provided the input of information). The last step in Process Mapping may be the most important. Hawke instructs the teams to brainstorm the five to seven highest level steps in the process as they exist today. Hawke shares several stories of Temojoe clients who succumbed to the temptation of creating the Process Map steps the way they want or desire the process to look. Hawke says this is eventually what we will do during the Improve phase of DMAIC work. However, creating how the process works currently is imperative during Define work. Hawke proceeds to craft the steps in his car-buying example and places them in the proper sequence. The results of his tutorial are found in Figure 5.7.

At the conclusion of the tutorial, Joe Hawke instructed the teams to work on Process Mapping. Hawke wanted the project teams to return to their breakout areas and create their impression of the current process. He stressed that this exercise did not complete Process Mapping. The breakout session, if done successfully, would indicate what the team thought the process looked like. Hawke indicated that one of the key responsibilities the teams had between training sessions was to verify the "As-Is" Process Map. This meant that between training sessions, the project team had to validate their Process Map through interviews with people currently operating in the process and/or following a product or service through the process.

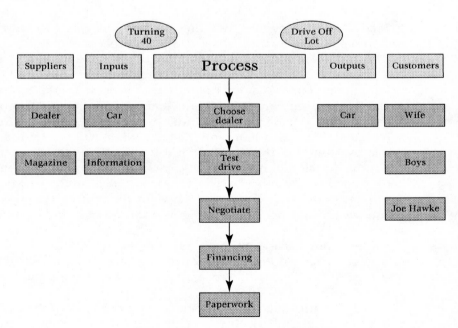

Figure 5.7 Car-buying process.

As the Call Center team assembled in the Cedar Room, it was just past 4:40 P.M. Hawke had indicated that the team could go as long as necessary in this last breakout and return on Thursday morning for training on the Measure phase of DMAIC at 8:30 A.M. Enthusiasm was running high and most Call Center team members wanted to put a major dent in the Process Mapping work before calling it a day.

Joy Schulenberg had Post-it notes available for all team members and reminded everyone of this breakout agenda's desired outcomes and ground rules before asking for ideas around the first step of Process Mapping; naming the process. She received several ideas that she captured on a flip chart and asked for discussion about the impact of them:

- The Call Center Reconcilement Process.
- The Customer Satisfaction Process.
- The Customer Complaint Process.
- The Call Center Information Process.
- The Customer Resolution Process.

All ideas generated had merit. Each author tried to create the case for his or her idea. Aaron Brown then came up with an idea that helped break the logjam. "Why not use the concept of the negative poll to see if we can eliminate any of these process names?"

With that suggestion, two of the listed names were agreed to be too expansive in Scope. Consensus was achieved that the Call Center Reconcilement and Customer Satisfaction Process would be similar to the Car Leasing name that Hawke had used as a lengthier process. It clearly would involve multiple other processes. While Jeff Seimonson argued that their Champion, Charles Zukor, had not resolved the Scope issue, most of the team said it was unlikely that Charles would make the decision to expand the Scope of the project. So not to lose Jeff's thoughts, Joy agreed to place these two ideas in the parking lot, so if Charles decided on a larger Scope for the project, these process names would not be forgotten. Seimonson seemed mildly pleased with this decision.

After more discussion, the group tentatively decided on the Call Center Information Process after deciding the Customer Resolution and Customer Complaint Process were too narrow for the type of work done in the Call Center.

With the title tentatively chosen (in Figure 5.8, all of the work for this breakout is shown), the team goes on to brainstorm where the

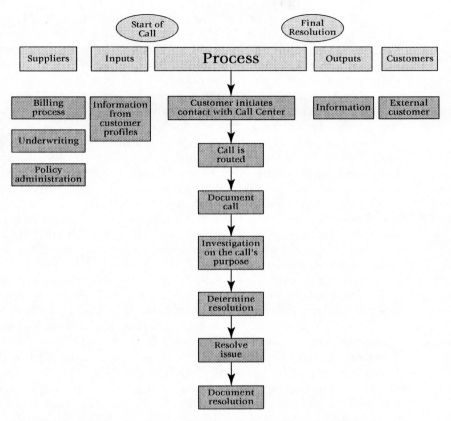

Figure 5.8   Call Center information process.

Call Center Information Process begins and ends. Within minutes, they had agreed that the process starts with the customer contacting an Alpha Omega customer service representative, and the process ends with final resolution of the customer's inquiry.

With these first two Process Map steps completed, the Call Center team moves on to the third step in Process Mapping: naming the output of the process. Indicating the output of the process as information was done quickly, with Suzanne Jackson noticing the output is equivalent to the customer's need.

The group continues by indicating the external customer as the customer. Aaron Gregson brings up an interesting question by stating he thinks management is a secondary customer. Kylie Madrid had been observing in the back of the room and jumped in when Gregson brought up his statement about management. Kylie went on to say that it is a rare event when management is actually the customer. Instead, she introduces the concept of the stakeholder, which she defines as someone affected by the team's project or someone necessary to implement the team's solutions. With this input, the Call Center team agrees that management is a stakeholder rather than a customer. Joy places a Post-it note of external customer under the customer column and moves toward the supplier and input section of the SIPOC.

"It's almost 5:30, shouldn't we call it a day?" Robert Wallace asks rhetorically. Unfortunately, for Robert and perhaps Jeff, Leroy Barney spoke representatively for the group saying he thought the group was on a roll and should continue until at least 6:00. Since Joy knew a negative poll wouldn't work here, she observed the back-up decision-making method for the group was a two-thirds-majority vote. She quickly posed the question of going to 6:00 and asked for a vote. All but Robert and Jeff voted to work until 6:00, and the work on the Process Map continued.

Deciding on the suppliers and inputs proved trickier than deciding on the output and customers. The next half hour was spent on discussions that reflected little knowledge of preceding processes that affected the Call Center. With time nearing 6:00, there was general agreement on the underwriting, billing, and policy administration functions as suppliers, with the customer profiles being the inputs coming from each of those functions, respectively.

With minutes left until 6:00 P.M., Joy concluded with a written pluses/deltas exercise. As the team left for the day, Joy and Kylie remained and talked.

"How do you feel about your team's efforts, Joy?"

"Overall, I think we have a vibrant team. I really like the enthusiasm and depth of thought among most of the team. I am worried about us eventually jelling as a team. I keep thinking what you just saw in that last half hour may be indicative of later problems with Robert and Jeff."

"It wouldn't be a Six Sigma team without potential problems among the team. There are always team members who see Six Sigma as something to do above and beyond their daily activities. I like the way you facilitated in the last half hour. Instead of trying to persuade Robert to work the last half hour, you used your back-up decision-making method knowing you weren't going to get consensus from the group."

"Thanks, that means a lot coming from a pro. Do you think I should have an off-line talk with Robert and Jeff about their commitment to this project?"

"I would wait for now. Friday afternoon Joe and I are going to review your intersession deliverables. Between Friday and when we return for Analysis training on April 8, you will need to assemble a detailed project plan. Specific assignments should be given. During the next few weeks, your assignment as the team leader will be to ensure that your individual team member work is done. If you begin to have trouble with Robert, Jeff, or anyone else for that matter, that would be the time to intervene. Any intervention done before then would be both premature and perhaps futile."

"Thanks for the suggestion. I'm sure it will come in handy." Both Joy and Kylie had been walking out of the hotel into the brisk February air. By the time they had said their goodbyes, the Colorado skies were spitting snow. As she drove off, Joy kept thinking her team might encounter the same cold weather in the coming weeks.

Thursday's training day began with Joe Hawke giving each team an additional 45-minute breakout to complete their high-level Process Map. In the Cedar Room, the Call Center team went quickly to work. Joy asked those who had given some thought to the five to seven high-level "As-Is" steps to write their ideas on Post-it notes. She recommended that the team's ideas should be put into one of three categories she had put on the wall labeled "Beginning," "Middle," and "End."

Within five minutes, the Call Center's team members had finished their furious scribbling on Post-it notes and had placed them on the wall. Joy clarified the ideas and over the course of the next 30 minutes the team had reached consensus on seven steps they believed were representative of the current process. These high-level steps are reflected on the Process Map in Figure 5.8.

■ MANAGING MEASURE—TOLLGATE #1 (CREATION OF THE DATA COLLECTION PLAN)

After the debrief of the breakout devoted to the creation of the Process Map, Joe Hawke begins his tutorial on the second element of Six Sigma, Measure. He presents a PowerPoint slide that shows the Data Collection Plan that he states is the first tollgate of Measure (Figure 5.9).

Hawke stresses that the completion of most of the Data Collection Plan can occur in the breakouts provided before noon on Friday. He states that a good Data Collection Plan is the what, where, and how of collecting data leading to the calculation of baseline sigma performance. He also states that work the team does between training sessions to validate the customers needs and requirements helps

What to Measure	Type of Measure	Type of Data	Operational Definition	Target	Specification	Data Collection Form(s)	Sampling	Baseline Six Sigma

Figure 5.9 Data Collection Plan.

the team start the work of the Data Collection Plan. He asks a volunteer team to share their work from the previous day to show them how easy getting started on the data collection can be. Joy quickly volunteers for the assignment and Hawke uses the Call Center team to show the teams how to create the first tollgate of Measure.

"Joy, it will be important to validate your customers' needs and requirements during your intersession work. For purposes here, let's say that what your team brainstormed has been validated. What were the more important requirements you brainstormed in your CTQ break-out?"

"We had three: accuracy, timeliness, and courtesy."

Joe Hawke moves to the wall where the nine columns of the Data Collection Plan were located. He takes out his flip chart pen and writes accuracy, timeliness, and courtesy in the first column with the heading labeled "What to Measure."

Hawke then moves to the second column with the heading labeled "Type of Measure." Hawke references the Process Map that all teams had recently completed in the last break-out. "You have just completed preliminary work on Process Mapping where we used the mnemonic device called SIPOC. In the Process Map, there are three major areas where measurement applies. First and foremost, there are measures regarding the output of the process. Next, there should be measures focused on your suppliers and the inputs to the process. Both output and input measures are measures of effectiveness, both yours and your suppliers. Finally, there should be measures of the process itself. These process measures are a measure of efficiency."

Hawke continues his tutorial on the second column of the Data Collection Plan. "Our second column on the Data Collection Plan determines if we have sufficient data from the first column. Six Sigma teams make two major mistakes around data. Collecting too little or too much data. Thus, our second column called 'Type of Measure' can aid us in determining whether we are collecting just the right amount of data. As I just indicated, a measure can be either an output, input, or process measure. Let's look at the Call Center team and use their measures to determine if their three measures are too much or too little. First, is accuracy an output, input, or process measure?"

While this question was aimed at the Call Center team, several other teams had listed accuracy as a Measure. Some participants indicated it was an output and others said it was an input. Hawke smiled wryly. "I have good news for those of you who said it was an output and I have good news for those of you who said it was an input. That is because it is indeed both. It is considered an output measure if it is important to our customer. It is an input measure if the accuracy eventually seen by the customer is dependent on previous processes that technically are your suppliers. This concept of one measure being more than one type of measure is called 'double-dipping.' A Six Sigma team should always be on the look out for when they can double dip. It means less time, effort, and money in the data collection phase of the project."

Hawke proceeds to the second column on the Data Collection Plan and places an "O"(for output) and "I" (for input) parallel to accuracy. He completes the second column after discussion with the participants where timeliness is an output measure (once it is validated as a customer requirement), but it is also a measure of how efficient the Call Center process is. Thus, Hawke labels timeliness as an "O" and "P" (for Process) measure in the second column. Finally, courtesy is labeled an output measure. Hawke goes on to say that traditionally, there are two or three output measures, one or two input measures, and one process measure. In the case of process measures, Hawke says that the four most popular measures are cycle time, cost, labor, or value. He further indicates that since all four are so strongly correlated with one another, there is no sense in measuring more than one.

The third column on the Data Collection Plan is called the "Type of Data." Hawke describes data as being two types. The first type is discrete data that is go/no go, pass/fail, good/bad, on/off. The other type of data is continuous data which, as the term implies, is data found on a continuum of values like weight, height, length, and so on. Again, Hawke uses the Call Center team to show that accuracy is typically measured discretely, either the information is accurate or not. Timeliness could be measured discretely (the information could be provided in a timely manner or not) or it could be measured on a continuum. Hawke advises that when possible, data should always be measured continuously if there is a choice. Thus, in the third column he puts discrete parallel to accuracy and continuous parallel to timeliness. Hawke describes the Likert scale and its use for courtesy. Here, customers could evaluate the degree of courtesy on a scale of 5 (extremely courteous) to 1 (not courteous at all). When the Likert scale is used, something like courtesy, which could be discrete (courteous/not courteous), can be transformed into continuous data, which is always preferred.

With three of the nine columns on the Data Collection Plan completed, Hawke reviews the fourth column called "Operational Definition." Hawke describes the operational definition as a description of something to be measured where those affected have a common understanding such that all parties involved experience no ambiguity over what is being described. Hawke receives nods of approval when he uses the 2000 Presidential election returns from

Florida as an example of both poor preparation and poor utilization of operational definitions. "Did a hanging chad or pregnant chad qualify as a vote?" Hawke inquired rhetorically. He further used the Florida vote as an example where if the teams don't get good clarity on their operational definitions, those negatively affected will not believe the results of the data.

Hawke reviews columns five and six that are taking each measure from the first column and finding the target (the ideal product or service in the eyes of the customer), and the specification (the least acceptable product or service in the eyes of the customer). He then tasks each team for their first Measure breakout. They are expected to work on their operational definitions, targets, and specifications.

The Call Center team retreats to the Cedar Room to work on their operational definitions for accuracy, timeliness, and courtesy. During the hour breakout, there was lively discussion about the operational definition of accuracy. Relative to the customers who utilize the Call Center, accuracy was in large part based on whether the customer needed to call back the Call Center. Thus, two suggestions were made relative to the operational definition of accuracy. One definition suggested by Maria focused on whether the same customer called back, and the other suggestion made by Suzanne was to create a Likert scale and periodically sample the customer base for the level of satisfaction with regard to how accurately the Call Center performed. Participation within the group was lively with two exceptions, Robert and Jeff. The same occurred during the Call Center's discussion of customer targets and specifications for each of their measures of accuracy, timeliness, and courtesy. The results of the breakout for the Call Center's operational definitions, targets, and specifications are shown in Figure 5.10

Thursday's afternoon tutorial on data collection forms (column 7 on the Data Collection Plan) and sampling (column 8 on the Data Collection Plan) was a lull in an otherwise exciting training week. Hawke discussed two different data collection forms, one for discrete data and the other for continuous data. Since the Call Center had both discrete and continuous data, Joy paid special heed to both types. The tutorial on sampling was a bit tedious but Joy recognized the importance of sampling for the Call Center customer base since they received literally hundreds of calls per week. When Hawke talked about the need to ensure that the sample was both representative and random, Joy took detailed notes. In regard to the Call Center, she knew more attention had to be spent on brainstorming type of call, region, type of contract being inquired about, and several other factors associated with ensuring the sample was representative. This was more important than the sampling formula to determine sample

What to Measure	Type of Measure	Type of Data	Operational Definition	Target	Specification	Data Collection Forms(s)	Sampling	Baseline Six Sigma
Accuracy	O	Discrete	Percent of return calls divided by total calls	100%	100%	Discrete Check Sheet	Representative/ random	*Unit* = Customer call. *Defect* = Callback or call length > 10 minutes or courtesy ranked < 3. *Opportunity* = 3
Timeliness	O,P	Continuous	Beginning of customer call to resolution of call	ASAP	5 minutes	Frequency Distribution Check Sheet	Representative/ random	*Unit* = Customer call. *Defect* = Callback or call length >10 minutes or courtesy ranked < 3. *Opportunity* = 3
Courtesy	O,I	Continuous	Likert scale of sampled customers where 5 = exceedingly courteous, 3 = courteous, 1 = not courteous	5	3	Frequency Distribution Check Sheet	Representative/ random	*Unit* = Customer call. *Defect* = Callback or call length greater than 10 minutes or courtesy ranked less than a 3. *Opportunity* = 3

Figure 5.10 Completed Data Collection Plan.

138

size. With regard to the latter, Hawke assured her that computer programs like mini-tab would be used so she didn't have to memorize the formula.

Friday morning was spent on learning how to calculate baseline sigma. During the morning break, virtually all the teams visibly sighed with relief after Hawke simply but effectively showed how to calculate sigma. Baseline sigma was simply determining what a unit, defect, and opportunity was. In the Call Center project, a unit was a customer call. A defect was when a customer requirement for a product or service was not being met. In the first case, it was a call back that was indicative of inaccurate information. The second way a defect could be created in the Call Center project would be when a call lasted more than five minutes. Last, when a customer survey ranked courtesy less than 3 on the Likert scale, that was a defect. Finally, the team needed to determine how many opportunities existed for the project. Hawke said that in the vast majority of cases the ratio of opportunities to validated CTQs would be 1:1. Thus, if during the intersession the Call Center validated accuracy, timeliness, and courtesy as the three most important CTQs to customers, the number of opportunities would be 3.

Hawke indicated that most project baseline sigma performance runs around 1.5 to 2.5 sigma. This would mean that for a baseline sigma of 1.5, nearly 500,000 defects per million opportunities were being generated. For a baseline sigma of 2.5, this would mean over 150,000 defects per million opportunities. Hawke used the concept of "low-hanging fruit" to describe how a team shouldn't be depressed when, during their intersession work, they find out their baseline sigma is so low. When baseline sigma is so low, the odds to harvest the low-hanging fruit is higher. Hawke even garnered some laughter from the participants when he said some of the teams in the room would find their projects would have fruit rotting on the ground, just waiting to be picked up.

■ INTERSESSION PLANNING—THE IMPORTANCE OF PROJECT MANAGEMENT

The last day of training had arrived and the group had been instructed on the tollgates of both Define and Measure. It was now past 1:00 and Hawke had turned the teaching over to Kylie Madrid. She was about to discuss two vitally important concepts. First, she was going to address the intersession work each team had to complete on the Define and Measure tollgates that they had begun during the breakouts in the training. Second, she was going to discuss the importance of several project management tools to use during the inter-session.

"Joe has just finished teaching the Define and Measure tollgates. You may be wondering what we are going to do with the half day remaining in the schedule." Madrid moves to a flip chart that was covered. "I have good news and bad news. First, the bad news. If you leave early today, chances are you will not have done the most important breakout of the week. The good news is that I am about to teach you some simple yet powerful tools that, once mastered, will allow your teams to work smarter, not harder."

As Madrid uncovers the flip chart, she begins the review of what each Alpha Omega team must complete by the morning of April 8, the day Temojoe Consulting returns for Analysis training. The list was long and comprehensive:

- Validate the project Charter with your team Champion. This includes modification of the Business Case, preliminary problem statement, project Scope, modification to the team member make up and goals/objectives.
- Validate the customers of your project, their need(s), and requirements. The customer needs and requirements should be validated through a combination of at least two of the following:
  —One-on-one interviews.
  —Focus groups.
  —Surveys.
  —Observing the customer use your product or service.
  —Customer complaints.
- Validate the high-level Process Map. This should include interviewing staff who "live" in the process as well as walking a product or service through the process.
- Complete the Data Collection Plan. This should include:
  —Confirm the operational definitions of all validated measures.
  —Gain agreement on the data collection forms to use.
  —Determine the factors that will go into making your sampling plan both representative and random.
  —Gain agreement on what your unit, defects, and opportunities are.

- Gather data and calculate your baseline sigma performance.

Kylie asks if anyone needs clarification because most class participants were taking notes furiously. She walks from the flip charts back to her PowerPoint presentation.

"The flip charts show what needs to be done between now and April 8. Now, I want to move into how you need to work between now and April 8.

"First, let me state that each of your teams needs to meet weekly. These weekly meetings should be a combination of status reports and decision-making forums. Most of the work completed by successful Six Sigma teams is done in subgroups, where tasks are subdivided among smaller groups of your team. To complete all of the above, you will need several simple project management tools that I now want to address."

Madrid continues her tutorial, "Project management is a way of thinking, communicating, and behaving. The first step in good project management is organizing your work. The flip charts on your intersession deliverables help you begin your organization. The second step in good project management is planning the work. Shortly, I will share with you tools to accomplish this important step. Finally, the third element of good project management is controlling the work to be done. This is the prime responsibility of your team leader.

"The elements of organizing and controlling are comprised of doing the tasks, comparing performance with the project plan, and fixing problems that occur. In addition, everyone must keep closely informed of both the elements of the plan and the performance to the plan. There are three key tools to help you become successful in accomplishing your intersession work; Work Breakdown charts, Linear Responsibility charts and Activity Reports."

➤ Work Breakdown Charts

Madrid describes three different types of Work Breakdown charts. She uses the example of validating customer requirements since all teams will have to do this activity. The first type of Work Breakdown chart is the organizational chart type. With the organizational chart type, the activities associated with your work are formatted in organizational chart form where larger tasks are subdivided and placed under the larger task. In the customer requirement validation example, the larger tasks include determining the methods of customer validation, determination of the customers to be contacted, development of the forms to be used to capture the customer's input, and organizing the results. Figure 5.11 shows how the organizational chart would look for the activities associated with customer requirement validation.

The second type of Work Breakdown chart is the indented outline type. This type of chart is preferred for those who are more comfortable with words and the details around them. Additionally, if your work breakdown is highly detailed with multiple subtasks, the indented outline approach may be preferred.

Using the customer validation example, Figure 5.12 shows how the same work to be done would be organized into an indented outline format.

The third type of Work Breakdown chart is the bubble chart. For those with simpler type activities, the bubble chart works nicely. Further, for those who respond favorably to visual depictions of work,

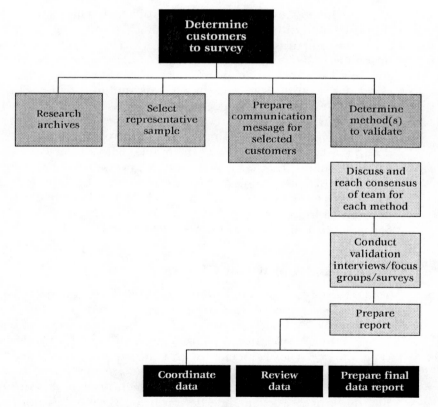

Figure 5.11 Validating customer requirements—organizational chart. Work Breakdown Chart

1.0 Determine Customers to Survey.
    1.1 Research archive
    1.2 Select representative sample of customers
    1.3 Prepare communication message for customers
    1.4 Notify customers of intent
2.0 Determine Method(s) to Validate Customer Requirements.
    2.1 Discuss and reach consensus of team for each method
    2.2 Conduct validation interview/focus groups/surveys
3.0 Prepare Report.
    3.1 Coordinate data
    3.2 Review data
    3.3 Prepare final data report

Figure 5.12 Validating customer requirements—indented outline format. Work Breakdown Chart

the bubble chart is often preferred. In Figure 5.13, we return to the customer validation work and show the activities and tasks in bubble chart form.

Madrid reviews some suggestions to make whichever Work Breakdown chart used more effective. First, the team leader/facilitator has the primary responsibility for creation of the Work Breakdown chart. However, better team leaders will solicit input from the rest of the Six Sigma team once a preliminary chart is created. Much like the exercise the Project Champion went through for project Scope, even the best team leader will not think of everything. Thus, taking a preliminary Work Breakdown chart and having it be reviewed by the team is strongly suggested. In addition, the external consultant and/or Master Black Belt should review the Work Breakdown chart to see if there are any gaps or redundancies. While there may be unique elements to each Six Sigma Work Breakdown chart, there will also be significant overlap and similarities.

Good Work Breakdown charts will change as work is done. Make sure these modifications are reflected in the most recent Work Breakdown chart. For example, once the project team completes item 2.1 (from the indented outline chart), they will have a specific method (or methods, as suggested) to obtain information on customer requirements. Once this determination is made, it is likely the Work Breakdown chart will be modified. In Figure 5.14, we show a Work Breakdown chart as an indented outline once the team decides to use a combination of a survey and focus group.

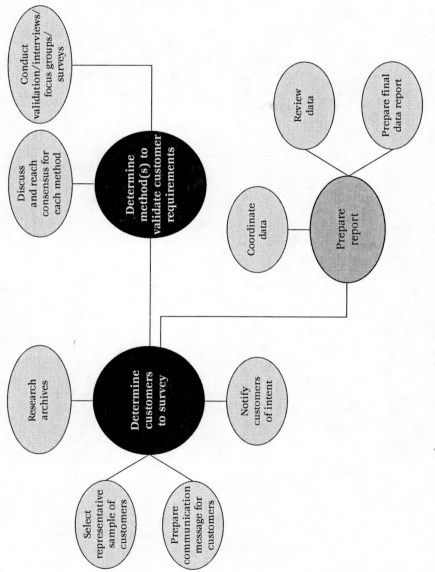

Figure 5.13 Validating customer requirements bubble chart.
Work Breakdown Chart

2.0 Determine Use of Focus Group to Validate Customer Requirements.
  2.1 Create list of customers for focus group
  2.2 Validate list to ensure customers selected follow basic sampling techniques
    2.2.1 Verify customer base being representative
    2.2.2 Verify customer base being random
    2.2.3 Determine appropriate sample size using mini-tab
    2.2.4 Select customers for focus group
  2.3 Notify list of customers to invite them to the focus group
    2.3.1 Draft letter of invitation
    2.3.2 Send letter of invitation
    2.3.3 Follow up with phone call
  2.4 Make arrangements for customers to visit Alpha Omega
    2.4.1 Make reservations
      2.4.1.1 Airlines
      2.4.1.2 Hotel
      2.4.1.3 Conference center for actual focus group
      2.4.1.4 Transportation arrangements to/from airport
  2.5 Create focus group questionnaire for focus group participants
    2.5.1 Create a 1st draft
    2.5.2 Have team review 1st draft
    2.5.3 Modify 1st draft based on input
    2.5.4 Complete finished draft
3.0 Determine Use of Survey to Validate Customer Requirements.
  3.1 Create list of customers (excluding focus group) for survey
  3.2 Validate list to ensure customers selected follow basic sampling techniques
    3.2.1 Verify customer base being representative
    3.2.2 Verify customer base being random
    3.2.3 Determine appropriate sample size using mini-tab
    3.2.4 Select customers for survey
  3.3 Create survey
    3.3.1 Create 1st draft of questions
    3.3.2 Have team review first draft
    3.3.3 Modify first draft based on input
    3.3.4 Compete final survey
  3.4 Send out survey
  3.5 Verify survey receipt
  3.6 Review survey upon return
  3.7 Compile data from survey

Figure 5.14 Indented outline.
Work Breakdown Chart

➤ Linear Responsibility Charts

Another major project management tool used successfully by Six Sigma project teams is Linear Responsibility charts. In some cases, Linear Responsibility charts are used in conjunction with Work Breakdown charts. In other cases, they are combined into one chart. Kylie Madrid reviews the importance of Linear Responsibility charts for Six Sigma teams.

"In any Six Sigma team, work needs to be delegated among team members. As we stated earlier, some decisions will be made in your weekly Six Sigma meetings but by and large your weekly meetings will be a time to status one another on your delegated work. The delegated work needs to be documented. This documented work must make those who it is delegated to accountable. Linear Responsibility charts allow this to occur. Let's go back to the customer validation work and see how the Linear Responsibility chart works around the work with creation and compiling data for a customer survey" (Figure 5.15).

Madrid reviews the legend at the bottom of the page. She stresses the importance of recognizing the difference between primary and

Task/ Activity	Team Leader	Champion	Member		All Other Members
			#1	**#2**	
Create survey	P				
Have team review first draft	S	A	P	P	P
Modify survey	P				
Complete final survey	P	A			
Send out survey	S		P		
Verify survey receipt	S			P	
Review survey upon return	P		S	S	S
Compile survey results	S		P	S	

P = Primary Responsibility; S = Secondary Responsibility; A = Approval

Figure 5.15 Linear responsibility charting.

secondary responsibility. In the case of primary responsibility, that person is responsible for actually doing the work, while secondary responsibility means either a supportive role or review and input to the person who has primary responsibility. Approval, as it implies, is strictly a review process for the person involved. In Six Sigma teams, this is the domain of the Project Champion.

The advantage of the Linear Responsibility chart occurs on several levels. First, in combination with the Work Breakdown chart, it clearly indicates both the activities and tasks to be completed but also specifies who has the accountability for the activity or task. In addition, it specifies at what level a person will be involved with the activity or task. Finally, it provides where the Project Champion will be involved. With regard to the Project Champion role, a good team leader will be as specific as possible and indicate where and when the approval of the Champion is requested. By doing a Linear Responsibility chart early in the project, a good team leader will sit down and get agreement from the Project Champion about their involvement in the team.

➤ Activity Reports

Madrid now addresses the last of the three project management tools typically used by Six Sigma teams, the Activity Report. Madrid reviews the three elements of project management that began her tutorial. "Again, we stated earlier that good project management is made up of organizing, planning, and controlling your intersession work. Work Breakdown charts and Linear Responsibility charts will help you with organizing and planning your work. The last tool we discuss, Activity Reports, assist you and your team leader with controlling the work to be done. Again, let's use the customer validation example to highlight how a team leader can control the intersession work associated with your Six Sigma project."

Madrid moves to the projector and reveals the Activity Report (Figure 5.16). Madrid states the Activity Report is self-explanatory. The Activity Report can be used by not only the team leader, but also the entire Six Sigma team. She stresses the second column should only hold the name of the primary responsible party for the task or activity. The third column indicates the start date that reflects the planned and actual date the task or activity is started, while the same is reflected for the finish date. Madrid indicates that it is not unusual for the start and finish dates to be the same, particularly for smaller tasks that can be done in one sitting. Team leaders were encouraged to review patterns in planned versus actual start and finish dates.

Task/ Activity	Primary Responsibility Held by	Start Date Planned/ Actual	Finish Date Planned/ Actual	Comments
Create survey	Team Leader	Feb. 10/	Feb. 10/	
Have team review 1st draft	Team	Feb. 15/	Feb. 18/	
Modify survey	Team Leader	Feb. 18/	Feb. 21/	
Complete final survey	Team Leader	Feb. 19/	Feb. 22/	
Send out survey	Team Member #1	Feb. 21/	Feb. 24/	
Verify survey receipt	Team Member #2	Feb. 25/	Feb. 26/	
Review survey upon return	Team Leader	March 7/	March 10/	
Compile survey results	Team Member #1	March 14/	March 17/	

Figure 5.16 Activity report.

Often, review of these reports will alert the project team leader to where there may be a problem with performance that the team leader will have to address.

The first training session had just been completed. The rest of the afternoon the teams begin to put together their intersession work plans that will take them from the end of the day to their report-outs the morning of April 8.

As the Call Center team exited the Omni Interlocken after an exhaustive week, Maria Carballo reminded Joy that things could get interesting during the intersession. "Joy, with all the personalities we have on this team, I don't envy you being the team leader."

As the sun set over the Front Range Mountains in nearby Boulder, Joy quoted Bette Davis from *The Three Faces of Eve,* "Fasten your seatbelt, Maria, it's going to be a bumpy ride."

■ SUMMARY

Chapter 5 begins the Alpha Omega's journey through the DMAIC methodology. Here, the teams get a chance to show their facilitative leadership skills relative to actual project work. In Chapter 5, we revisit the Project Champion and review at a detailed level the work expected of the Champion to assure the project team's dynamics remain strong. We discuss in detail such Champion's responsibilities as validating the Charter, monitoring the various tollgates of the DMAIC methodology, and removing the roadblocks that act as impediments to the project team's work. In Chapter 5, we also introduce the importance of project management tools such as Work Breakdown charts, Linear Responsibility charts, and Activity Reports that help the project team maintain momentum.

KEY LEARNINGS

➤ The DMAIC process improvement methodology is made up of Define, Measure, Analyze, Improve, and Control.

➤ Each phase of DMAIC is made up of a series of tollgates. These tollgates are opportunities for a formal review between the Team Leader and Project Champion.

➤ The Define tollgates are made up of the Project Charter, Customer Focus, and the High Level Process Map.

➤ The Measure tollgates are made up of the creation of the Data Collection Plan, and implementing the Data Collection Plan that results in the calculation of baseline sigma performance.

➤ A key success factor in the management of the Six Sigma project is the active involvement of the Project Champion. The Project Champion's responsibilities during the project team's existence include:

—Validating the Project Charter.
—Monitoring and approving all project team tollgates.
—Meeting regularly with the team leader/facilitator.
—Removing barriers or roadblocks to the team's success.
—Maintaining the momentum of the team and keeping them on task.
—Dealing with resistance among the team members.
—Communicating progress to upper management.
—Continuing education.

(continued)

(Continued)

—Recognizing the team's efforts.

—Re-evaluating Scope during the project.

➤ Six Sigma teams need to practice good project management. Good project management includes organizing, planning, and controlling the DMAIC methodology.

➤ There are three project management tools that every Six Sigma team should strongly consider using: Work Breakdown charts, Linear Responsibility charts, and Activity Reports.

Chapter

Dealing with Maladaptive Six Sigma Behaviors

"Every unhappy family is unhappy in its own way."

Leo Tolstoy

The work a Six Sigma team does in achieving improved sigma performance includes dealing with maladaptive behaviors. In Chapter 6, we spend time with the Alpha Omega Call Center team as they begin to deal with working on the DMAIC methodology away from the training atmosphere. We address specific forms of resistance and communicate how a team leader and Champion can provide interventions that can assist the team in moving through their difficulties to achieve lasting improvement on the project. We discuss how to diagnose the more common problems a Six Sigma team encounters from the resistor to the person who doesn't follow through on assignments.

■ MANAGING INTERSESSION WORK

As stated in Chapter 5, an effective Six Sigma team leader puts together a detailed breakdown chart of the work to be done between training sessions. The Alpha Omega teams had between early February and April to complete all their work in the Define and Measure portion of DMAIC. Toward that end, Joy Schulenberg made a detailed Work Breakdown chart using the indented outline method referenced in Chapter 5 (see Figure 6.1).

Joy Schulenberg began her work in earnest by meeting with Charles Zukor early in the week following the Define and Measure

1.0 Validate Project Charter with Champion.
    1.1 Review Business Case
    1.2 Review preliminary problem statement
    1.3 Review project Scope
        1.3.1 Reconcile whether other processes will be included in this project work
    1.4 Review if other team members need to be added
    1.5 Review goals and objectives.
2.0 Validate Customers, Needs, and Requirements.
    2.1 Determine method(s) for validation of customers needs and requirements
3.0 Validate High-Level Process Map.
    3.1 Walk through current Call Center process
    3.2 Interview current Call Center member participants to validate process map
    3.3 Review with team members results from above
4.0 Complete Data Collection Plan.
    4.1 Gain agreement on data collection forms
    4.2 Brainstorm elements to assure sampling plan is representative
    4.3 Brainstorm elements to assure sampling plan is random
    4.4 Review criteria for assurance of unit, defect, and opportunity
    4.5 Develop plan for sampling of customers to determine baseline sigma
        4.5.1 Assign six sigma team members to collect data
        4.5.2 Determine list of customers to sample
        4.5.3 Collect data
    4.6 Organize data in baseline sigma form
        4.6.1 Perform baseline sigma calculation
        4.6.2 Review sigma calculation with consultants
        4.6.3 Modify if necessary

Figure 6.1 Detailed intersession work breakdown chart.

training. She quickly addressed the input the Call Center team provided to both the project Scope and preliminary problem statement. Charles complimented the team and Joy specifically for coming up with ideas that he hadn't initially addressed in his brainstorming prior to the formation of the Call Center team. Zukor decided that the Call Center team should not preclude examining other processes for answers to the Call Center's current problems and said he was unaware of the market research data around the index. Remembering his Champion training, he noted that when possible a Six Sigma team should always use currently available data. Thus, he approved the use of the index as part of the preliminary problem statement and said that improvement of the current index number of 42 percent should be a goal of the Call Center team. Improving courtesy would still be in Scope for the time being. His only concern was that the expansion of the team's project Scope should not go into other processes until the data warranted it.

This first intersession work by Joy did not escape Charles Zukor. "Joy, I am really excited about this project and your leadership. I got great feedback from people like Suzanne, Aaron, and Maria. I really am glad I made you the project leader. I also received a packet from Temojoe Consulting about my role as Champion during your existence as a team. I vow to do everything possible to make this project a success. Do you have any concerns as we move forward?"

"Well, I am concerned that Robert and Jeff are not on board like the others. Kylie Madrid indicated that during this first intersession, I need to monitor the situation closely. She said that in all likelihood I should expect to have some intervention on behalf of either Robert or Jeff. I may need your help and I will not hesitate to call on you if necessary."

This first meeting went well from both Joy's and Charles' perspective. Both knew that problems existed on the horizon. What both didn't know was how quickly the need to address maladaptive behaviors was going to occur.

■ MANAGING MALADAPTIVE BEHAVIORS IN THE SIX SIGMA TEAM

The Call Center team had agreed to meet Monday afternoons from 3:30 to 5:00. Since Joy had indicated to the team her action item to meet with their Project Champion the week after their Define and Measure training, the Call Center's first intersession meeting was to occur 10 days after the end of training. Other than Joy, no one had any action items to report on. Joy created an agenda for their first meeting (Figure 6.2).

During the last afternoon of training over a week ago, the Call Center team had agreed to several project management approaches. They agreed through consensus to use the indented outline form for the Work Breakdown chart structure combined with a Linear Responsibility chart, and they would use an Activity Report for all items where primary responsibility had been assigned.

The appointed meeting time came and went with only Aaron Gregson, Leroy Barney, Suzanne Jackson, Aaron Brown, and Joy in the conference room assigned to the Call Center team. Joy began to experience frustration as the clock neared 3:40. Those in attendance

Element	Desired Outcome	Method	Responsible Party	Time Allotted
Review agenda and ground rules.	Agreement on agenda and ground rules.	Discussion and consensus	Joy and Team	5 min.
Review changes to Project Charter.	Communicate changes to Six Sigma team.	Status report	Joy	10 min.
Review Work Breakdown chart for Define and Measure work.	Gain agreement on work breakdown chart.	Discussion and consensus	Joy and Team	15 min.
Develop activity reports for customer validation items and validation of high-level "As-Is" map.	Gaining agreement on timelines for completion of define toll-gates.	Discussion and consensus	Joy and Team	30 min.
Plus/Delta	Review pluses and deltas of meeting.	Brainstorming	Team	5 min.

Figure 6.2 Agenda for Call Centers first intersession meeting.

had come into the conference room just past 3:25 and had engaged in small talk. The two Aarons were debating the latest hockey news while Suzanne and Leroy were discussing the increasing traffic problems along the Denver-Boulder corridor. Both discussions were of such intensity that all parties except Joy were unaware of the clock until Joy finally called the meeting to order without the three absent team members.

"All right, even though everyone is not here, we should get started. If this team is going to be successful, we need to be punctual."

Joy's first comments didn't sit right with Suzanne. "I don't know why you said that. We were all here on time."

Suzanne's comment went without response but Joy was aware of the futility of her input. She reviewed the agenda for the meeting and was well into the changes to the Charter that had been approved by Charles Zukor. At 3:50, midway through her status report, Maria Carballo rushed into the meeting, apologizing profusely as she took her chair. As Joy continued with her report, Maria interjected with a question about project Scope.

"What about the decision regarding our project as it affects other processes?"

Aaron Brown glared at Maria who was unaware that Joy had just covered that point moments ago. Suzanne wasn't as shy about sharing her thoughts. "Maria, we just covered that point. If you had been here only 15 minutes late instead of 20, you would know what decision was made."

Joy observed Maria's sincere regret at her error and knew she had to save this moment, otherwise she could lose Maria's future involvement. She decided to ignore Suzanne and Aaron's frustration and swiftly reviewed the decision made by Charles to keep the current Scope but to re-examine the need to expand work into other processes if the data led the way. While she did this expediently, she could see the growing ire of Suzanne and Aaron who sighed noticeably.

The rest of the meeting went by without further interruption. When Joy was reviewing the Work Breakdown charts, Robert and Jeff's absence became discussion points as both of them had primary responsibility for elements associated with validating the high-level "As-Is" Process Map.

"So what do we do with Wallace and Seimonson's action items, Joy?" Leroy Barney inquired. "The rest of us have our plates full. I'm certainly not going to cover for them."

"I guess this is why I get paid the big bucks, Leroy," Joy said jokingly. "I will handle this situation before our next meeting."

At the close of the meeting that started late and ended early, Joy contemplated her options. She first was tempted to call Charles and have him handle the situation. She resisted the temptation, afraid it was too much like calling Dad when her two brothers were fighting. She remembered the discussion she had with Kylie during the first week of training. She looked in her Palm Pilot for Kylie's number and called her.

"Kylie, I just had my first meeting without the training wheels and it was a near disaster. Two people were no-shows and another was 20 minutes late. What do you suggest I do with my no-shows."

"Hmm, let me guess. Robert and Jeff?" Kylie asked rhetorically. "What was their reason for not showing up?"

"Well, I haven't asked them yet. I was hoping to get your ideas on how to handle it."

"First, use DMAIC on them. Find out the root cause of their no-show status. I would also suggest a two-prong attack to regain the momentum of the group."

Madrid went on to mention a person named Tuckman who came up with a model of stages of team development. Madrid mentioned that Tuckman has shown that any team goes through four stages: *Forming, Storming, Norming,* and *Performing.*

Madrid suggested several approaches that included icebreakers and team building exercises. Icebreakers are a way to learn about those around you by asking some question far removed from the work at hand. Madrid indicated that since the group had been formed, they were quickly moving into the storming phase of Tuckman's model. Icebreakers and team building exercises were ways that a group could migrate through the storming phase into establishing norms for each other's behavior and ultimately into the performance that would make them a true Six Sigma success story.

Joy Schulenberg took notes on some of the more popular icebreakers and team building exercises. She mulled over the ones Madrid had recommended, and which she would use.

First, she needed to check in with Robert and Jeff and determine the root cause for their failure to show up. What she found was two similar excuses. Jeff said he had "forgotten" the meeting and offered superficial apologies. Joy reminded him of the next meeting the following Monday. Robert said he thought the meeting was on Tuesday at 3:30. Robert was less apologetic and seemed to blame Joy for this "miscommunication" even though no one else had been mistaken about the meeting time.

With the first tollgate of Define validated, Joy went through her subtask assignments for customer validation. She had obtained agreement from Aaron Gregson and Maria Carballo to take primary responsibility to deal with the customer validation work for the second tollgate of Define. Agreement on the methods to validate customer requirements was to be the primary agenda item for next Monday's meeting. But before the Call Center team was to dive into this important agenda item, Joy had prepared a detailed icebreaker to help her team move into Tuckman's norming and performing phase of team development.

Figure 6.3 shows the agenda for the February 25 meeting where Joy ensured that all participants were to be in attendance. That morning, Joy called each member to verify his or her attendance. During the

Element	Desired Outcome	Method	Responsible Party	Time Allotted
Review agenda and ground rules.	Agreement on agenda and ground rules.	Discussion and consensus	Joy and Team	5 min.
Icebreaker.	Improve Call Center team dynamics.	Icebreaker exercise and debrief	Joy and Team	55 min.
Customer validation exercise.	Determine methods to validate customer needs and requirements.	Discussion and consensus	Joy and Team	25 min.
Plus/Delta	Review pluses and deltas of meeting.	Brainstorming	Team	5 min.

Figure 6.3 Call Center agenda for February 25.

prior weekend, she had e-mailed the agenda (Figure 6.3). When Jeff Seimonson had indicated he would be at a meeting in the afternoon from 1:00 to 3:00, she even offered to walk over to the meeting room with him. He hastily said that would not be necessary and that he would be in attendance when the February 25 meeting started at 3:30.

Joy moved through the agenda and ground rules for the February 25 meeting. While inwardly nervous, she portrayed an outward confidence as she moved to a premade flip chart with the following instructions:

Think about the person you consider your personal hero. In five minutes, be prepared to share who that person is and why he or she is your hero.

The reaction to this icebreaker was diverse. Maria, Suzanne, and the Aarons almost immediately went to work. Jeff, Robert, and Leroy vocally indicated their displeasure as Leroy said, "I got into this project thinking it would help all of us reduce the workload of the Call Center. I didn't sign up for psychotherapy, Joy."

"Leroy, we didn't get off to a great start last week. We need to recognize that, like any other team, we have issues that result in poor performance. If we see each other as people instead of just a pair of hands, then our chances of working together as a cohesive unit increases dramatically. I will make the following offer to you, Leroy. Indulge me this exercise. If, after the next hour I have wasted your time, I will take over your primary responsibility for customer validation."

With that tangible offer that showed Joy was putting her money where her mouth was, Leroy immediately moved to writing about his hero and why. At the same time, Leroy's successfully managed resistance forced Robert and Jeff to perform the exercise as requested.

Within five minutes, Joy announced the random order for report-outs. Maria went first.

Maria

"My personal hero is my older sister, Tania. She is eight years older than I am. She was the first person from my family to attend college. She taught me what hard work and perseverance could do to change your life. Without her guidance, I don't know what I would have done career wise. I would have perhaps ended up like many of my relatives who worked in low-paying jobs. I wouldn't have aspired to as much in life. While sometimes I have had trouble getting assignments done, I eventually get them done. I never would have had that drive without my sister showing me how to be achievement-oriented."

Aaron Gregson

"When I think of heroism, I think of my grandfather who was in World War II. He was in the Battle of Bastogne and survived overwhelming odds to eventually be part of the Allied Forces who stormed Hitler's mountain hideaway. He gave me his Army helmet when I was a small boy. He was a legitimate war hero, but he never tooted his own horn. That's how I want to be remembered. I want people to know I did my job quietly and efficiently but without a lot of fanfare. That is why I think so highly of being on this team. I will get a chance to improve my work with tried and true methods and get to use skills I don't normally get to exhibit."

Suzanne

"I guess I am going against the norm to say something about someone who is not in my family. Jack Welch is my hero. I worked for

General Electric for several years and got to meet him twice. Not only do I think he's a great leader, I worked on a small project that he reviewed; he sent me a personal letter of thanks. That letter means more to me than all the annual increases in pay I received."

Jeff

"I thought long and hard on this. I am not one to be into hero worship or even participate in exercises like this. But, finally I came up with my son, Jason. He just turned 12 and has overcome dyslexia that apparently runs in the family. I had it but it just wasn't diagnosed when I was a child. He has worked very hard and I am proud of him. It makes me recognize nothing is more important than family and, in the large scheme of events, you shouldn't take yourself too seriously."

While everyone was learning about one another in a different light, Jeff's comments made him more of person in Joy's eyes. It helped Joy see him as a person rather than the impediment to the team she was beginning to think he was.

All eyes were on Robert who was next.

Robert

"Well, I really didn't give it too much thought. Maybe someone in my family. I guess we all have heroes who have influenced us in our lives. I guess my parents would be considered my heroes but I really don't think too much in terms of heroes or their effect on my life. It's just too busy a time to get wrapped up in that sort of thing."

Joy thanked Robert for his effort though she noticed his physical discomfort as he literally squirmed in his chair and his voice level was barely audible in answering the question.

Aaron Brown went on to state his hero was his wife for being so supportive, though he did put in a plug for Winston Churchill as someone who overcame adversity. Leroy mentioned his father who overcame semiparalysis to still provide a living for his family while Joy concluded with her hero being her grandmother who helped raise her and send her to college.

The reaction to this exercise didn't seem impressive right away. The Call Center team didn't use all 55 minutes allocated for the discussion period. At first, Joy thought she had taken too much of a risk in being "touchy-feely." The rest of the meeting was uneventful though the team did detail the work around validating the customer requirements and determined to use a combination of a focus group and a survey. Aaron Gregson and Maria Carballo again committed to completion of this activity by mid-March. With the additional time remaining on the agenda, the team worked on validation of the high-level map with Jeff having primary responsibility for interviewing Call Center employees. Jeff tapped Robert for having secondary responsibility in assisting him. Other secondary assignments were given to the entire team (Figure 6.4). Joy assured all that she would be meeting with the persons having primary responsibility between regular Call Center meetings.

The pluses/deltas at the end of the day did show a negative reaction to Robert's less-than-enthusiastic response to the exercise.

Over the course of the next six weeks, Joy spent much of her time working in subgroup team meetings. She practiced her pluses/deltas exercises relative to her team and its work. On the plus side, the customer validation went well and was slightly ahead of schedule in mid-March when both the focus group and survey had been completed. It was somewhat surprising that Aaron Gregson had also taken such a strong support role in Maria's work, but Joy assumed that this was due to Aaron's true commitment to process improvement.

By mid-March, she also recognized a significant team problem. While some of the work associated with data collection had begun in earnest, the work around validating the high-level process map had begun to lag. Both Robert and Jeff had offered several excuses about their lack of progress on validation. Joy couldn't help but think of her college training at Notre Dame. She had learned more at the University of Notre Dame than just her Bachelor of Arts. She had learned commitment to excellence. She had learned that successful people overcame obstacles and did not let adversity overcome them. She was coming to the conclusion in the business world that, much like college, people who let adversity get in their way end up holding "whine parties" and blame everyone else for their dilemmas when a good look in the mirror would explain their current plight.

Joy was looking forward to the March 18 Call Center status meeting. It was the day that Kylie Madrid was to be in town for Temojoe's intersession consulting. Joy had lunch with Kylie that day and told her of the lagging performance around validation of the high-level process map in general and the substandard work of Robert and Jeff in particular.

Kylie had asked to facilitate the meeting of the 18th. Joy didn't need to be asked twice to agree to this request. She was puzzled when Kylie asked Joy to obtain four large Evian water bottles and a funnel. She complied and they were ready when Kylie took center stage at the meeting that started promptly at 3:30.

Task/Activity	Team Leader Joy Schulenberg	Champion Charles Zukor	Members Aaron Gregson	Suzanne Jackson	Maria Carballo	Robert Wallace	Jeff Seimonson	Aaron Brown	Leroy Barney
1.0 Validate project charter with Champion	P	A							
1.1 Review Business Case									
1.2 Review preliminary problem statement									
1.3 Review project Scope									
1.3.1 Reconcile whether other processes will be included in this project work									
1.3.2 Review if other team members need to be added									
1.3.3 Review goals and objectives									
2.0 Validate customers, needs, and requirements	2.0P								
2.1 Create survey	2.1P	2.1A						2.1S	
2.2 Modify survey	2.2P							2.2S	
2.3 Send out survey	2.3P							2.3S	
2.4 Verify survey receipt	2.4P							2.4S	

Figure 6.4 Call Center's linear responsibility chart.

Task/Activity	Team Leader Joy Schulenberg	Champion Charles Zukor	Aaron Gregson	Members Suzanne Jackson	Maria Carballo	Robert Wallace	Jeff Seimonson	Aaron Brown	Leroy Barney
2.5 Review survey on return	2.5P							2.5S	
2.6 Compile survey results	2.6P							2.6S	
3.0 Validate customers, needs, and requirements part 2 (Focus Group)	3.0P				3.0S				
3.1 Determine customers for focus group	3.1P	3.1A			3.1S				
3.2 Invite customers to Alpha Omega	3.2P				3.2S				
3.3 Determine questions for focus group	3.3P	3.3A			3.3S				
3.4 Make travel arrangements for focus group	3.4P				3.4S				
3.5 Conduct focus group	3.5P				3.5S				
3.6 Collect data on focus group	3.6P				3.6S				
3.7 Compile data from focus group	3.7P				3.7S				
4.0 Validate high-level "as-is" process map	4.0P								

Figure 6.4 *(Continued)*

Task/Activity	Team Leader Joy Schulenberg	Champion Charles Zukor	Members Aaron Gregson	Suzanne Jackson	Maria Carballo	Robert Wallace	Jeff Seimonson	Aaron Brown	Leroy Barney
4.1 Develop questions about current	4.1P					4.1S			
4.2 Interview current employees	4.2P					4.2S			
4.3 Compile data/reconcile Process Map if needed	4.3P						4.3S		
4.4 Walk through current Process Map as a customer	4.4P						4.4S		
5.0 Complete Data Collection Plan	5.0P	5.0A	5.0S						
5.1 Gain agreement on data collection forms	5.1P		5.1S						
5.2 Brainstorm elements to assure sampling plan is representative	5.2P		5.2S						
5.3 Brainstorm elements to assure sampling plan is random	5.3P		5.3S						
5.4 Review criteria for assurance of unit, defect, and opportunity	5.4P		5.4S						

Figure 6.4 *(Continued)*

Task/Activity	Team Leader Joy Schulenberg	Champion Charles Zukor	Members						
			Aaron Gregson	Suzanne Jackson	Maria Carballo	Robert Wallace	Jeff Seimonson	Aaron Brown	Leroy Barney
5.5 Develop plan for sampling of customers to determine baseline sigma	5.5P		5.5S						
5.5.1 Assign six sigma team members to collect data									
5.5.2 Determine list of customers to sample									
5.5.3 Collect data									
6.0 Organize data in baseline sigma form	6.0P	6.0A		6.0S					
6.1 Perform baseline sigma calculation	6.1P			6.1S					
6.2 Review sigma calculation with consultants	6.2P			6.2S					
6.3 Modify if necessary	6.3P			6.3S					

P = Primary Responsibility; S = Secondary Responsibility; A = Approval

Figure 6.4 (Continued)

Madrid said that the meeting was going to begin with an exercise that was going to be a "gut-check" for the team. Silence pervaded the room as Kylie, dressed in a black and gray pinstriped business suit, three-inch heels, and off-black hose proceeded to the front of the conference room where the four Evian water bottles had been placed. Robert Wallace had taken a seat near the front. Prior to the meeting, Kylie had removed the cap of one of the bottles and emptied its contents.

"Think of these water bottles as being you. I am about to have you do a self-perception check but moreover also ask you to evaluate your fellow team members. First, think of this project and your openness to the ideas we are trying to impart. We at Temojoe Consulting are bottle #1. The water bottle I am holding represents both our Six Sigma knowledge and experience, which we are attempting to share with you. Bottle #2 as you can see is empty of Six Sigma knowledge and experience. But its cap is on. Watch what happens when I try to pour my knowledge and experience into a water bottle with its cap closed."

With that admonition, Kylie pours water from her bottle onto an empty Evian water bottle with its cap on. Water splashes in all directions hitting those near the front including Robert Wallace.

"Hey! Watch it, I'm getting wet," Wallace says with the most emotion he has shown since the team was formed two months ago.

Laughter pervades the room seeing the biggest Six Sigma resistor get his due. Madrid goes on with her presentation. "Or are you like bottle #3?" With Robert at a safe distance, Kylie proceeds to pour water from bottle #1 into bottle #3 which had its cap off. Some water trickles into bottle #3 but most hits the floor. The team is speechless but concentrates on Madrid's exercise. "Finally, are you the type of Six Sigma team member that results in Six Sigma success." With that admonition, Madrid takes out the funnel and proceeds to put it over Evian bottle #4. This time she pours the entire contents of bottle #1 into bottle #4.

As soon as Madrid finishes the exercise, she circulates a handout with the Call Center team member names and three columns next to each name labeled bottle #2, #3, and #4. She asks each team member to anonymously fill out a review of not only themselves but also each other Call Center team member. At the end of the meeting, Joy and Kylie review the assessments and find some surprises. Figure 6.5 shows the results. The number is the average provided by all ratings.

Doing the math in her head, Kylie communicated to Joy that even Robert and Jeff ranked themselves "3" while it was obvious everyone else rated them a "2." The big surprise was Maria being rated a 3.2. Kylie indicated to Joy that a special meeting should be scheduled to

Call Center Team Member	Bottle #2	Bottle #3	Bottle #4
Aaron Gregson			4.0
Maria Carballo		3.2	
Leroy Barney			4.0
Robert Wallace	2.8		
Suzanne Jackson			4.0
Joy Schulenberg			4.0
Aaron Brown			4.0
Jeff Seimonson	2.8		

Figure 6.5   Results of water bottle experiment.

handle what could become an on-going problem without intervention. Joy had several choices. She could meet with each person individually. She could meet with the entire group. She could have a meeting with just Maria, Robert, and Jeff. Kylie reviewed the positive and negatives of each approach. In the final analysis, the approach that was best was the one Joy was most comfortable with since she was going to play a pivotal role in its implementation.

Joy decided to hold a special team meeting. Prior to that meeting, she planned to meet with Maria, Robert, and Jeff, separately. She felt surprised by Maria's vote and felt personally responsible that she didn't see that one coming, having spent time on the lack of work by Robert and Jeff. She wanted an entire team meeting in the unlikely event another team member might lag in the future. At the same time, she wanted to collect data on her three laggards to see if there was anything to avert the type of confrontation that was likely in the large team meeting.

Kylie agreed with her strategy and offered to help in whatever way Joy wanted. Joy asked that Kylie coach her on the tools to use with this intervention. In addition, Kylie helped structure the agenda for this special meeting that was to be held March 25, the next scheduled meeting for the Call Center team.

Figure 6.6 shows the agenda for the meeting on March 25. Joy knew her work was cut out for her prior to March 25. Kylie had agreed to spend additional time the next day coaching Joy on the intervention tools while Joy was busy scheduling individual meetings with Maria, Robert, and Jeff.

She met with Maria first. On some level, she was sure it was due to the curiosity about Maria's ranking which came as such a surprise. On another level, Joy wondered if she was avoiding the inevitable

Element	Desired Outcome	Method	Responsible Party	Time Allotted
Review agenda and ground rules.	Agreement on agenda and ground rules.	Discussion and consensus	Joy and Team	5 min.
Creating the need for the Call Center project.	Creating the threats/ opportunities for the Call Center project.	Threat/ opportunity matrix	Joy and Team	30 min.
Shaping the vision of a new improved Call Center.	Create the vision, mindset, and results of a new Call Center.	More of/less of exercise	Joy and Team	25 min.
Identifying the sources of resistances to the Call Center Six Sigma effort.	Identification of the issues preventing the Call Center team from being further ahead on its project.	Stakeholder analysis and planning for influence chart	Joy and Team	30 min.
Update on the process map validation.	Report on the validation of the brainstormed "As-Is" Process Map.	Report out	Jeff and Robert	10 min.
Plus/Delta	Review pluses and deltas of meeting.	Brainstorming	Team	5 min.

Figure 6.6 Call Center agenda for March 25.

dreariness that awaited her when it came time to meet with Robert and Jeff off-line.

Joy had agreed it might be better to meet with Maria away from Alpha Omega and scheduled lunch the next day. Maria was clearly nervous as they drove to the restaurant for lunch.

Maria preempted Joy's questions about her rating. "Joy, I know why we are having lunch. It's likely that I didn't register a four on the bottle test. You are probably the only one on the team that doesn't know that Aaron Gregson covered for me on the survey on which I was supposed to be the secondary responsible party. Every time you met with me, I was showing you Aaron's work and taking credit for what he was doing."

Joy's shock almost made her drive off the road. Maria had clearly dropped a bombshell. She tried to think of something professionally appropriate to say but the silence was becoming deafening. She finally decided to be a friend instead of the team leader/facilitator.

"It must have taken a lot for you to just make that admission so directly and honestly, Maria. I give you credit for taking responsibility for your actions. My only question is why?"

"I could give you a million excuses. I can see you are far busier with the team leader role than I could ever have imagined. You haven't complained once. My problem with what we are doing wasn't like Robert and Jeff. They are nonbelievers. My problem was a combination of time management and lack of confidence. I thought I couldn't deal with the statistics of a survey plus I am not as well organized as I should be. Not only did Aaron cover for me, he also kept saying how relatively easy creating, administering, and compiling the data for the survey was. He actually said it was fun and very informative. He even thinks the data from the survey and focus group could be used to help in calculating baseline sigma. Joy, I am ashamed. I clearly didn't carry my weight on this project and my guilt has been massive. Just give me another chance and I promise I will make it up to you and the team."

By now Joy and Maria were at the restaurant and had already ordered lunch. Maria acknowledged Joy's next comments as she ate her lunch. "I appreciate the apology, Maria. But in all honesty, it doesn't seem like your behavior will be a problem in the future. What I am most concerned about now is Robert and Jeff. What do you anticipate their issues will be when I talk with them?"

"I haven't spent much time with them directly. But the word on the street is that they think this is TQM warmed over. I saw a couple of the Dilbert cartoons on Six Sigma posted in Robert's office with your name and Joe Hawke's name penciled over Ratbert, the consultant."

Over lunch, Maria and Joy went on to work out a communication plan that would alert Joy to any problems Maria had with future assignments. Joy contracted with Maria that she would give Maria additional assignments during the course of the DMAIC methodology but Maria would inform her if she was encountering time management problems or was uncomfortable with the assignment. Joy left the restaurant with Maria, certain that one of her problems had been addressed.

Unbeknownst to Maria and Joy, Robert and Jeff were seated at the same restaurant that same day. Robert had asked Jeff to lunch to commiserate about the Six Sigma project.

"This project is a waste of our time. I just wish it would go away."

"I agree with you, Jeff. This is a waste of time and money. They don't really understand our business. I have a hundred other things to work on. I tell you one thing, if I had been in charge and they had done what I wanted, we wouldn't have so much inefficiency. We don't need Six Sigma, we just need better workers in the Call Center and better management in the portfolio management function and management in general." With those comments, Robert dived into his lunch and Jeff finished his meal. Both discussed how they could dodge the meeting on the 25th.

"One thing about the TQM effort we had years ago, Jeff, it died of its own weight. I just wish we could have the same thing happen here. I will have to admit that this has the attention of management more than our previous effort. I still think it will die a natural death. I just wish I could help it along some. I really don't want to attend this meeting on the 25th. It will be another touchy-feely session if Joy is running it. Just like that icebreaker session."

"I know what you mean. It made me feel uncomfortable. Maybe if we just cooperate, we can get this over quickly. I know I don't want to be there on the 25th, Bob."

The rest of their lunch was spent in similar fashion but no decision was made about dodging the March 25 meeting.

Joy attempted to meet with both Jeff and Robert. Efforts to schedule these meetings were always met with excuses.

On March 25, Joy began what would later prove to be the most important Six Sigma meeting she would lead by reviewing the desired outcomes. She began the meeting promptly with all in attendance except Robert and Jeff. She acknowledged their absence but indicated both the amount and importance of the work around gaining greater team cohesion could not wait.

Joy referenced the copious notes she had taken from several coaching sessions on the topic from Kylie. Reviewing the agenda, ground rules, and expectations had become routine. This time the group didn't just rubberstamp what Joy had created. They asked for clarification on much of the agenda and desired outcomes and asked for clarification on the concepts within the agenda. Joy provided a high-level conceptual review and promised more detail on the tools and techniques as they were introduced throughout the agenda.

Joy first explained that any project will provide a change to the targeted area. She briefly explained that the word change is associated with the word "loss." If people perceive change as loss, this will lead to resistance to the project because people will link the project to the loss of the status quo.

➤ Creating the Need for a Project

To ignore these natural feelings of resistance will ultimately spell the doom of the project. Resistance ignored is resistance that wins. To overcome resistance involves simple but effective tools. The problem is while the tools associated with overcoming resistance are simple to understand and use, they are tools and techniques that are applied not to processes but people. As a result, using these tools can become complicated. The approach to overcoming resistance to change at the project level is as follows:

➤ Create or establish the need for the change.

➤ Shape a vision of what the change will bring to those affected.

➤ Review current and desired commitment to the change among those who will either be affected by the change or need to implement the change.

➤ Continuously measure the acceptance of the change.

➤ Monitor and modify the systems and structures within the organization that either support or constrain the acceptance of change.

As it affected the Call Center team, the first three items needed to be addressed were within the team itself. That was because it was becoming apparent that there was resistance to change within the Call Center team itself. Since during the Improve phase of DMAIC this same team would be required to impact change among other stakeholders, it was critical to get all the Call Center team members on the same page in terms of support for the project.

Kylie's water bottle exercise had begun the journey for the Call Center team to do a self-evaluation. A significant number of the team members were not in a position to be called advocates of the project. Consequently, it was now time to work on the first three elements of overcoming resistance.

The first three elements associated with overcoming resistance are not linear. Therefore, you don't necessarily have to first create the need, then shape a vision, and then review commitment. However, Joy picked creating the need for the Six Sigma team. On two flip charts, Joy wrote two questions she wanted everyone to ponder seriously and answer.

Question 1

What will happen if the Call Center is successful in its Six Sigma efforts to improve effectiveness and efficiency?

Question 2

What will happen if the Call Center does not take Six Sigma efforts to improve effectiveness and efficiency?

In a brief tutorial, Joy reviews what is behind each question. She says that the need for any change is created through two venues. First, the threats to the organization for maintaining the status quo must be established. People change when a threat is felt. If I threaten you with the loss of something you value, it is highly likely that will motivate your behavior. The concept works with the behavior of children. If I threaten my boys with withholding their skateboard time if they don't clean their room, it is highly likely they will comply with my request to change behavior.

However, the reliance on threats to assure the need for change is created will result in short-lived results. Relying on threatening your children to create a need for change will ultimately result in either passive compliance, rebellion, or increased resistance. Threats are great motivators for change in the short term.

The best way to create a need for change is to identify the opportunities that will occur as a result of the change. People will be far more motivated to see the need for change if they can witness the positive advantages associated with moving from the status quo.

By answering the two questions, the Call Center team can create the need for their project. Each of the participants worked on Question 1 and wrote one idea per Post-it in answering that question.

After clarifying and duplicating like ideas, Joy has the Call Center team multi-vote. The list of those receiving the most votes were:

➤ Improved first call resolution.

➤ Decrease in the Call Center Index.

➤ Less frustration.

➤ Less overtime.

The same process was used for Question 2. The team posted their answers on the wall. After clarifying and duplicating like ideas, Joy once again had the Call Center team multi-vote. The list of those receiving the most votes were:

➤ Continued increase in the Call Center Index.

➤ Greater overtime.

➤ Greater stress among employees.

➤ Greater dissatisfaction with Alpha Omega.

➤ Greater chance of customers leaving Alpha Omega for competition.

➤ Increased turnover due to stress and unwanted overtime.

Joy reviews the list and has the Call Center team challenge all ideas. She indicates that no idea should be used unless it can be proven through data or demonstration, the latter of which is described by anecdote or best practice. She also describes the importance of communicating each threat or opportunity in the language most important to the stakeholder to whom the message is directed. Using this criteria, such threats or opportunities as "improved first call resolution" or "continued increase in the Call Center Index" would have to be more personalized. For example, improved first call resolution could reasonably be expected to improve customer satisfaction, which in turn could improve job security for Alpha Omega employees.

After a discussion of which threats and opportunities could either be proven or shown to be a best practice, the Call Center created the "Threat/Opportunity Matrix" shown in Figure 6.7. The last thing the Call Center team does is determine which of the threats will occur in the next 12 months (these are labeled short-term threats) and which threats will occur beyond 12 months (these are labeled long-term threats). They next do the same thing for opportunities.

Just as the Call Center team was completing their Threat/Opportunity Matrix, Jeff and Robert joined the meeting. They were greeted

Short-Term Threats	Short-Term Opportunities
Continued increase in the Call Center Index Greater overtime Greater stress among employees	Improved first call resolution Decrease in the Call Center Index Less frustration Less overtime
Long-Term Threats	**Long-Term Opportunities**
Greater dissatisfaction with Alpha Omega Greater chance of customers leaving Alpha Omega for competition Increased turnover due to stress and unwanted overtime	Greater job security

Figure 6.7 Threat/Opportunity matrix.

with silence from the rest of the Call Center team—the "cold-shoulder treatment." Joy knew she had to provide some intervention but wasn't sure what to do immediately. She bought time by nodding casually to both men as she went on to the next agenda item. However, without a well-timed and high-level intervention soon, the Call Center team was subject to "The Dead Elk Syndrome."

"The Dead Elk Syndrome" is something that Kylie Madrid had warned Joy about during her last visit. She said that maladaptive behavior that goes unaddressed is similar to a dead elk in the middle of the family room. A dead elk is not supposed to be in the middle of a family room. To ignore a dead elk in the family room results in further maladaptive behavior. First, you have to go around a dead elk to go into the kitchen. Most importantly, after a time of ignoring a dead elk, it really smells up the house. The analogy of the dead elk in a Six Sigma team is obvious: An event or situation left ignored smells up the entire team. Joy knew a high-level intervention was needed for her dead elks, Jeff and Robert, but proceeded with shaping the vision of the Call Center team, simultaneously contemplating what her intervention would be.

➤ Shaping the Vision for a Project

Once the need for change has been established for a project team, a vision of where the successfully implemented project team will take the organization needs to be developed. To accomplish this task, Joy indicated this scenario:

Team, suppose you met someone in the elevator who works in the Call Center. Further suppose they are skeptical of our project and want to know why you are participating. What I would like you to script out and be ready to read is a 90-second or less statement that answers the following:

➤ *What is Six Sigma?*

➤ *Why has the Call Center team been chosen for a Six Sigma project?*

➤ *What is expected of the Call Center team relative to the project?*

➤ *What are the benefits to the Call Center team participants for being a part of this team?*

As she finished administering the assignment, she also had determined her intervention. "Once you have scripted your answers, we will share our individual answers starting with Robert and Jeff."

Neither Robert or Jeff seemed phased by the request. When it came time to hear their "Elevator Speech," their poor performance was evident. Neither man had speeches that would have convinced their potential listener how important or vital the Call Center project work was. In keeping with giving feedback that was constructive, pluses and deltas were given. In short order, Joy had the other Call Center members give their Elevator Speeches. Over the course of several report-outs, she asked for the most motivating answers for each of the four questions (see Figure 6.8). Leroy had a great response for what is Six Sigma. Aaron Gregson had the most motivating answer for why the Call Center team had been chosen for a Six Sigma project. Suzanne Jackson gave a good answer for what is expected of the Call Center team relative to the project. Aaron Brown provided the preferred answer to what are the benefits to the Call Center team participants for being a part of this team.

Joy encouraged every Call Center team member to begin memorizing this Elevator Speech in an effort to communicate to other Call Center employees what the project was and why they were doing it. She next moved to her last issue associated with dealing with the project team's resistance.

➤ Identifying the Sources of Resistance to the Call Center Project

So far during this meeting, the Call Center team had been working on the periphery of issues dealing with resistance. While creating a

Six Sigma is a management philosophy that focuses on improving the effectiveness and efficiency of an organization. Effectiveness is the degree which we meet customers needs and requirements while efficiency is the resources consumed in being effective, whether it's measured in time, money, or labor. The Call Center project team has been chosen as one of Alpha Omega's first project's due to the excessive call index of 42%. It is expected that the Call Center Six Sigma team will reduce the Call Center Index which would result in greater customer satisfaction, less stress to the Call Center employees, and greater job security through increased customer expansion, the latter of which will occur in part once customers and potential customers realize that Alpha Omega is the easiest financial and card holder organization to deal with. To achieve these goals the Call Center team members are required to spend upwards of 20% of their work time collecting data on the current process, determining root causation for the extent of the current problems, and generating and implementing a set of solutions that will reduce the Call Center Index.

Figure 6.8 Call Center's cumulative elevator speech.

need for the Call Center project and then shaping a vision were critical first steps to overcoming resistance, Joy was now about to deal with resistance issues head on. She started out having everyone answer a simple question on Post-it notes:

What are your personal concerns that prevent you from being 100 percent behind the project?

This simple but forceful question was meant to elicit issues that prevented each team member from being 100 percent behind the project. Of course, a hidden agenda behind this question was determining if there was resistance on the part of a Call Center team member. Only after each team member had written down his or her answer did Joy begin her tutorial on resistance.

First, Joy indicated that there were five categories of support (or nonsupport) for a Six Sigma project as it applies to the team members who are the most important stakeholders of the project. Stakeholders as earlier described are those individuals who are affected by change or are necessary to implement the change. The Call Center team members are stakeholders who are both affected by the change (since they are Call Center employees) and also necessary to implement the change since they are team members.

Figure 6.9 indicates the Stakeholder Analysis chart where each stakeholder (i.e., Call Center team members) is listed down the left-hand column and the five potential levels of support are to the right. First, there is the strongly supportive column. The strongly supportive team member is sometimes known as the "Make It Happen" person. The operational definition of someone in this category would be someone on the Linear Responsibility chart who not only does what is asked of them but also helps others accomplish their tasks. Clearly, Aaron Gregson's assistance of Maria Carballo on the customer validation action items would place him in this category. This would also be someone who when trying to answer the question about what prevents them from being 100 percent behind the project couldn't come up with an answer.

The second category is the moderately supportive stakeholder. This would be someone who "Helps It Happen." In other words, they do what is asked of them but probably have some mild issues associated with the project. The neutral column refers to stakeholders who have more significant issues that prevent their involvement but will not get in the way of the general momentum of the team's work. The next column refers to stakeholders who are considered moderately against the project. This refers to people who have significant issues around why they can't support the project. Finally, there is the strongly against category. This refers to people on the project team who are so virulent in their resistance, they not only will not do what is asked of them in terms of project action items, they will try to recruit others to join their resistance.

Key Stakeholder	Strongly Supportive	Moderately Supportive	Neutral	Moderately Against	Strongly Against

Figure 6.9 Stakeholder analysis chart.

Once Joy had described the stakeholder analysis chart, she reviewed the Post-it notes with the issues that prevented the team from being 100 percent behind the project. They included the following:

➤ The amount of time devoted to the project.

➤ Uncertainty around rewards and recognition.

➤ Uncertainty that the goals and objectives could be accomplished in the time allotted.

➤ Lack of confidence relative to what to do to achieve results.

➤ This is just a fad.

➤ This is just a way to get the Call Center team to work harder.

➤ We have tried this before and failed.

➤ I was drafted, I didn't volunteer.

Instead of trying to deal with these important issues herself, Joy decided to have their Champion, Charles Zukor, address them formally before their next meeting in keeping with his responsibilities. The last thing Joy requested is that the preprinted Stakeholder Analysis forms be filled out by each individual, ranking themselves and the other team members. The meeting ended with a report-out from Jeff and Robert on the validation of the Process Map. While the report-out was short, it did seem to validate through interviews with current Call Center employees and observation of the process that the work done brainstorming in the training class was indeed accurate. With a sense of relief that the Call Center resistors had completed their tasks, Joy collected the stakeholder analysis handouts and proceeded to the pluses/deltas. The reaction to the exercise around resistance was very well received and, aside from time management as a delta, there were no other issues. Unfortunately, the "dead elk" of the tardiness of Jeff and Robert was neither brought up by the team nor explained by Jeff and Robert.

Anxiously, Joy retreated to her office and compiled the stakeholder analysis chart. Figure 6.10 is the stakeholder analysis chart for the Call Center project team.

Joy scheduled a meeting with Charles to discuss his formal responses to the Call Center's team issues and to develop a strategy to deal with Robert and Jeff. Relative to dealing with Robert and Jeff, there was some level of apprehension but she knew she could rely on Charles to provide assistance. When she looked at her linear response plan, she knew that during the April 8 morning report-outs, her team

Key Stakeholder	Strongly Supportive	Moderately Supportive	Neutral	Moderately Against	Strongly Against
Aaron Gregson	X				
Maria Carballo		X			
Leroy Barney	X				
Robert Wallace					X
Suzanne Jackson	X				
Joy Schulenberg	X				
Aaron Brown	X				
Jeff Seimonson				X	

Figure 6.10 Completed stakeholder analysis chart.

would be in good shape to complete all the Define and Measure deliverables.

➤ Champions and Interventions

The meeting between Joy and Charles was short. In reviewing the list of concerns that prevented total support of the Call Center team, he was struck by which of the concerns could be addressed by a large group meeting with the Call Center team and if any individuals on the team should have a separate meeting. After a review of the stakeholder analysis chart, Charles was certain that two people on his team needed one-on-one coaching.

Even before Joy raised the issue of Robert and Jeff, Charles took control, "It's clear that we need at least three meetings, Joy. A separate meeting should be scheduled with Robert and Jeff. I will address remaining items at your next meeting. I want to meet with Robert and Jeff alone. I will schedule them within the next day or so and get back to you if there are unresolved issues."

"But what if they try to fabricate things that may mislead you about why they hold their current positions? You may need me there just as a reality check."

"I appreciate your concern, Joy, but if I can't smell a bull shitter at my age then I don't deserve to be your Champion. Besides, they may speak more freely without you present. If between you and them a giant pissing match starts, then I really can't intervene effectively."

With that, the meeting between Joy and Charles was concluded. Joy left the meeting with further respect for Charles' leadership. No sooner had Joy left Charles' office then he called Robert and Jeff. It was past 5:00 P.M. and both had apparently left for the day. He left messages that they were to call him the first thing the next morning. Not wanting to cause undue alarm, Charles showed both of them the respect of indicating what he wanted to see them about; issues facing the Call Center Six Sigma team and their perception of the problems and their solutions to the problem.

Robert was the first to call back. Charles wanted a relaxed atmosphere for their conversation so Robert would be as candid as he possibly could. He suggested lunch at Red Robin, an upscale restaurant chain. Within hours, they were placing their orders. Charles started the discussion with asking how the project was going, "What is your opinion of Six Sigma?"

"Why do you ask, Charles. Would it matter if I told you it's another bureaucratic task that just gets in the way of people doing real work. But, of course, Charles, that's straight talk from a straight guy. And it doesn't really matter what I think of Six Sigma, does it? I mean, Brenda Sexson isn't going to stop her Six Sigma commitment in its tracks just because Robert Wallace thinks Six Sigma is a giant waste of time and resources, is she?"

Charles soon realized for all Robert's talents, skills, intelligence, and accomplishments, his attitude kept him from having Charles' job.

"No, Robert, your opinion won't determine the future course of Six Sigma at Alpha Omega. But the success or failure of these first projects will determine the future of Six Sigma at Alpha Omega. If they succeed, Six Sigma will likely end up being a way of life here. And if these first projects are failures, then its likely Six Sigma will be dumped. Is that what you want?"

"I don't agree with that opinion. I think like any other quality initiative, Six Sigma will fade here, just like TQM or Statistical Process Control or Just in Time. It will die of its own weight."

"I could argue with your basic premise, Robert. None of those initiatives have generated the kinds of results or management involvement like Six Sigma. But, I'm not going to argue the merits of Six Sigma with you, Robert, because unlike others who may feel that way who I could persuade to change their minds, I don't really think that is your issue. For all your skills, you have developed a reputation of being a naysayer within Alpha Omega. You certainly are aware through your performance reviews that this has been a problem for you. Participation in this project would be a way for you to correct this developmental need. Yet, looking at this stakeholder analysis chart, it looks like you aren't interested in being a team player."

"I'll do what is asked of me."

Charles found this comment lacking in commitment. "Is there any issue raised in the last meeting that you genuinely need me to help you with. I plan to formally address the team in next week's meeting. Issues such as other work and reward and recognition are legitimate issues that I plan to have solid answers for. If you want me to comment on any of these now, I will gladly and fully answer. But, I also advise you that resistance to Six Sigma is not a wise career move."

"I'll wait for the meeting next week, Charles. I am sure your wisdom will provide additional motivation for all of us."

Charles couldn't help but hear the sarcasm in Robert's answer. It was frustrating to Charles to know his first comments to Robert were perhaps the most important. It was his theory that Robert's attitude had precluded him from being promoted into the position that Charles now occupied. That embittered attitude had only worsened since being passed over and now he was negative to anything Alpha Omega's management pursued. Therefore, Robert could take an "I told you so" approach if Six Sigma was not successful in the first wave of projects. Yet, it was dependent on people like Robert to make it successful. Robert was in a traditional chicken-and-egg scenario. Charles left the lunch with his jaded employee knowing this would probably not be the last intervention between the two.

On his return from his less than successful lunch with Robert, there was a message waiting from Jeff. He called and arranged to have a meeting at the end of the day, promising Jeff to stop by his office. The rest of the day went quickly and before he knew it Charles was in Jeff's office.

"I know why you are here, Charles. I really do have some issues with this Six Sigma thing. I appreciate you taking time to try to answer them."

"Jeff, the experts have taught me smart people sometime are skeptical of Six Sigma but if their issues are addressed they become the best leaders. List out your concerns as specifically as you can and I will do my best to bring you into the fold."

Unlike the meeting with Robert, the meeting with Jeff was spent on a variety of issues that were specific and legitimate. The biggest issues for Jeff were the time it took away from his normal work and the fact that the issues affecting the Call Center came from other processes. More general issues related to what was in it for him to pursue such a large scale project.

Charles spent the better part of an hour answering the questions. First, he made note of the amount of inefficiency in the Call Center that could be improved allowing for greater work life balance. Aware of Jeff's closeness to his family in general and dyslexic son in particular, he stressed the lower overtime that would come by putting in more work now on the Six Sigma project. He also emphasized that the Call Center would have a less stressful atmosphere if the Call Center Index was reduced. Most importantly, he agreed that if the data pointed to other processes he would expand the Scope of the project in the direction the data led the team. Some of these other processes such as portfolio management, dispute resolution, and order fulfillment were part of the first wave of Six Sigma projects as well. He didn't overstate this case, saying not every problem associated with Alpha Omega would be solved in these first wave projects. Jeff seemed genuinely pleased by Charles' efforts to appease him. His interest in dispute resolution was raised as an issue and Charles promised him input into that project, going so far as to say that if it was necessary, Jeff could even be an ad hoc member of the dispute team or at a minimum be the Call Center liaison to that team if the data showed that the two projects were related. Of course, by giving Jeff this promise, he expected something in return.

"Jeff, if the data shows a relationship between the Call Center team and dispute resolution, I want you deeply involved. However, this can only occur if you are seen doing the work associated with the Call Center team. How does this sound to you?"

"For years, I have been saying that one reason the Call Center Index was as high as it is was due to problems our customers have related to the billing statement design. If the dispute resolution team goes in that direction, I would like to be of assistance to them based on the data we have to help them with that redesign. Of course, if you were to let me assist them, I understand the need to be a team player for the Call Center. That would only be fair."

Amazingly, through this discussion Charles felt that additional work, albeit not directly associated with the Call Center, was a key to get Jeff on board with his Call Center responsibilities. Charles left work that day feeling he had done his job effectively as a Champion, at least with Jeff. It remained an open question if there was any hope for Robert.

Over the course of the next week, Charles prepared answers to the formal issues raised by the Call Center team relative to why they couldn't be 100 percent behind the Call Center project. During the meeting he attended the following week, the team responded favorably to his responses to their inquiries that are discussed next.

The Amount of Time Devoted to the Project

Six Sigma teams average about 20 percent of their time dealing with project work. Good project and time management can reduce that time, but not significantly. Six Sigma teams must first realize that Business Process Management processes that have the highest impact and worse performance have been targeted for improvement. A typical process has over 50 percent inefficiency associated with it. One major method to measure inefficiency is cycle time. For the Call Center team, a Call Center Index registering 42 percent means a great deal of unnecessary overtime, stress, and unnecessary work. Thus, while the extra work to improve the process may seem burdensome, if the team is successful, they can dramatically reduce the amount of time associated with excessive cycle time associated with the current process. While the short-term pain of improvement cannot be denied, the best and brightest of the Call Center have been chosen to generate the solutions to create lasting gain for the entire Call Center operation.

Charles went on to explain that when a person finds out they are not physically fit, that person needs to change their lifestyle which may require more work (i.e., exercising more which may mean getting up earlier or going to the gym rather than heading right home), but that those additional hours spent doing the right things are necessary for survival.

Uncertainty Around Rewards and Recognition

While it may be nice to have your ego stroked as being the best and brightest, it is also true that the best and brightest are always chosen for special projects. Six Sigma is no different. Of course, those that are the best and brightest in an organization should also be those that are most recognized and rewarded in an organization. Thus, the next statement by Charles Zukor turned this issue on its head.

"Most of the Champions have been talking among themselves about the time it takes to be a part of the team. This has been a ubiquitous issue for all Champions. At Brenda's last staff meeting, we brainstormed various rewards and recognition. They ran the gamut from a pizza party to gain sharing. Pizza parties were quickly ruled out. Personally, I haven't had a good pizza since moving out to Colorado. It's a great place to ski but the pizza is terrible. Instead, I am authorized to inform you today that achieving improvement in the Call Center Index will result in all people on the team receiving an additional week of vacation. That means getting the Call Center Index down to 35 percent from its current level of 42 percent. Brenda has approved my request of an additional two weeks of vacation if we can match the national industry standard of 30 percent."

Reaction was swift and positive. Leroy Barney was the first to comment. "Darn, that extra week of vacation would go over well with the family. Okay, Charles. I am psyched. Let's wrap up this discussion so we can get on with our data collection implementation and baseline sigma calculations."

"I just have a few more questions to answer and I will be out of your hair, Leroy." Charles saw the energy in the room rise conspicuously, even for Jeff. Robert remained stoic as always.

Charles moved to the last items on the list provided by Joy the week before.

Uncertainty That the Goals and Objective Could Be Accomplished in the Time Allotted

Charles emphasized the concept of tollgates and the milestones through the end of September. He stated that the Call Center team was off to a good start despite some team dynamic issues. With the last statement, Charles made sustained eye contact with his nemesis, Robert Wallace. He emphasized the reasonable goal of reduction in the Call Center Index down to 35 percent. There was no objection to this as a goal, particularly after his proclamation of the vacation reward.

Lack of Confidence Relative to What to Do to Achieve Results

Charles began discussion of this issue by asking what he could personally do to increase either an individual's confidence or the team's confidence. Without waiting for an answer, he indicated that everyone is in a learning mode during this first-wave project. He also stressed that the contract with Temojoe Consulting included intersession consulting with individual teams. Charles continued by indicating that he would personally make Kylie Madrid available if necessary. As he concluded his offer, Maria spoke up. "I just don't feel comfortable with a lot of the math. I would feel embarrassed if Kylie just came in for me. I think it would be nice if we had some intersession tutorials. But not if I'm the only one who needs the work. If that is the case, Joy and I have agreed to work closer."

Joy intervened with a suggestion. "I heard Kylie will be here at the end of March for a general review. I will make sure everyone on the team gets an invite."

This Is Just a Fad

Charles seemed short-tempered with this one, speculating that Robert Wallace is the author of this idea. "Hula hoops were a fad. Pet rocks and mood rings were fads. Improving the way something is done is more than a fad. It's all of our jobs to make sure that Six Sigma becomes our method of achieving greater improvements in effectiveness and efficiency. One fact is indisputable. Many other organizations have used Six Sigma to save millions of dollars and assist them in achieving their business objectives. If we don't do the same, then there is something wrong with us, not Six Sigma. These first 11 projects of which we are a part will determine if this is a fad at Alpha Omega. If you believe it is a fad, then it will become a self-fulfilling prophecy."

This Is Just a Way to Get the Call Center Team to Work Harder

Charles discussed this issue by asking how hard the project team works in the Call Center. He talks of the excessive overtime, stress, and the impact an inefficient Call Center has on everyone. Through Six Sigma, these issues that currently contribute to the excessive hours can be positively impacted. The goal of Six Sigma is not to work harder but smarter.

We Have Tried This Before and Failed

Charles first acknowledges a fact. "Yes, Alpha Omega has engaged in improvement efforts in the past. Yes, those efforts have failed. The key reason behind our previous efforts failing was that previous efforts at quality were without a strategy, they were without a connection to our overall business objectives and thus were without management support. Each of these situations is different with this initiative. Yes, we failed with previous efforts, but this is not going to be the case with Six Sigma."

I Was Drafted, I Didn't Volunteer

Charles' perspective on this was a twist on what was initially meant by the statement. "When I first read this I had a different take than the person who brought it up. I thought to myself, of course, you were drafted; not only drafted but you all are #1 draft choices. I was thinking of football draft choices and the writer was thinking of the military. I want you all to understand that we were advised to choose the best and the brightest. I did that without qualification. Recognize that your being drafted for this assignment means something to other managers and leaders in this organization. What it means is that you are seen as current or future business leaders of the organization."

The feedback from this meeting with Charles was highly positive. He answered questions directly and motivated the team in the process, particularly when he discussed the vacation reward. With less than a few days before the Analysis training and data yet to be collected, it was just the tonic needed to move the team through the rest of the Measure phase of their project.

■ SUMMARY

Six Sigma teams go through a series of stages before actual work can begin. Tuckman created a model of four stages of team development: forming, storming, norming, and ultimately performing. Chapter 6 was devoted to various interventions that should take place as teams begin storming.

In the storming phase, various maladaptive behaviors begin to exhibit themselves. The focus of Chapter 6 was on the more serious maladaptive behaviors a Six Sigma team can encounter; namely, the failure of certain team members to want to be a part of the Six Sigma effort. We discussed general ideas to counter this problem. First, Six Sigma teams that begin to see each other as people rather than just someone conducting action items can be helpful. Therefore, we introduced the importance of icebreakers. An icebreaker is an activity that allows a Six Sigma team to know others in a more direct personal manner. The assumption of the icebreaker is once a person is known in this manner the chances of progressing past the storming phase increase dramatically.

Unfortunately, many Six Sigma teams will encounter more serious problems. Thus, the concept of gaining acceptance among the team for the project must be formally developed. The tools to accomplish this are simple in nature. However, they deal with highly personal issues. The tools of creating the need for the project, shaping a vision, analyzing current support among the team to Six Sigma, and ascertaining what prevents the team from wholeheartedly supporting the project must be established. This becomes the responsibility of both the team leader and Project Champion. Once the issues preventing the team from being a high-functioning team are determined, it is the responsibility of the team leader and Champion to intervene in such a way that the team moves into the performance necessary to achieve greater Six Sigma success.

■ REFERENCES

Tuckman, B. W. (1965). Developmental sequences in small groups. *Psychological Bulletin, 63,* 384–399.

Tuckman, B. W., & Jensen, M. A. C. (1977). Stages of small group development revisited. *Group and Organizational Studies, 2,* 419–427.

KEY LEARNINGS

➤ Tuckman's model of team development (forming, storming, norming, and performing) applies to Six Sigma teams.

➤ A Six Sigma team must be in the performing phase of Tuckman's model if they expect to achieve goals of improved sigma performance.

➤ Icebreakers are a great way for the team to understand each other on a more personal level.

➤ The concept of gaining acceptance to the project by the team should be seen as a formal set of activities.

➤ Resistance to the project is to be expected.

➤ Resistance must be formally managed by the team leader and the Project Champion.

➤ The first step in dealing with team member resistance is to create the need for the Six Sigma project. The need for the project can be created through determining what threats and opportunities are facing the project. Two questions can be asked to identify the threats and opportunities. First, what will happen if we don't successfully apply the concepts of Six Sigma to the project (the threats)? Second, what will happen if we successfully apply the concepts of Six Sigma to the project (the opportunities)?

➤ Threats and opportunities must be proven. An unproven threat or opportunity that sounds good but is unproven does damage rather than overcoming resistance within the team.

➤ A vision of the new process must be established to assist the team members develop support for participating in the project. This should include what is to be gained by participation in the project.

➤ Issues that prevent total support for participation in the project must be clearly identified and addressed by the team leader and Champion if the project team is expected to ultimately achieve greater sigma performance.

Chapter

Completing the Six Sigma Project

The Never–Ending Responsibility of the Champion

"Fool me once, shame on thee, fool me twice, shame on me."

Native American proverb

In Chapter 7, we look at the performance of the Alpha Omega Call Center team as they progress through the critical DMAIC phases of Analyze and Improve. Most importantly, we examine the vital role the Champion plays with team dynamics, showing that a Champion's leadership never ends. We examine how a proactive Champion reviews tollgates through the DMAIC process, and how he or she must recognize that the people issues surrounding the project they sponsor sometimes will call for tough decisions.

■ ALPHA OMEGA'S BASELINE SIGMA PERFORMANCE AND ANALYZE TRAINING

In the first week of April, baseline data had been collected on the Call Center project. The Call Center team now had four confirmed customer critical to quality (CTQs) characteristics. Through customer

Alpha Omega	Six Sigma Project Charter

Business Case (Connection to SBOs)

Alpha Omega has experienced significant decline in its operating profits and customer satisfaction, both of which are strategic business objectives. To positively influence both, improvement must occur across all business processes. Currently, the Call Center could positively impact customer satisfaction and operating profits through improvement of first call resolution, timeliness of response, and improvement in courtesy to the customer.

Project Scope

IN	OUT
External calls	Policy issues with customers
Issues related to first call resolution	Organization structure
Job descriptions	
Process redesign	
Other processes	
Customer index	
Customer courtesy	

Goal and Objectives	Subject Matter Experts
Reduce the call index from 42% to 36%	

APPROVAL

Champion:

Date:

Team Leader:

Date:

Six Sigma Director:

Date:

Figure 7.1 Completed charter template.

Problem Statement			
Since ___, Alpha Omega's Call Center has experienced a Call Index of 42% versus the industry standard of 30%. This has negatively impacted customer satisfaction and operating expenses placing Alpha Omega at a competitive disadvantage in meeting its strategic business objectives for operating profit and customer satisfaction.			

Expected Benefits	Target		Stretch
Total Savings	$ –	$ –	

Milestones Start Date	Plan	Actual
Define	February 6, 7, & 8	
Measure	February 6, 7, & 8	
Analyze	April 8, 9, 10, 11, & 12	
Improve	May 21, 22, & 23	
Control	June 25, 26	
Team:		
Champion	Charles Zukor	
Team Leader	Joy Schulenberg	
Master Black Belt		
Team Members	Role	Percent of Time
Aaron Gregson		
Maria Carballo		
Leroy Barney		
Robert Wallace		
Susan Jackson		
Aaron Brown		
Jeff Seimonson		

Figure 7.1 *(Continued)*

validation, they had determined the *call index, first call resolution* (measured by dividing percent of return calls by total calls), *call resolution time* (measured by the beginning of the call to the final resolution), and *courtesy* were the top four customer requirements. The team was now prepared to calculate baseline sigma performance, and there are multiple ways this can be accomplished. One method to calculate sigma is to perform calculations of each of the CTQs individually. The other method is to use a formula that combines all four CTQs into one measure. This "mother" sigma, as it is sometimes called, was determined not to be as useful as four separate calculations. As the poker players say, "Read 'em and weep." The baseline sigmas for the four CTQs were:

Call Index	1.2 sigma
First call resolution	1.3 sigma
Call resolution time	0.9 sigma
Courtesy	2.8 sigma

Fortunately, the Call Center team had plenty of company with the other ten Alpha Omega teams. Virtually all of the teams registered 2.0 sigma performance or lower. Kylie Madrid and Joe Hawke stressed that low sigma performance was expected since the strategic selection of these first wave projects was based on low performance. It would have been more of a surprise if baseline sigma performance in these first wave projects had been three or higher. Selecting processes with good sigma performance would have been counter to the concept of selecting processes where there was currently available "low-hanging fruit."

Figures 7.1–7.4 show the Call Center team's presentation of their Define and Measure tollgates that had been completed during the intersession—February 9 through April 7.

■ MANAGING *ANALYZE*—TOLLGATE #1: DATA ANALYSIS

Project teams felt chastened by their baseline sigma performance. As a result, their attention to the tutorial by Joe Hawke the afternoon of April 8 was particularly focused, even more so when Hawke said that if done right, Analyze would pave the way for a significant improvement in sigma performance.

First, Hawke illustrated the relationship of the first two tollgates of Analyze, *Data Analysis* and *Process Analysis,* and the third tollgate,

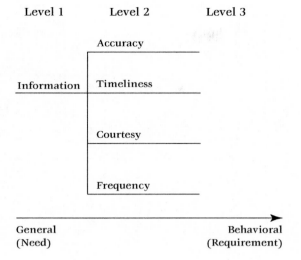

Figure 7.2   Call Center CTQ tree.

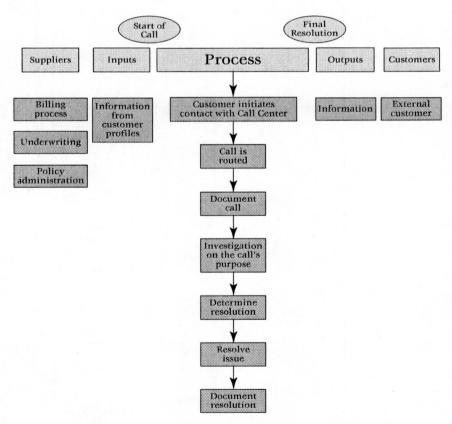

Figure 7.3   Call Center information process.

What to Measure	Type of Measure	Type of Data	Operational Definition	Target	Specification	Data Collection Forms(s)	Sampling	Baseline Six Sigma
First call resolution	O	Discrete	Percent of return calls divided by total calls	100%	100%	Discrete Check Sheet	Representative/ random	1.3
Call response time	O,P	Continuous	Beginning of customer call to resolution of call	ASAP	5 minutes	Frequency Distribution Check Sheet	Representative/ random	0.9
Courtesy	O,I	Continuous	Likert scale of sampled customers where 5 = exceedingly courteous, 3 = courteous, 1 = not courteous	5	3	Frequency Distribution Check Sheet	Representative/ random	2.8
Call index	O	Continuous	Market research definition	0	30	Market Research Definition	Representative/ random	1.2

Figure 7.4 Completed Data Collection Plan.

Root Cause Analysis. He used the analogy of Root Cause Analysis being a house, and Data and Process Analysis were two doors that could be used to enter the house of root cause. He emphasized that there are multiple doors that can be used to enter a home, but one door is usually used more often than the others. For projects that had predominantly *effectiveness-based* goals, the data door would be the door of choice. The process door would be used if the project team had predominantly *efficiency-based* goals for their project. Regardless of which door is used, it was stressed that micro-problem questions would be the "key" to entering the root cause house. Figure 7.5 shows the path through the data door leading to the creation of the micro-problem question or questions.

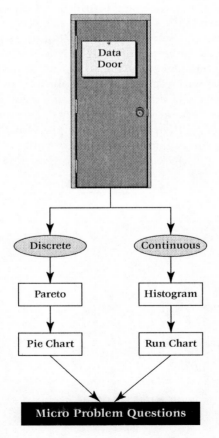

Figure 7.5 Process flow through data door.

Figure 7.5 also shows that data can be either *discrete* or *continuous*. As we learned in the Data Collection Plan Creation tollgate, discrete data is pass/fail, on/off, good/bad type data. Continuous data is data that exists on a continuum such as weight, time, length, and so on. The short-term goal of Data Analysis is to create a visual display of the data, revealing the variation in the process that would lead to the creation of the micro-problem question. Hawke quoted his mentor, W. Edwards Deming, as saying, "Variation is the enemy, and it is easier to fight an enemy you can see."

During the first breakout, the Call Center team created visual pictures of the variation in its process. Figure 7.6 shows the *histogram* the Call Center team created to observe more readily the variation in its process. A histogram is a bar graph, or frequency distribution that shows the number of times a given event occurs in a set of observations.

Data had been collected for the Call Center Index, which is the percent of return calls, along with first call resolution and courtesy. While this data was of some value, the histogram, or "picture" of call resolution time was the most interesting (Figure 7.6). There is an old saying that "customers feel variation in a process, not the average." This is especially true with regard to call resolution time. While the average call length to the Call Center was 13 minutes, you can see on the histogram that over 20 percent of Alpha Omega's customers experience 20 minutes or more on the phone, or have to call back until final resolution.

During the breakouts on the afternoon of April 8 and the morning of April 9, the Call Center team worked on Data Analysis, with

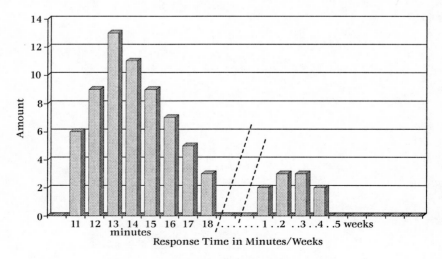

Figure 7.6 Histogram.

the short-term goal of generating a micro-problem question. While the team considered all of the data, the histogram on call resolution time generated the most attention. What made this histogram more important to the team was the clear correlation between resolution calls in the 20-minute plus range and call backs. This correlation meant that the customers who were on the phone 20 minutes and longer with a customer representative *also* had to call back since their problem was not rectified during the first call.

By the morning of April 9, the Call Center team was in a position to take the macro-problem statement (also called the preliminary problem statement) it created in the Define phase of the DMAIC methodology and make it more granular through the creation of the micro-problem question. Hawke and Madrid had encouraged the teams to create a question beginning with the word "Why."

The original macro-problem statement was:

Since January 2000, Alpha Omega's Call Center has experienced a call index of 42 percent versus the industry standard of 30 percent. This has negatively impacted customer satisfaction and operating expenses placing Alpha Omega at a competitive disadvantage in meeting its Strategic Business Objectives for operating profit and customer satisfaction.

After a review of all the relevant data, particularly the call resolution histogram, the Call Center team had created the following micro-problem question:

Why are over 20 percent of our customers spending 20 minutes or more on the phone with call center representatives?

■ MANAGING *ANALYZE*—TOLLGATE #2: PROCESS ANALYSIS

The afternoon of April 9 was devoted to Hawke's tutorial on Process Analysis. While the Call Center team felt invigorated by their work in Data Analysis, Joy and company were aware that call resolution time was an efficiency measure. Remembering Hawke's statement that Process Analysis is used predominantly for efficiency goals, the team knew they would be using Process Analysis for call resolution time.

Hawke explained that the first step of Process Analysis is highly dependent on how well the teams had validated the high-level Process Map they had created in the Define phase of DMAIC. The first step of

Process Analysis is to take the validated high-level "As-Is" map and do what he called *subprocess mapping*. Subprocess mapping is taking the five to seven high-level "As-Is" steps in the process and drilling down to the next, more granular level. Ideally, each of the five to seven steps should be subprocess mapped. However, Hawke indicated that if the team has fallen behind in its work, then the team should use their expertise to theorize which one or two of the five to seven high-level steps are most likely to hold the most inefficiency.

Like the high-level map completed in Define, the subprocess map also had to be validated. Hawke pointed out that during the afternoon breakout the teams would be given a chance to brainstorm what they thought the subprocess map would look like. He encouraged the teams to brainstorm the subprocess steps but not to assume that their brainstormed map was reality until it had been validated. As in high-level mapping, Hawke underscored the vital importance of creating the "As-Is" subprocess map, or the way it operates *today.*

For its breakout assignment, the Call Center team decided to pick the fifth step, *determine resolution,* from their high-level *call resolution* map. The team consensually decided this step took the longest and merited investigation because of what the histogram had shown them in Data Analysis.

The Call Center team determined that the following 13 subprocess steps constituted the *determine resolution* step in the call resolution process:

1. Customer is on hold waiting for a Call Center rep.
2. Customer is greeted and preliminary data is collected on the customer issue.
3. Call Center rep repeats the issue information back to the customer for verification.
4. Issue is either handled by the Call Center rep or, more likely, the customer is put on hold to gather further information.
5. Call Center rep verifies that the conversation is being taped in compliance with SEC regulations.
6. Call Center rep reconnects with customer to assure them their issue is under consideration.
7. Preliminary information for the customer is verified and reviewed by Call Center rep for accuracy of message.
8. Issue resolution is communicated to the customer.
9. Further clarification is requested by the customer, or the customer calls back.

10. Call Center rep emphasizes Alpha Omega's commitment to quality.

11. Further investigation of customer issue is conducted.

12. Complicated issues are queued for special treatment and held in the "urgent bin."

13. Communication of the resolution to the customer and verification with the customer of administrative paperwork.

Temojoe Consulting had taught the teams that once they brainstormed the subprocess map for at least one high-level step, it was necessary for them to categorize the subprocess steps as either adding value or not adding value, as well as estimating the time each subprocess step took. A value-added step was defined as meeting each of the following three criteria. First, it had to be important to the customer. Second, there had to be some physical change to the product or service going through that step. Third, it had to be done right the first time.

By the time the first breakout was over, the Call Center team had determined that, of the 13 *determine resolution* subprocess steps, only three of those steps added value according to the above definition. As had already been established through Data Analysis, the process could take as long as two weeks, and most of that time was spent in the *determine resolution* step.

Figure 7.7 shows a Process Summary Analysis Worksheet for the Call Center team. It shows the 13 subprocess steps in the first row and the best case and worse case times for each step in the second row. The third row indicates the three process steps that add value and the remainder of the grid indicates the type of nonvalue-added steps of the activity.

Process Analysis had confirmed the micro-problem question created through Data Analysis. In addition, Process Analysis had tentatively located the area where the greatest delays were occurring. From this Process Summary Analysis Worksheet, you can see *delays* are the biggest problem, whether you measure them as a percentage of the overall time of the subprocess steps or the percentage of the overall quantity of nonvalue-added steps. As a result of Process Analysis, the Call Center team created an additional micro-problem question: "Why are there so many delays in the *determine resolution* subprocess?"

The Call Center team knew that only through validation of the subprocess map would the second micro-problem question be worthy of its time and effort. While Hawke stressed the importance of not jumping to premature conclusions, most, if not all, of the Call Center

Process Step	1	2	3	4	5	6	7	8	9	10	11	12	13	Total	%
Time (minutes or days) Best/Worst	30 sec./ 1 hr.	2 min.	1 min.	1 min./ 1 wk.	30 sec.	30 sec.	30 sec.	2 min.	1 min./ 1 wk.*	10 sec.	1 day/ 3 days	1 hr./ 1 day	10**	†/ ‡	
Value add		x						x		x				3	23%
Nonvalue add	x		x	x	x	x	x		x		x	x	x	10	77%
Internal failure/rework														0	0%
External failure														0	0%
Control/ inspection			x				x						x	3	23%
Delays	x			x					x		x	x		5	38%
Preparation/ set up						x								1	8%
Moves														0	0%
Value enabling					x									1	8%

*If step 8 is successful, the rest of the steps are not seen.
**Administrative step not seen by customer.
† 1 day/1 hr./6 min./10 sec.
‡ 2 wks./4 days/1 hr/6 min./40 sec.

Figure 7.7 Process summary analysis worksheet.

team members felt confident that there would be no big surprises during the subprocess map intersession validation.

■ MANAGING *ANALYZE*—TOLLGATE #3: ROOT CAUSE ANALYSIS

Joe Hawke began his tutorial on the third tollgate of Analyze by indicating his belief that Analyze is the most important phase of DMAIC work, and that Root Cause Analysis was the most important tollgate in Analyze. He returned to the analogy of the data door and process door being used to enter the "house of root causation." The "keys" to this house were the micro-problem questions that could only be used accurately once intersession validation occurred on the subprocess map.

Nonetheless, Hawke instructed the class participants to use their unvalidated micro-problem questions to assist them in learning the tools of root causation. Algebraically, root causation is stated as $Y = f(x_1, x_2, x_3...x_n)$, where Y is the micro-problem question, which is a function (f) of a series of process variables, or xs. The goal of Root Cause Analysis is to solve this formula. At the advent of root causation, the Six Sigma project team used its technical expertise to generate as many xs as possible. The tool of choice for generating these process variables (xs) is the Cause-Effect Diagram. Located in Figure 7.8, the micro-problem question is positioned in the box to the far right. Attached to the micro-problem question is a horizontal line with six diagonal lines coming out of the horizontal line. These six lines represent the major sources of variation in any process, called *process variables:* Machines, Materials, Methods, Measurements, Mother Nature (environment), and People (sometimes called the 5 Ms and 1 P). In the case of the Call Center project team, their third breakout was devoted to brainstorming as many of the process variables, or xs, as possible that could explain the micro-problem question. In Figure 7.8, we see a partial list of the process variables the Call Center team believed would explain the micro-problem question. The team believed there was significant overlap in the two proposed micro-problem questions. Therefore, they combined their brainstormed ideas into one micro-problem question. This combined micro-problem question was:

> *Why are delays in the determine resolution subprocess resulting in 20 percent of customers spending more than 20 minutes on the phone with Call Center representatives?*

Upon the return of the project teams to the large group, Hawke instructed them to use the concepts of the Affinity Diagram to narrow

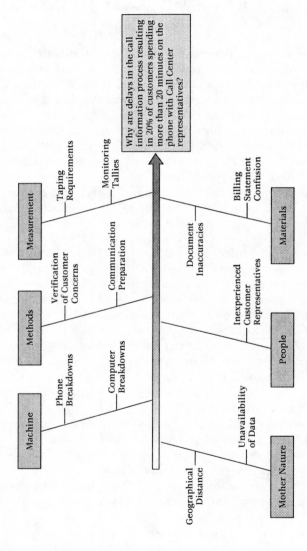

Figure 7.8 The Cause-Effect diagram.

their list to the more likely root causes that could explain the micro-problem question. These concepts include clarifying, combining duplicates, and ultimately the utilization of the team's expertise to multi-vote the list of process variables, resulting in a prioritized list of possible explanations for the micro-problem question.

This breakout proved to be the liveliest of all the Call Center team's breakouts. Uncharacteristically, but clearly welcomed, was the more active involvement of Jeff Seimonson. During the clarification step of the process variables, Jeff discussed the issues around billing statement confusion. Jeff had once worked in billing and claimed that the billing statement had been modified informally over the years to address customer concerns. However, it was Jeff's belief that these modifications had done more harm than good. Joy welcomed Jeff's input and allowed his advocacy of the idea more than is typically allowed during the clarification step. Normally, clarification is simply an opportunity for the author of an idea to clarify the process variable for others on the team. Joy could see Jeff's enthusiasm for his idea flourishing and didn't want to dampen his involvement.

The Call Center team was soon multi-voting. Their narrowed list of root causes for the micro-problem question, "Why are delays in the *determine resolution* subprocess resulting in 20 percent of customers spending more than 20 minutes on the phone with call center representatives?" included the following:

➤ Billing statement confusion.

➤ Computer breakdowns.

➤ Inexperienced customer reps.

In the language of Root Cause Analysis, the Call Center project team's $Y = f(x)$ looked as follows:

Delays in the determine resolution subprocess resulting in 20 percent of customers spending more than 20 minutes on the phone with Call Center representatives (the Y) are a function (the f) of billing statement confusion, computer breakdowns, and/or inexperienced customer reps (the three xs).

$$Y = (x_1, + x_2, + x_3)$$

Billing Statement Confusion	Computer Breakdowns	Inexperienced Customer Representatives

$Y = f(x)$ formula.

The last tutorial Hawke provided was on validating root causation. He introduced three basic approaches. The first approach he introduced was the concept of using basic data collection methods to verify root causation. The second method is correlation. He defined the concept of the scatter diagram—a simple tool that establishes correlation between one process variable (x) and the micro-problem question (Y). He went on to explain design of experiments (DOE), the third validation method, as a more sophisticated method that can be used to verify root causation.

A special course on design of experiments was to be taught to selected Alpha Omega project teams once they had verified their micro-problem questions and formally identified their xs for $Y = f(x)$. For the Alpha Omega teams with multiple xs who could not validate through either basic data collection and/or scatter analysis, a separate three day design of experiments class was to be provided. It was unlikely that the Call Center team would need the design of experiments training since they had readily available data that could be used for scatter analysis.

■ THE CALL CENTER TEAM'S ANALYZE INTERSESSION

The last breakout of Analyze training on April 10 was devoted to intersession project management planning. The Call Center team prepared a Linear Responsibility chart for the work the team would need to complete before the next formal training that was scheduled for May 21, 22, and 23 (Figure 7.9).

■ THE CALL CENTER'S HIGHEST LEVEL INTERVENTION

Joy Schulenberg's weekly meetings with Charles Zukor resumed after the Analyze training was completed. Charles' zeal continued to grow as he saw his interventions with Jeff bearing fruit. He was excited when Joy reported Jeff's renewed interest in the project. Unfortunately, reports of Robert Wallace's passive compliance to action items was not a surprise. He was keenly aware that the moment of truth for Robert was eminent. From reviewing the Linear

Task/Activity	Team Leader Joy Schulenberg	Champion Charles Zukor	Members						
			Aaron Gregson	Suzanne Jackson	Maria Carballo	Robert Wallace	Jeff Seimonson	Aaron Brown	Leroy Barney
1.0 Validate subprocess map	1.0P	1.0A							
1.1 Interview current employees	1.1P							1.1S	1.1S
1.2 Compile data/ reconcile process map if needed	1.2P								
1.3 Walk through current subprocess map as a customer									
2.0 Reconfirm micro problem statements	2.0P	2.0A							
2.1 Data analysis micro problem statement verification	2.1P						2.1S		
2.2 Process analysis summary worksheet verification	2.2P						2.2S		
2.3 Process analysis micro problem statement verification	2.3P						2.3S 2.4S 2.5S 2.6S		

Figure 7.9 Call Center teams linear responsibility plan.

Task/Activity	Team Leader — Joy Schulenberg	Champion — Charles Zukor	Members — Aaron Gregson	Suzanne Jackson	Maria Carballo	Robert Wallace	Jeff Seimonson	Aaron Brown	Leroy Barney
3.0 Validate $y = f(x)$	3.0P	3.0A	3.0S	3.0S	3.0S	3.0S	3.0S	3.0S	3.0S
3.1 Reconfirm cause effect diagram	3.1P		3.1S	3.1S	3.1S	3.1S	3.1S	3.1S	3.1S
3.2 Reconfirm clarification, duplication, and multi-voting done during analysis training	3.2P		3.2S	3.2S	3.2S	3.2S	3.2S	3.2S	3.2S
4.0 Validate $y = f(x)$ formula	4.0P	4.0A							
4.1 Basic data collection	4.1P						4.1S		
4.2 Scatter diagram if necessary	4.2P						4.2S		

Figure 7.9 *(Continued)*

P = Primary
S = Secondary
A = Approval

Responsibility chart created the last day of Analyze training, he was saw that Robert's involvement was limited to the validation of the Cause-Effect Diagram and the narrowed list of potential root causes. Charles knew that such limited responsibilities for a resistor was not too much to ask. Failure to abide by this minimal expectation would bring dire consequences.

Intersession work for the Call Center team proceeded smoothly. The first two major elements of the intersession were validated quickly and accurately, with no surprises or changes resulting from the validation work. While Hawke and Madrid had cautioned that work done in the Analyze breakouts is often modified during intersession validation, this was not the case for the Call Center team. In short order, the Call Center team had not only validated their subprocess map with nary a change, but also had accurately estimated the best case scenario and worse case scenario times for each of the steps in the *determine resolution* subprocess map.

This work had been properly delegated to Aaron Brown, Leroy Barney, and the new star of the team, Jeff Seimonson. In the case of Jeff, his turnaround was truly something to behold. Joy was reminded of the advice she received from Kylie during the first intersession work. Kylie had said that those who are initially resistant to the Six Sigma project should not be dismissed summarily. Many times their resistance comes from an issue that, if properly addressed, will not only bring that resistor on board but will also make him or her among some of the greatest contributors to the Six Sigma team. In many cases, he or she will bring ideas to the project that will dramatically improve the chances of project success.

While it was too early to tell, it was possible that improvement in the billing statement could dramatically improve not only the Call Resolution process but also Alpha Omega in general. Joy tried to restrain her optimism and excitement about the potential of being among the first Six Sigma success stories at Alpha Omega.

Despite this enthusiasm, Joy was still keenly aware of what awaited not only her and her team but Charles Zukor as well. Robert Wallace's involvement was still a vital factor during the root causation section of intersession work. During the first weeks of intersession, Robert participated, but only passively.

As Joy sat in her cubicle preparing the agenda for the critical root cause validation meeting, she saw an e-mail from Charles Zukor and opened it immediately.

To: Schulenberg, Joy

From: Zukor, Charles

Re: Mid-project performance review

Joy,

In the interest of improving my Champion performance before the completion of the Call Center project, I would like for you to prepare answers to the following three questions relative to my Champion role:

1. What are two things you would like for me to continue doing?
2. What are two things you would like for me to stop doing?
3. What are two things you would like for me to start doing?

Either e-mail a reply or stop by with your feedback.

Thanks, Charles

Joy was impressed with Charles' commitment to improvement. Frankly, she didn't have much in the way of suggestions for questions two and three. Relative to the first question, she clearly expected ongoing intervention with Robert if his resistance continued to be an issue. She also wanted Charles to keep his regular weekly meetings with her since they helped to maintain her momentum in leading the group.

In casual discussions with other team leaders, she had become aware that Charles did not ask as many detailed questions about the tollgates as some of the other Champions. Joy remembered three team leaders of other first wave Alpha Omega teams sharing notes about the types of questions their Champions had been asking. This prompted her to suggest a "clearinghouse" of all the questions team leaders had gotten from their Champions. The team leaders convened a conference call with Joe Hawke and Kylie Madrid regarding the subject, and the Temojoe consultants agreed to augment the questions that might be asked throughout DMAIC projects. These questions were then typed and circulated to all Champions during the intersession. (The complete list of Champion questions is found in Appendix B.)

Over the course of the next several days, Joy finalized both the agenda for her Six Sigma team and the performance evaluation for Charles. She decided to prepare a written document to hand to Charles and review it with him in person. Joy also had been contacting team members to get updates of the subgroup meetings she had been having with Aaron Brown, Leroy Barney, and Jeff Seimonson. Most updates had been over the phone and had gone well.

It was a different matter altogether with Robert Wallace. In recent weeks, Wallace had not been returning Joy's calls. When she would drop by his office, Robert was always busy and rebuffed her. During Joy's weekly meetings with Charles, he always inquired about the team dynamics in general and Robert in particular. Charles had indicated to Joy that he was close to making a decision with regard to Robert's future involvement. He let Joy know that his decision would be between himself and Robert, and Joy would be the first to know how it went. On the Friday before the Call Center team's big root causation validation meeting, Charles and Joy met to review the agenda, as well as conduct Charles' mid-session performance review.

"Joy, I have some news for you. This morning after consulting with Brenda Sexson about my decision, I met with Robert Wallace. After a brief dialogue with him, I removed him from the Call Center team. I had asked him to affirm his commitment to Six Sigma, and specifically to the Call Center team. I also instructed him that his failure to do so would result in his removal from the team, along with a negative performance review relative to special project support, which is 15 percent of his review. Since he technically is also in the bonus pool because of his years of service, I thought this would bring him on board. Unfortunately, it did not. Sadly, I didn't think I would have to take this action.

"I'm asking you to speak candidly with your team on Monday about this development. I also informed him that I would not mince words about the cause of his departure. You are free to inform your team that his removal was based on his lackluster performance in the Six Sigma endeavor."

Still in a state of shock, Joy was at a loss for words. When she had gathered her thoughts, she expressed her appreciation. "Charles, I appreciate you taking the bull by the horns. Quite frankly, this will be addition by subtraction. Team members had talked to me one-on-one about Robert but they never thought this would happen because of Robert's stature and previous standing within Alpha Omega. I can assure you that the news, while shocking to some, will come as good news to most."

"Great. I really need a victory here to show Robert how fatal a decision it was for him to not support Six Sigma. However, we need to get back to the business at hand. Today's meeting is for you to tell me how I'm doing. Give it to me straight, Joy."

"Charles, here's my list. Today, you showed your leadership qualities in spades. I, along with the other team leaders, created a list of questions good Champions should ask their teams. It's a mild suggestion for improvement. Overall, I couldn't ask for better support than what you've given to me. And thanks again. Your decision today just made my job easier." With that said, the weekly meeting ended. Both the Champion and the leader of the Call Center team were breathing a little easier.

The following Monday afternoon meeting began with the status of Robert's removal. Joy was surprised that the announcement of his removal didn't cause more of a ripple among the team members. She allowed some time for discussion about Robert before moving forward with the agenda items relative to root cause.

In characteristic fashion, Suzanne went straight for the jugular: "He made his bed, let him lie in it." With a little more empathy, Aaron Gregson offered his opinion: "I'm truly sorry that Robert didn't see the value of Six Sigma and our project. He could have been a valuable addition to our efforts. I'm sorry it ended up this way."

Aaron Brown went with a sports analogy: "Robert Wallace was our Carl Everett." Since many of the Call Center team members were unaware of who Carl Everett was, Aaron continued, "Carl Everett is a talented major league baseball outfielder. The problem is that he can't get along with either his teammates or his manager. He has been traded to multiple teams because of his talent but always gets into fights or is a no show for team meetings. Sometimes he doesn't even show up for games. They punish him, fine him, and ultimately trade him. It's addition by subtraction and that's what we have here. Aaron Gregson is right. Robert's talents could have helped us but we've been inefficient in our work because we've been waiting for him to come to bat. Now we don't have to worry about him being in our line up."

While some team members got lost in the Carl Everett story, the concept of addition through subtraction rang true through the group. However, Leroy Barney pointedly reminded everyone of the new challenge that awaited them: "Now there's even more pressure on us to perform well and get improved sigma performance results. If we fail, Robert will be going around like a rooster crowing, 'I told you so.' I take that as a personal challenge. I want him on the outside looking in."

Joy had noticed Jeff's silence. She wasn't sure if it would help the group to hear his perception, but she felt obligated to get his input. "Jeff, what are your thoughts?"

All eyes focused on Jeff. "Robert has been and will always be my friend. I can't help but think we all could have done more to make him feel welcome. But frankly, and most importantly, Robert didn't go halfway in making a connection with this team. During the first few weeks of the project, I had some of the same feelings he had. But in the final analysis, Robert's the one who's responsible for his departure. Speaking of analysis, I really have some interesting things to share about our root causation."

While Joy didn't wholly agree with Jeff's comments about doing more to make Robert feel welcome, she was pleased to hear that he was now clearly part of the team. She also liked his segue back to the issues of analysis. She took Jeff up on his offer. "Sounds good, Jeff. Unless any one else has something else to say, let's go ahead with your report-out."

Jeff showed the data he had collected from his subgroup work. His data collection showed that over 93 percent of calls to the center were with regard to billing statement confusion. He was quick to point out the calls were *not* disputes. Further, the data he had collected also showed a statistically significant difference between experienced and inexperienced Call Center reps and the length of calls. Joy was highly impressed when Jeff showed a *t*-test where the probability of the difference between experienced and inexperienced workers being a random event was less than 1 percent.

When Jeff was finished with his informative report-out, Aaron Brown and Leroy showed data for computer breakdown and length and frequency of calls. The data was inconclusive at best. The scatter analysis they had done between the number of computer breakdowns and length of call and delays showed very little correlation. After a brief discussion, the Call Center team agreed that two of the three theorized *x*s that explained *Y* had been validated. They agreed to drop computer breakdown from their $Y = f(x)$ formula. Further, with only two *x*s under consideration as they entered the Improve phase of DMAIC, a call to Kylie verified that the Call Center team was exempted from the design of experiments training. Kylie expressed some disappointment that she would be missing her favorite team leader during the design of experiments training. (Madrid told every team leader that they were her favorite, but this time she really meant it.) She told Joy that she looked forward to seeing her and her team during Improve training that was scheduled to begin the morning of May 21.

■ ALPHA OMEGA'S IMPROVE TRAINING

The morning of May 21 began with report-outs from each of the 11 project teams' ever-important Analyze intersession work. Joy and her team received major kudos for their root cause validation work. Charles beamed as both Kylie and Joe recognized the statistical validation of the work they had done since early April. Five of the other teams received similar positive feedback on their report-outs. The other five teams were struggling a bit. Joe Hawke gave some encouragement along with some strong suggestions to help the struggling teams.

As Joe was offering his suggestions, Joy noticed his sartorial elegance for the first time. He was dressed in a three-button dark brown suit and recently shined shoes. For some reason, Joe's appearance seemed to make his feedback more credible. Meanwhile, Kylie Madrid's black business suit didn't escape attention, either, not the least of which was the attention of the new Champion star of Alpha Omega, Charles Zukor.

■ MANAGING *IMPROVE* —TOLLGATES #1 AND #2: GENERATING SOLUTIONS AND SELECTING SOLUTIONS

As Madrid began the Improve tutorial immediately after lunch, it was a cold, blustery day in Westminster, Colorado. Temperatures were hovering in the mid-30s. The weather tends to be unpredictable in Colorado at this time of the year. The aspen trees had budded and spring had sprung, but a freak late spring snowstorm was on its way, despite what the Denver weather forecasters had predicted.

Madrid talked about following the same methodology when using brainstorming to generate solutions that were used for determining root causation. Kylie informed the teams that by affinitizing a set of solutions, they could then use the most highly prioritized solutions to soften or dampen common cause variation, and preferably eliminate special cause variation of the validated root causes.

Once the teams had reached agreement on a set of solutions in the Generating Solutions tollgate, and had narrowed the list using the tools discussed previously, they would then begin the process of Selecting Solutions. When Selecting Solutions, they were expected to compare the solutions against a set of "solution criteria." There are two types of solution criteria. The first type is called "Must" criteria. Must criteria are an either/or test of a solution. Typical Must criteria include *adherence to budget* or *not adding to headcount*. Must criteria emanate from the Champion, and they either approve or preclude further consideration of each of the Six Sigma team's prioritized solutions.

Charles Zukor and the other Champions had been briefed prior to May 21 in the hopes that there would be some commonality in the Must criteria for the Alpha Omega teams. With rare exceptions, the Must criteria for all teams included:

➤ Must be within budget.

➤ Must not add to current Alpha Omega headcount.

➤ Must be implementable by September 30.

The goal of the project teams was to compare their proposed solutions against the Must criteria. A solution must generate a "yes" against the criteria in order for the solution to be further considered against the "Want" criteria that will be discussed next. In the case of the Call Center team, they had three prioritized solutions: *redesign the billing statement, create a routing system for certain calls to more experienced call center reps, and develop a new training program for the Call Center reps to truncate the time it took for an inexperienced rep to become experienced* (Figure 7.10).

Temojoe Consulting had advised against an exclusive focus on "people" or "training" related solutions. In over 20 years of consulting, Temojoe had not seen a significant improvement in sigma performance when the exclusive remedy was focused on training alone.

The Call Center team's proposed solutions had all passed the Must criteria. Want criteria are then used to prioritize the order of implementation of the solutions that pass the Must criteria. Want criteria are usually consensually determined by both the Champion and the project team. For the Call Center team, the Want criteria are:

➤ Impact on root causation.
➤ Impact on stakeholders.
➤ Cost to implement.

Application of the Want criteria is statistical in nature. The most important Want criterion, according to the team's expertise, is given a weight of "10." Next, the remaining Want criteria are also rated between 1 and 9 in terms of their importance. The team then compares the compliance (scored from 1=low compliance to 10=high compliance) of each of the prioritized solutions to each of the weighted Must criteria, and the team members average rating is multiplied by the weight of the criterion by which it was rated. Finally, each solution's scores are totaled and the highest scored solution is implemented first. Other prioritized solutions can be implemented at a later time if the implementation of the first solution does not result in the team achieving its goal. During the Improve training, the Call

	Musts		
	Budget	Headcount	September 30
Statement redesign	Yes	Yes	Yes
Call routing	Yes	Yes	Yes
Training program	Yes	Yes	Yes

Figure 7.10 Call Centers Must Criteria results.

Center team accomplished this task in a breakout. The results of its work are found in Figure 7.11.

Based on the above calculations, the order of solution implementation was *redesigning the billing statement* followed by *changing the procedure for call routing,* and finally, *implementing the training program.* Both Kylie and Joe indicated that the impact of the each implementation should be evaluated by doing a sigma calculation after full implementation of each prioritized solution. By doing the sigma calculation, many teams discover that the first or second solution implementation helps them to achieve their goal. The benefit of this strategy is that teams do not necessarily have to implement all of their solutions, thus being able to either disband the team earlier than anticipated or reduce the cost of solution implementation.

Interestingly, the Call Center team's number one ranked solution, *redesigning the billing statement,* was very similar to the work of another Alpha Omega team, the Application Submission team. As a result, on the last day of Improve training, the Call Center team and the Application Submission team joined forces on the billing statement redesign effort. Joy became the de facto team leader because she had done such an outstanding job of applying the project management tools, such as the Linear Responsibility chart. Joy designated Jeff as the one with the primary responsibility for the solution implementation plan. Jeff worked in conjunction with Joan Snyder of the Application Submission team.

Part of their solution implementation plan included gaining acceptance to the newly designed statement. This included using many of the same tools referenced in Chapter 6 as they applied to overcoming stakeholder resistance. Jeff took the lead on this action item since he was living proof of the efficacy of tools such as creating the need, shaping a vision, and mobilizing commitment to the newly formed solutions. Jeff and Joan created a large-scale Stakeholder Analysis chart, and over the next few months worked to overcome the resistance to the newly created billing statement. The resistance

	Statement Redesign	Call Routing	Training Program
Root causation 10	10/100	8/80	7/70
Stakeholders 9	9/81	8/72	8/81
Cost 8	6/48	8/64	8/64
Total	229	216	215

Figure 7.11 Call Centers Want Criteria results.

primarily came from internal customers, such as the Call Center reps. In the case of the Call Center reps, many of the more experienced reps had developed skills in the interpretation of the old statement, and therefore were resistant to the new design.

Fortunately, Jeff and Joan developed specific strategies to overcome the key stakeholder reps' resistance, and by late summer the newly designed billing statement had dramatically improved the Call Center Index. From the initial Call index of 42 percent, the newly designed statement had driven the index down below the national average of 30 percent. In addition, the length of the average call improved from a baseline sigma performance of 0.9 to well over 3.0 sigma, and first call resolution went from 1.3 to 3.5 sigma. Even courtesy, which was not directly addressed during the Analyze and Improve phase of the Call Center project, benefited by the new billing statement. The baseline sigma performance of 2.8 improved to over 3.5 as less frustrated customers no longer "killed the messenger" as a result of their frustration with the old billing statement.

While implementation of the new billing statement was the primary solution that drove improved sigma performance, the Call Center team also went ahead with their other two solutions: a new call routing procedure and the training program to expedite experience among the Call Center reps.

As a result of the Control training the teams received June 25 and 26, the Call Center team was able to develop a Response Plan that became the formal document Charles Zukor approved prior to the completion of the project. Figure 7.12 shows the completed Response Plan from the Call Center team. A good Response Plan includes the type of controls that are in place, along with the process improvements that helped to drive the improved sigma performance.

A good Response Plan also allows the other employees that work in the process to monitor the new process once it has been subjected to DMAIC, even if those employees were not a part of the Six Sigma process improvement team. A cursory examination of the Response Plan shows some similarities to the Data Collection Plan, along with some distinct differences. (For a complete description of the Response Plan, see our first book, *The Six Sigma Revolution*.)

■ THE CHAMPIONS' RESPONSIBILITIES *AFTER* THE TEAM DISBANDS

In Chapter 2, we reviewed the responsibilities of a Champion *before* the formation of the team. In Chapter 5, we discussed the responsibilities

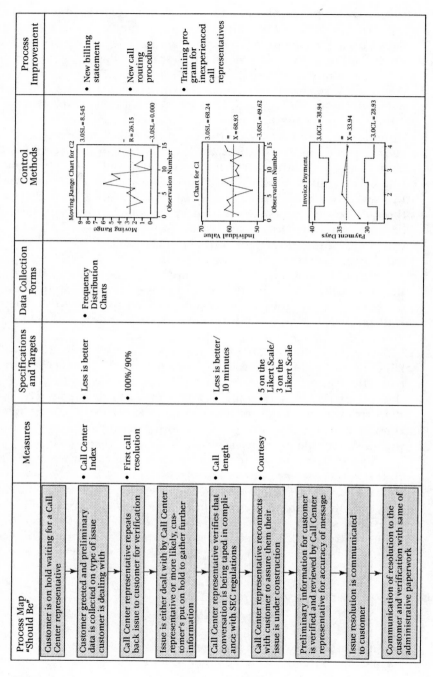

Process Map "Should Be"	Measures	Specifications and Targets	Data Collection Forms	Control Methods	Process Improvement
Customer is on hold waiting for a Call Center representative	• Call Center Index	• Less is better	• Frequency Distribution Charts	Moving Range Chart for C2 3.0SL = 8.545 R = 26.15 −3.0SL = 0.000	• New billing statement
Customer greeted and preliminary data is collected on type of issue customer is dealing with	• First call resolution	• 100%/90%		I Chart for C1 3.0SL = 68.24 X̄ = 68.93 −3.0SL = 49.62	• New call routing procedure
Call Center representative repeats back issue to customer for verification				Invoice Payment 3.0CL = 38.94 X̄ = 33.94 −3.0CL = 28.93	• Training program for inexperienced call representatives
Issue is either dealt with by Call Center representative or more likely, customer's put on hold to gather further information	• Call length	• Less is better/ 10 minutes			
Call Center representative verifies that conversation is being taped in compliance with SEC regulations	• Courtesy	• 5 on the Likert Scale/ 3 on the Likert Scale			
Call Center representative reconnects with customer to assure them their issue is under construction					
Preliminary information for customer is verified and reviewed by Call Center representative for accuracy of message					
Issue resolution is communicated to customer					
Communication of resolution to the customer and verification with same of administrative paperwork					

Figure 7.12 Process improvement hand-off: The Response Plan.

of a Champion *during* the time a Six Sigma team works on the Six Sigma improvement project. In this chapter, we conclude with the last set of Champions' responsibilities. These are responsibilities of a Champion *after* his or her team disbands.

Once the project team implements its solutions and creates the Response Plan, the team is ready to disband. In the case of the Alpha Omega Call Center team, while their last training session on Control occurred in late June, the implementation of their solutions and the ability to observe improved sigma performance did not materialize until late September.

The last formal activity Joy Schulenberg completed as part of her team leadership was the hand-off of the Response Plan to Charles Zukor. The hand-off that occurred in September officially ended the Call Center team's Six Sigma improvement project. There were several responsibilities Zukor, along with each of the other Champions, had once the team disbanded. They were:

1. *Communication of the improved process and the results, to the Business Quality Council.* Through the use of the Response Plan, the Champion is expected to communicate the new process and its associated results to the Business Quality Council. In the case of the Call Center where the solutions are part of another project, and more importantly another process, it is essential that these communications are orchestrated so that the strategic component of Six Sigma is maintained and managed. (See the *Six Sigma Revolution*, pp. 230–241.)

2. *Capture the lessons learned.* Regardless of the extent of success or failure of a project team, the Champion should conduct a poll of the Six Sigma project team. Using the plus/delta concept, the Champion should gather data on what went well over the course of the team's existence and what could have been done better. This information could apply to the team's results, its methods of achieving the results, or the role of the Champion or the executive team.

3. *Monitor the performance of the new process.* The Champion, in more cases than not, is also the Process Owner. As such, the process owner has the long-term responsibility of assuring that the Response Plan becomes standard procedure. When the Champion and Process Owner are one and the same person, the transition of monitoring the new process is simple. However, when the Champion and the Process Owner are two different people, the Champion needs to contract with the Process Owner the duration and extent of his or her involvement. The involvement will include the transition of monitoring methods, managing the new process, and implementation of the Response Plan.

4. *Recognize, reward, and celebrate both success and effort.* Particularly in first wave projects, it is imperative that Champions recognize, reward, and celebrate both the success and the effort of their teams. These activities should focus on the collective team. Many organizations sponsor a combination of a science fair and a banquet. At this gathering, the entire organization can review the storyboards and templates of the various projects. As the day progresses, a banquet is held where the business leader and Champions pay special recognition to the teams. Sometimes special note of individual performance is given. In most cases, the teams are recognized and the lessons that were learned from the first wave of projects are captured.

■ THE ALPHA OMEGA CELEBRATION BANQUET

On November 4, Brenda Sexson invited the 11 first wave Six Sigma project teams, their Champions, and Temojoe Consulting back to the "scene of the crime," the Omni Interlocken. An all-day science fair was attended by a significant number of Alpha Omega employees whose curiosity had been piqued by the first wave of projects. During the science fair, Alpha Omega employees were regaled by project team members who shared not only the lessons they learned, but also the solutions that helped generate over $2,332,000 in cost savings.

The enthusiasm from the science fair continued into the hospitality session that evening. The team members and their spouses were invited for a dinner of rack of lamb with fig-port sauce, herbs de provence, and grilled polenta. Brenda gave a stirring speech, thanking everyone for their extra effort since the teams were formed back in January. She reported the collective results both in terms of monetary savings and improved processes, stressing that the ultimate result will be less stress, greater job security, and greater prominence of Alpha Omega in the financial community. All 11 of the Champions also gave brief speeches, thanking their teams for their hard work. When it was time for Charles to speak, he complimented everyone on his team, leaving the last two tributes to Jeff Seimonson and Joy Schulenberg. By prior arrangement, Jeff gave the last speech of the night.

"When I was first chosen to be a part of the Call Center project improvement team, I had serious reservations. I thought Six Sigma was like previous efforts associated with improving our performance. Only when I saw the quiet but effective efforts of people like Aaron Gregson, did I start to think this might be different. Ultimately, it was seeing the commitment to Six Sigma, starting at the top of this organization and cascading all the way through management, that convinced me this might be different. In addition, my Champion, Charles Zukor, actually listened to me and my ideas. I learned that I was just another person with an opinion unless I could support my ideas with facts and data. When my opinion was substantiated through our data collection, I could see that Six Sigma was going to be a cultural phenomenon at Alpha Omega. I'm excited about the future of this company, and I'm excited about Six Sigma being a part of our future. Because of the great experience I've had under Charles' leadership, it's my hope to be a Champion in the second wave of Six Sigma projects." Jeff's ringing endorsement of Six Sigma was sure to positively influence future waves of "would be" skeptics at Alpha Omega.

As the evening drew to a close, a few people were still milling about in the ballroom. Charles caught the eye of Kylie who was sitting with Joe Hawke at the main table. Several class participants were approaching Joe and remarking about his extraordinary teaching skills. Charles took a seat next to Kylie and thanked her for her efforts in helping his team.

"Another successful client, eh, Kylie?"

"We don't take the credit and we don't take the blame, Charles. We just take your money," Kylie said as she sipped her wine.

"We couldn't have done it without you. Thanks for getting us, and me specifically, on the right track."

"You showed great leadership, Charles. Not just in the way you handled things with Robert, but in a number of other ways as well. You asked for feedback on your performance, as well as receiving the feedback from Joy to expand your questions during the weekly meetings." By this point in the conversation, Charles and Kylie had left the ballroom and were nearing the elevators.

"Thank you, Kylie. When are you heading home?"

"I have meetings with Brenda tomorrow to plan out the next six months of strategic Six Sigma. I head back home the next morning."

"If you're interested, I'd love to take you to dinner in Denver tomorrow evening?"

"I am honored, Charles. But I am married to a brilliant, funny, and loyal Italian business writer. In fact, one of his books was just chosen as one of the 25 best business books of the new millennium. It's tough when we both travel as much as we do, but, I don't want to do anything to lose him. If I ever cheated on him I would forfeit something I could never have with anyone else. And he is far too important in my life for me to ever hurt him."

"I understand totally, Kylie. I trust no offense is taken. All I can say is, he's one lucky man."

■ SUMMARY

Chapter 7 takes us through the critical steps of Analyze, Improve, and Control with our Alpha Omega Call Center team. Most importantly, we address the highest level intervention of a project team member— the removal of a member from the Six Sigma team. We also discuss the responsibilities of the Champion once the formal Six Sigma team disbands. We finish the chapter with a discussion and example of the importance of reward and recognition for the Six Sigma team.

KEY LEARNINGS

➤ The Analyze step is the most important phase of the DMAIC methodology.

➤ Data and Process Analysis should help create detailed, micro problem questions that in turn will assist the Six Sigma project team become more granular in their project work.

➤ Micro-problem questions are the "keys" to open the most important door of DMAIC, the tollgate known as root cause analysis.

➤ Solving the formula $Y=f(x)$ is the most important work a Six Sigma project team will attempt.

➤ Removal of a project team member may result in "addition through subtraction." Like divorce in a marriage, it should be the option of last resort in an attempt to maintain Six Sigma team dynamics.

➤ Good Champions will ask for feedback on their performance as a Champion during the existence of the Six Sigma team.

➤ Improvement can be one of the easiest steps in DMAIC when root causation has been done successfully.

➤ Champions have responsibilities once the team disbands. Namely, communication of the new process to those affected; capturing lessons learned; monitoring the new process; and rewarding, recognizing, and celebrating both the results and efforts of their teams.

Chapter 8

Pitfalls to Avoid in Creating Six Sigma Team Dynamics

"Living is easy with eyes closed."

John Lennon

As we have in our previous books on Six Sigma, we devote the last chapter to the pitfalls to avoid in creating Six Sigma team dynamics. Throughout the Alpha Omega case study, we have emphasized that the role of the Champion is vitally important if the project team is expected to accomplish its goals and objectives. In this chapter, we further discuss this all-important Champion role that helps shape the dynamics of the teams they sponsor. In addition, we focus on the importance of selected project management tools we introduced in *Six Sigma Team Dynamics: The Elusive Key to Project Success.* Further, we discuss such issues as reward and recognition being established prior to the team achieving their goals.

In the Alpha Omega case study, we saw several examples of resistance that occur in "real life" project improvement teams. We not only discuss the importance of bringing these resistors into the fold, but also listening to these skeptics as a way to make your project team dynamics more vibrant. Finally, we talk about the concept of "addition through subtraction" that we saw in the Alpha Omega case study. Using the analogy of divorce, we stress that the decision to remove a person from your team may become necessary, and we elaborate on how to do this effectively and efficiently.

■ PITFALL #1—FAILURE OF THE CHAMPION TO BE INVOLVED IN EACH STEP OF THE TEAM'S WORK

Appendix C captures the specific responsibilities of a Project Champion before, during, and after a Six Sigma team exists. In Chapter 2, we discussed the 11 things that a good Champion must do *before* the Six Sigma team is formed. Having responsibilities ranging from *selecting the best and brightest* for team members and a team leader to *creating* and *communicating the Business Case,* a Champion must recognize the prework necessary to enhance his or her team's chances for success.

In Chapter 5, we reviewed the 10 responsibilities that a Champion must practice *during* the Six Sigma team's project work. A Champion must have multiple skills to guide the team in its work. As our Alpha Omega case study showed us, some of these skills include *project management skills* (keeping the team on track through the team's weekly meetings), *strategic interventions* (removing roadblocks and providing resources), and possibly the most important skill, *management of the actual team dynamics, including individual team member resistance.*

Finally, in Chapter 7, we reviewed the responsibilities of the Champion *after* his or her team disbands. This postwork includes responsibilities ranging from *implementing* the Response Plan created by the team, to *rewarding, recognizing,* and *celebrating both the team's effort and success.*

When our clients ask us about the critical factors for team success, we always stress the importance of the Champion's involvement. Our previous books revealed that we have had overwhelming success and overwhelming failure with clients. Let's look at an exemplary failure that will highlight the importance of the Champion role.

The client, located in the Southwest, had selected a set of low-performing, high-impact projects through Business Process Management, a part of the strategic piece of Six Sigma. The Champions were selected and matriculated through Champions' training, similar to the training mentioned in Chapter 2. While two of my senior associates conducted DMAIC training for project team members, it soon became apparent that the client was likely to experience difficulty meeting their goals and objectives. During intersession work, when my staff asked the team leaders how often they had been meeting with their Champions, they reported that the frequency of meetings was sporadic at best. One team leader reported that he didn't even know who his Champion was.

Sadly, our best efforts to convince the client of the importance of providing strategic leadership fell on deaf ears. During intersession report-outs, the Champions would be in and out of the room. Intersession report-outs revealed that the teams were always behind in their work, and complaints about competing priorities were common. However, requests for special intersession meetings with the Champions never resulted in a quorum. As a result, not a single project in the first wave generated a substantiated cost savings. If you asked this client what they thought of Six Sigma, both management and the general workforce would tell you that it was bogus or it didn't work in their business.

Imagine the Robert Wallaces within this organization. Their resistance had won. Any subsequent effort to improve productivity would be met with derision. It was without bemusement that one of my staff called me, a year after we completed our work with this client, to inform me that he had read in *The Wall Street Journal* that the company was up for sale and near bankruptcy. I am firmly convinced that if their first-wave projects had been successful, we would not have been reading of their demise. Unfortunately, because the 11 Champions didn't do their jobs in the ever-important first wave of Six Sigma projects, not only did the improvement effort fail, but the organization failed as well.

■ PITFALL #2—FAILURE TO WRITE IT DOWN

In Six Sigma training, we discuss the importance of "What gets measured, gets done." The same aphorism, "What gets written down, gets done," could apply. In this context, we refer to the project management tools we discussed in Chapter 6. Project management has become popular in recent years—understandably so. In this text, we discussed the minimum tools, like Work Breakdown charts, Linear Responsibility charts, and Activity Reports that can be used. We did not address several other project management tools, such as Critical Path Reporting, since these are covered in other books.

Teams and team leaders who develop a written plan for intersession work are far more likely to meet intersession milestones than those who don't. Moreover, when business executives ask me about skill sets for their internal Six Sigma hires, I strongly recommend they examine the employee's current project management skills. For example, in the fall of 2000, Wells Fargo Financial committed to a Six Sigma management philosophy. Dan Porter, their CEO, is known as a charismatic, no-nonsense, results-driven leader from the Jack Welch-type mold.

I first met Dan when he was a business leader for General Electric's Business Development Unit in London. When he took over the reins at Wells Fargo in 2000, he designated Mark Aeilts, his project management guru, as his Six Sigma quality leader. This wise decision helped Wells Fargo achieve over seven figures in cost savings in their first wave of projects. While Eckes and Associates provided the first-wave training and intersession consulting, we were impressed with Mark Aeilts and his staff as they utilized many of the tools we have discussed here to further enhance their project work relative to their DMAIC intersession deliverables.

A key variable of good project management is detailed, documented, and reviewable action plans. Mark Aeilts and his associates, Greg McWilliams, Shelley Brotherton, and Brent Johnson, assisted the 11 project teams as they developed detailed action plans similar to the plans we showed in Chapters 5 and 6. These plans not only helped the project teams, but they also benefited Mark's team and Eckes and Associates since the action plans enabled us to provide specific feedback on performance. Additionally, proper use of good project management tools provides Champions with a reference point from which to review, comment, and modify what their teams should be working on during the all-important intersessions.

■ PITFALL #3—FAILURE TO FORMALIZE AND COMMUNICATE REWARDS AND RECOGNITION FOR THE SIX SIGMA TEAMS

When I travel, I commonly have my shoes polished at the airport. As part of my shoeshine ritual, I always tip the shoeshine person (in Denver, the shoeshine person is more likely to be a woman) in advance. I have never regretted my pre-tip policy. My theory is that when they know what their total compensation will be prior to doing the work, they provide a better shine than if I tip them after they are done. I have a similar suggestion for executives with regard to project teams.

As I said in *Making Six Sigma Last*, first-wave projects must bear fruit to showcase the application of Six Sigma principles within an organization. Executives must maximize the potential for bearing fruit in a variety of ways. Since far too many Robert Wallaces exist in organizations, I recommend they establish and formalize a reward and recognition plan for first-wave project participants *before or shortly after* the project starts. Doing this can help to offset the jaded view of Six Sigma in an organization. I recommend a combination of a week's vacation and an awards banquet. Let's examine each of these recommendations separately to discuss the value of this approach.

First, a common complaint among even the most dedicated Six Sigma team members is the amount of time required for first projects. Although this complaint has merit, in many cases, it is both overstated and exaggerated. However, why not take action to offset this concern of the project teams? Organizations that embrace Six Sigma usually register inefficiency scores of 50 percent or higher. First wave-project team members who are accustomed to wasting half of their day on rework activities are sure to see Six Sigma as extra work. Thus, create an opportunity for these first-wave "pioneers" to benefit from their perception that Six Sigma is extra work. Offer them an extra week of paid vacation if they meet a set of predetermined goals and objectives for their projects. Having established this reward in advance will encourage teams to perform better, realizing that the extra time required to complete the project will result not only in short-term benefits (e.g., vacation time), it will also result in the longer term benefit of working in more efficient processes.

The concept of the banquet has an equal opportunity to motivate teams. As we discussed in Chapter 7, we suggest that the banquet include spouses. The extra hours spent in first-wave projects may have resulted in more than one burnt casserole. Extending an invitation to spouses and companions is a thoughtful acknowledgement and recognition of the sacrifices they made as well. For many team members, knowing that their significant other will be included in the celebration of a professional accomplishment tends to strengthen their focus. In addition, when teams are aware the banquet is coupled with a science fair that will showcase their project, their performance is improved even more. No one wants to look bad in the eyes of others, particularly fellow workers. Thus, while the intent of the banquet and science fair is to celebrate the teams' work, it also provides a secondary benefit—the competitive element that motivates teams to work even more diligently to complete their projects on time and successfully.

■ PITFALL #4—IGNORING THE POTENTIAL OF "CONVERTED" RESISTORS

In 20 years of consulting, I have encountered hundreds of resistors. In the early years of my consultation work, they were a source of major frustration. I felt as though my reputation with the client was being thwarted by these naysayers. However, during later years, I learned that the majority of resistors are much like our friend, Jeff Seimonson. Jeff had very legitimate reasons behind his resistance. Over the course of our work with clients, I have learned that the odds of resistors changing are high. Our formal data analysis shows that 80 percent of resistors become supporters when the sources of their resistance are taken seriously. We have found that when these issues are correctly addressed, the resistor may even become a true Champion of change. Thus, resistors must be carefully managed. When handled correctly, they can become significant contributors to the success of the project and their input can result in greater project success.

Sadly, not all resistors are like Jeff Seimonson. Our data has shown that 20 percent of the people who are resistant to Six Sigma will remain resistant, even to their professional deaths. These resistors are probably representative of people who are hard and fast resistors to *any* change. However, whenever working with resistors we always recommend playing the odds that you are dealing with one of the "80 percenters." If they prove to be one of the "20 percenters," at some point, as we've shown in this text, they must be dealt with directly and swiftly.

Just as we discussed in Chapter 7, the stakes for project success are raised when a die-hard naysayer is removed from a team. If the first wave of projects ends up a disaster, the ejected resistor is thought of as the Osama bin Laden of the organization. If the project turns out to be successful, the resistor's career, for all intents and purpose, is over.

■ PITFALL #5—FAILURE TO ASSIGN YOUR BEST AND BRIGHTEST

Household Retail Services contracted with Eckes and Associates to assist in their Six Sigma effort in late 2000. At the time we were extremely busy, but Household's new business leader, Sandy Derickson, had requested my involvement with her Six Sigma launch. I had the pleasure of working with Sandy when she was the highest ranking woman at General Electric Capital, having been at the helm of the ill-fated General Electric Capital Auto Financial Insurance business. It was my belief that Sandy was one of the five best business leaders I had worked with at General Electric. When she asked me to be involved in the Six Sigma effort in her new job at Household Retail Service, I couldn't resist. I was confident that the Six Sigma effort would be successful under Sandy's leadership. Despite our busy schedule, no consulting firm can ignore working with a client where success is virtually assured.

There were several reasons why I had high confidence in Household Retail Services' eventual Six Sigma success. First and foremost was Sandy Derickson herself. She is an amazing business leader who embodies the traits of great leaders—traits I rarely see in other business leaders. She clearly knows how to establish a vision for her organization. And she knows how to delegate responsibility, allowing the people she puts in charge to do their work. Additionally, she possesses high confidence in herself and others. Thus, she doesn't spend the time some leaders spend trying to make herself look good. Sandy also hires the best and the brightest.

In the initial weeks of the Household initiative, I worked with their financial director, Joe Hoff. Joe took an active role in the Six Sigma initiative, first administratively, then becoming one of the first Project Champions. I anxiously awaited Sandy and Joe's choice for the Six Sigma director at Household. I didn't have to wait long to know that they had made an excellent choice. In early 2001, Brian Zempel was the Call Center Director for Household. Bright, energetic, and ambitious, Brian was tapped by Sandy to be the Six Sigma leader. Shortly after meeting Brian, I knew that Household could be a record-setting client. Indeed, they have proven this to be true. Failure is not in Zempel's vocabulary, and he would be a success in any endeavor. When Household executives selected nine first-wave projects, I remember telling them that in typical initiatives two or three of the projects would be "home run" projects, two or three would be successful with a return on investment, and two or three projects would be unsuccessful.

Brian publicly informed the executives and project teams that Household would be the first Eckes and Associates client to achieve success in *all* of the first-wave projects. Our data shows that an average cost savings of $175,000 to $200,000 per project can be expected in typical Six Sigma initiatives. In December 2001, Household Retail became the first client to generate success in each of their first wave projects.

This impressive first-wave success was due to the excellent people involved at Household—Sandy, Joe, Brian, and the Champions and teams in their first wave. One thing was certain about their effort—Household had not fallen prey to just back-filling key positions with warm bodies. The Six Sigma people we worked with were all winners.

The advantage of populating key positions—business leaders, Champion's roles, and teams—with your best and brightest is two-fold. First, you dramatically increase the chances for success in your first projects. We have repeatedly said that your first-wave projects must produce results if Six Sigma is to be seen as a viable source of improvement in your organization. Second, by choosing your best and brightest, you send a strong message to the entire organization that you are serious about Six Sigma being a cultural phenomenon in your organization.

In the business world, there is no more important voice that supports this theory than the voice of Jack Welch. In his popular autobiography *Straight from the Gut,* Welch indicates that Six Sigma was one of only three formal initiatives he spearheaded during his 20 years at the helm of the GE worldwide conglomerate. In a September 5, 2001, *Wall Street Journal* article, he talked about tapping the best and brightest for Six Sigma posts. "We could have had Six Sigma quality, but if we hired 26 statisticians to be the leaders of this and put them in a room it wouldn't have happened. We had to take the best and brightest and put them there, so the whole organization says, 'They took Mary or Joe off this key assignment and they put them in quality. They (GE) must mean it.'"*

■ PITFALL #6—FAILURE TO UTILIZE GROUND RULES IN SIX SIGMA MEETINGS

In Chapter 3, we introduced the importance of Six Sigma teams recognizing the two critical components of their work: the *content* of their work and the *method* they use to achieve the content. Method was described as having two components—preventions and interventions. While interventions are more dramatic, preventions are probably more fundamentally effective in helping teams stay on track and achieve their goals and objectives.

Several years ago, I was about to begin work with a division of General Electric. I had been warned of the dominance of a particular vice president with whom I would be consulting. According to my sources, this vice president would attempt to dominate the meetings and turn everything that was discussed toward him and his function. Even before the meeting began, it was predicted to be a disaster. With the knowledge of this person's likely attempt to derail my work, I began the meeting by listing some ground rules for all of us to follow. Through the negative poll, "Is there anyone who disagrees with . . . ?" I established the ground rule, "Balanced participation of the entire group." I went on to operationally define this ground rule as "Everyone participates, with no one person dominating the meeting." While I was explaining this ground rule, I noticed furtive glances aimed at the vice president in question.

Over the course of that day and the next, there was true balanced participation. The vice president actively participated in the meetings and it was obvious he had an ego the size of Texas. However, he abided by the ground rule of balanced participation and was never a problem for me or the rest of the group. Later, the Six Sigma leaders expressed amazement at his behavior. One of the Master Black Belts

---

*Interview with Jack Welch, *Wall Street Journal,* September 5, 2001.

complimented me by suggesting my personality must have neutralized the behavior that had been a problem for them in the past. While I love being complimented, I shared my secret of the ground rule being my key to success in managing this person's domineering tendencies. A simple prevention had helped to keep the meeting on track.

Unfortunately, many Six Sigma teams either ignore or rush through the creation of ground rules. Some teams believe that it is beneath them to go through the exercise. However, I believe it is perhaps the most important of the preventions that help teams stay on track and achieve results. I know firsthand how the failure to establish ground rules can cripple your Six Sigma team dynamics.

My consulting work calls for sessions to take place over a period of several weeks, or even months. Therefore, it is incumbent on me to revisit, or at least repost, the ground rules that had been established in a previous meeting. I once neglected this critical prevention with a client in Europe. The audience was populated by a group of Type A hard-charging sales and marketing folks. After nearly the entire group was in the back of the conference room talking on their cell phones during the meeting, I realized I had neglected to formally start our meeting by posting the ground rules, specifically including "no cell phones." Recognizing the importance of ground rules is one of the simple but highly effective facilitative behaviors that can go a long way toward ensuring project success.

■ PITFALL #7—USING FACILITATIVE LEADERSHIP TO ELIMINATE PERSONALITY DIFFERENCES

Six Sigma Team Dynamics: The Elusive Key to Project Success is devoted to increasing the probability of project success. A key component of team dynamics is dealing with maladaptive behavior—something that the teams will certainly encounter. We discussed multiple ways to handle maladaptive behavior, including both preventions and interventions. While we are confident that applying the practical tips in this book will dramatically improve your chances of Six Sigma success, we also know that no set of principles will eliminate all behaviors considered maladaptive.

It should be noted that facilitative leadership should not be used to eliminate personality differences among the teams. As we stated in Chapter 1, assembling a group of people into a team is similar to gathering a large family for the holidays. By definition, people are a diverse lot. In the Six Sigma teams, there will be a host of people with a wide variety of backgrounds, both environmentally and culturally. The team members bring a host of differing values, beliefs, and personalities with them to the Six Sigma teams. We are not suggesting that team dynamic tools can, or should, be used to eliminate the behaviors that others in the group find offensive simply on the basis of personality differences.

One of the revelations that has come from being a consultant is seeing the vast differences between organizational cultures. I have learned that what is accepted as normative behavior in one culture is seen as abnormal behavior in another. For example, one CEO I worked for swore like a sailor, and the scatological outbursts occurred even when he was not angry. Expectedly, others in the organization were also prone to four-letter adjectives. When I facilitated their meetings, I found my language becoming profane even though that is not my normal language.

In another client situation, I found that my personality strongly clashed with the "personality" of the organization. The client was located in Silicon Valley. They not only dressed casually (unlike their consultant who likes suits and ties) but their collective personality was also casual in nature. When I began facilitating the meetings with agendas, ground rules, and desired outcomes, their reaction was a collective yawn. The team's disapproval of the preventative structure was formalized at the end of the day when I was given a delta for being "too inflexible and Gestapo like." If I had been a full-time employee of this organization (after all, the employee acquisition process will always be flawed on some level), my personality would always clash with others no matter how well facilitative behaviors were practiced.

Regardless of the frustration that personality differences may cause within the team, facilitative tools should not be used to eliminate these differences. As a former psychologist and marriage counselor, I saw firsthand that appreciation for the other's uniqueness contributed to a better "team" in terms of a marriage relationship. In both marriage and Six Sigma teams, an appreciation for the individual differences of one another contributes to compatibility of values and beliefs. None of the ideas shared in *Team Dynamics* are intended to be misused to eliminate the divergent personalities that are brought to the Six Sigma team.

■ PITFALL #8—JUMPING TO "DIVORCE" TOO EARLY

Probably one of the largest factors that prompted my transition into the business world was the multitude of failures I witnessed in my previous career as a marriage counselor. While divorce is often a sad reality, all too often I saw troubled relationships where one spouse or the other was unwilling to give therapy an opportunity to salvage the marriage. Because of my Italian heritage where divorce was shunned, observing these divorces impacted my values and beliefs. A part of the impact was the way I thought about resistance and team dynamics.

As we said earlier, there are many times when much can be learned from those who are initially resistant to the Six Sigma project. We shared an example of an ardent resistor who made a costly career decision and was jettisoned from the project team. It cannot be stressed enough that these decisions, like divorce, should be few and far between. Remember that the odds are good (80%) that a resistor will change and become a valuable member of the team. Champions and team leaders must be cognizant of these odds when dealing with the resistor.

In our work with pro-active Champions and team leaders, we have had multiple experiences of encouraging them to give the resistor more time to get on board before making the final decision to remove the resistor from a team. It should be remembered that the stakes of project success increase significantly when someone is removed from the team. Once something as visible as removal from the team occurs, there is no longer a win-win scenario. The ejected person must save face.

Unless the reason for the removal of the team member is painted over with a lie, the person who was removed will become what Jack Becker, the Six Sigma vice president at Lithonia Lighting, calls a "permanent resistor." If the team does not achieve its desired results, the resistor essentially "wins," gaining confirmation that Six Sigma was a waste of valuable time. However, if the project team achieves its goals, and the project is proven to be a success, then the ejected person's career in the organization is all but over. We believe that there will be times when the removal of a person from the team will be necessary but, like divorce, the option should be exercised only as a last resort.

■ PITFALL #9—EXPECTING SIX SIGMA TEAMS TO SOLVE ALL ORGANIZATIONAL ISSUES

The excitement that Six Sigma has generated in the business world has been a true joy to witness. Unlike other quality issues that have come and gone, I am confident that Six Sigma as a true management philosophy is here to stay. While we cautioned in *The Six Sigma Revolution* that the adoption of Six Sigma in an organization must be more than just improvement projects, the importance of vibrant projects will always be a significant contributing factor to an organization's decision to commit to a Six Sigma initiative.

Having said that, it is important for executives to be careful not to mistakenly diagnose poor Six Sigma management as poor team dynamics. For example, a recent client had completed the eight steps of creating the Business Process Management system. As my readers know, the short-term goal of the first four days of this critical step in strategic Six Sigma is the selection of projects based on high-impact, low-performing processes. The client dutifully picked nine projects that needed attention. However, as we created the project Charters in Define, it became apparent that one of the projects that had been selected was poorly chosen for DMAIC. As the Champion worked with us to craft the project Scope, it became obvious that this was a bureaucratic issue that could be improved through a "work-out" approach. The work-out approach, also dubbed "Six Sigma Lite" by some, was first used by General Electric. It is an intensive two- or three-day training session for subject matter experts. The work-out team goes through Defining a problem, Analyzing its root cause, and making Improvements by generating and implementing a set of solutions. As you can see, it parallels the steps in DMAIC, with the exception of Measure and Control, which is the significant difference between using a three-day process versus a four- to eight-month improvement process.

The adage "When your only tool is a hammer, every problem looks like a nail" applies to Six Sigma as well as it does to many other areas in life. Whether it is a work-out improvement process or a full-scale DMAIC improvement process, management must be on the lookout to avoid making Six Sigma projects become the "be all and end all" of their organizations. Without proper knowledge about when and where to apply DMAIC, teams that are formed may have difficulty with their dynamics for one major reason—they never should have been formed in the first place.

■ PITFALL #10—INTERVENING TOO MUCH

In the summer of 1977, I was psychologist intern in a mental health clinic in Saginaw, Michigan. Motivated to make a difference in people's lives, I had chosen the same career path as my father. During that summer internship, I was given a limited client caseload. Every Friday afternoon I spent time with my mentor as he reviewed my cases and provided feedback (yes, feedback is ever present in all professions). During one review session, I remember indicating that there were many times when I wasn't sure what to say in response to a client. To this day I remember my mentor's feedback, "George, at times it is more important to know what *not* to say to a client."

This sage advice also applies to team interventions. Often, an inexperienced facilitator will jump too quickly to an intervention when certain behaviors are just the normal course of events for a large gathering of people. I will share with you one of the most painful events in my professional career that highlights this point.

Early in my career I was consulting with an automotive client. During a meeting I was facilitating, one of the executives received a message from his secretary. As he was leaving, I reminded the group about the importance of the meeting and that we had all agreed to stay. He told me the note was marked "urgent" and offered his regrets about leaving. Unbeknownst to us, this executive was being called out of the meeting to hear the crushing news that his wife had just been killed in an auto accident. Painfully, I learned that day that with few exceptions interventions should be done judiciously, and usually only after repeated behaviors have been determined to be maladaptive.

■ REFERENCE

Jack Welch with John A. Byrne. (2001). *Jack—Straight from the Gut.* New York: Warner Books.

KEY LEARNINGS

There are several pitfalls in creating Six Sigma Team Dynamics

➤ Failure of the Champion to be involved in each step of the team's work.

➤ Failure to write it down.

➤ Failure to formalize and communicate rewards and recognition for the Six Sigma team.

➤ Ignoring the potential of "converted" resistors.

➤ Failure to assign your best and brightest.

➤ Failure to utilize ground rules in Six Sigma meetings.

➤ Using facilitative leadership to eliminate personality differences.

➤ Jumping to "divorce" too early.

➤ Expecting Six Sigma teams to solve all organizational issues.

➤ Intervening too much.

Appendix A

Alpha Omega Call Center DMAIC Templates

Alpha Omega	Six Sigma Project Charter

Business Case (Connection to SBOs)

Alpha Omega has experienced significant decline in its operating profits and customer satisfaction, both of which are strategic business objectives. In order to positively influence both, improvement must occur across all business processes. Currently, the Call Center could positively impact customer satisfaction and operating profits through improvement of first call resolution, timeliness of response, and improvement in courtesy to the customer.

Project Scope

IN	OUT
External calls	*Policy issues with customers*
Issues related to first call resolution	*Organization structure*
Job descriptions	
Process redesign	
Other processes	
Customer index	
Customer courtesy	

Goal and Objectives	**Subject Matter Experts**
Reduce the call index from 42% to 36%	

APPROVAL	
Champion:	
Date:	
Team Leader:	
Date:	
Six Sigma Director:	
Date:	

Figure A.1 Completed charter template.

Problem Statement

Since January 2000, Alpha Omega's Call Center has experienced a Call Index of 42% versus the industry standard of 30%. This has negatively impacted customer satisfaction and operating expenses placing Alpha Omega at a competitive disadvantage in meeting its strategic business objectives for operating profit and customer satisfaction.

Expected Benefits	Target	Stretch
Total Savings	$ –	$ –

Milestones Start Date	Plan	Actual
Define	February 6, 7, & 8	
Measure	February 6, 7, & 8	
Analyze	April 8, 9, 10, 11, & 12	
Improve	May 21, 22, & 23	
Control	June 25, 26	
Team:		
Champion	*Charles Zukor*	
Team Leader	*Joy Schulenberg*	
Master Black Belt		
Team Members	**Role**	**Percent of Time**
Aaron Gregson		
Maria Carballo		
Leroy Barney		
Robert Wallace		
Susan Jackson		
Aaron Brown		
Jeff Seimonson		

Figure A.1 *(Continued)*

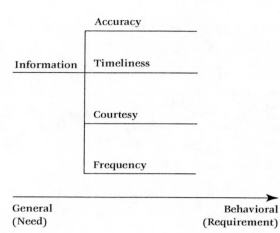

Level 1   Level 2   Level 3

Information

Accuracy

Timeliness

Courtesy

Frequency

General   Behavioral
(Need)   (Requirement)

Figure A.2 Call Center CTQ tree.

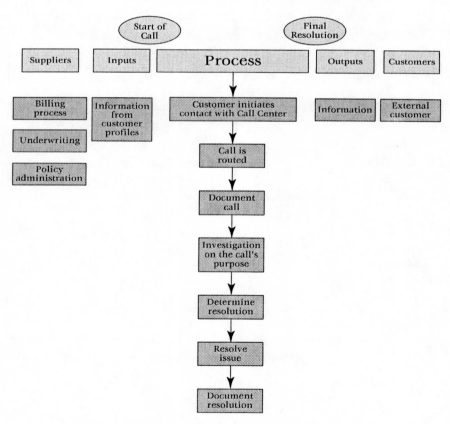

Figure A.3 Call Center information process.

What to Measure	Type of Measure	Type of Data	Operational Definition	Target	Specification	Data Collection Forms(s)	Sampling	Baseline Six Sigma
First call resolution	O	Discrete	Percent of return calls divided by total calls	100%	100%	Discrete Check Sheet	Representative/ random	1.3
Call response time	O,P	Continuous	Beginning of customer call to resolution of call	ASAP	5 minutes	Frequency Distribution Check Sheet	Representative/ random	0.9
Courtesy	O,I	Continuous	Likert scale of sampled customers where 5 = exceedingly courteous, 3 = courteous, 1 = not courteous	5	3	Frequency Distribution Check Sheet	Representative/ random	2.8
Call index	O	Continuous	Market research definition	0	30	Market Research Definition	Representative/ random	1.2

Figure A.4 Completed Data Collection Plan.

237

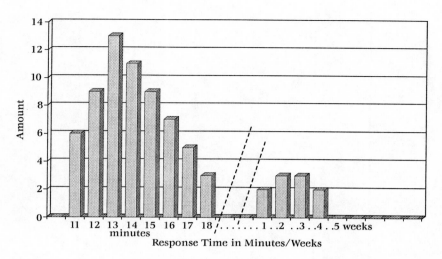

Figure A.5 Histogram.

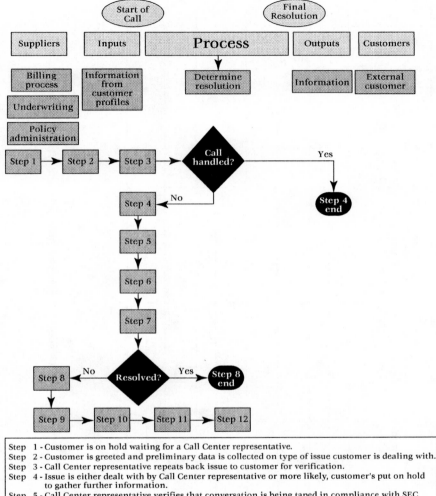

Step 1 - Customer is on hold waiting for a Call Center representative.
Step 2 - Customer is greeted and preliminary data is collected on type of issue customer is dealing with.
Step 3 - Call Center representative repeats back issue to customer for verification.
Step 4 - Issue is either dealt with by Call Center representative or more likely, customer's put on hold to gather further information.
Step 5 - Call Center representative verifies that conversation is being taped in compliance with SEC regulations.
Step 6 - Call Center representative reconnects with customer to assure them their issue is under consideration.
Step 7 - Preliminary information for customer is verified and reviewed by Call Center representative for accuracy of message.
Step 8 - Issue resolution communicated to customer.
Step 9 - Further clarification requested by customer or this is where customer calls back.
Step 10 - Call Center representative emphasizes Alpha Omega's commitment to quality.
Step 11 - Further investigation of customer issue is conducted.
Step 12 - More complicated issues are queued for special treatment and held in the "urgent bin."
Step 13 - Communication of resolution to the customer and verification with same of administrative paperwork.

Figure A.6   Determine resolution—Step 5 subprocess map of high-level Call Center information process.

Process Step	1	2	3	4	5	6	7	8	9	10	11	12	13	Total	%
Time (minutes or days) Best/Worst	30 sec./1 hr.	2 min.	1 min.	1 min./1 wk.	30 sec.	30 sec.	30 sec.	2 min.	1 min./1 wk.*	10 sec.	1 day/3 days	1 hr./1 day	10**	†/‡	
Value add		x						x		x				3	23%
Nonvalue add	x		x	x	x	x			x		x	x	x	10	77%
Internal failure/rework														0	0%
External failure														0	0%
Control/inspection			x				x						x	3	23%
Delays	x			x					x		x	x		5	38%
Preparation/set up						x								1	8%
Moves														0	0%
Value enabling					x									1	8%

*If step 8 is successful, the rest of the steps are not seen.
**Administrative step not seen by customer.
† 1 day/1 hr./6 min./10 sec.
‡ 2 wks./4 days/1 hr./6 min./40 sec.

Figure A.7 Process summary analysis worksheet.

240

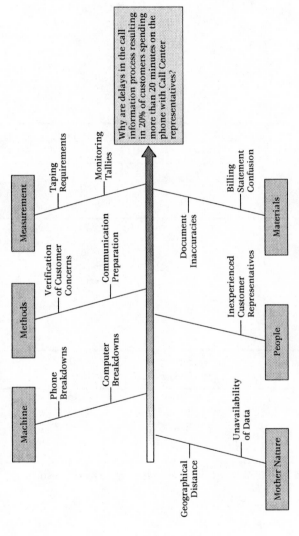

Figure A.8 The cause-effect diagram.

$$Y = (x_1, + x_2, + x_3)$$

Billing   Computer   Inexperienced
Statement Breakdowns   Customer
Confusion   Representatives

Figure A.9 Y is a function of $Y=f(x)$ formula.

	Musts		
	Budget	**Headcount**	**September 30**
Statement redesign	Yes	Yes	Yes
Call routing	Yes	Yes	Yes
Training program	Yes	Yes	Yes

Figure A.10 Call Centers Must Criteria results.

	Statement Redesign	**Call Routing**	**Training Program**
Root causation 10	10/100	8/80	7/70
Stakeholders 9	9/81	8/72	8/81
Cost 8	6/48	8/64	8/64
Total	229	216	215

Figure A.11 Call Centers Want Criteria results.

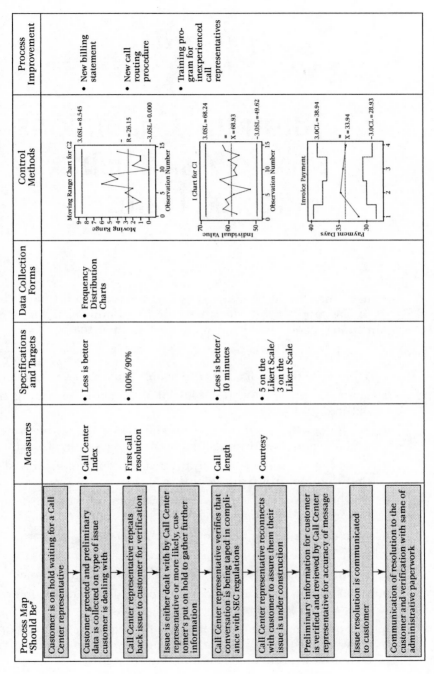

Figure A.12 Process improvement hand-off: The Response Plan.

Appendix B

95 Questions Champions Should Ask Their Project Teams

These questions should be starting points for any good Champion. Following the "audit trail" should result in hundreds of follow-up questions that a good Champion should ask of their team.

Define

1. What does the team see as the business case for the project?

2. Does the team have any additional thoughts regarding the defined problem?

3. What does the team think is outside the Scope of the project and what do they think is inside the Scope of the project?

4. Does the team believe that any team members are missing that were not originally identified?

5. Do the team members know their various roles and responsibilities?

6. Who does the team believe is the customer(s) of the project?

7. What are the needs of the customer(s) of this project?

8. What are the requirements of the customer of this project?

9. What methods did the team use to validate the customer(s) needs and requirements?

10. Did the team use a combination of interviews, focus groups, surveys, customer complaints, and observing or being the customer to validate needs and requirements?

11. Has the team validated their high-level "As-Is" Process Map?

12. Which employees of the current process have been interviewed to validate the process?

13. How has the team simulated the product or service going through the process to modify the brainstormed Process Map?

14. How has the Process Map been changed as a result of validation?

Measure

15. What are the one to three measures that the team has validated from customer data that will act as our effectiveness measures?

16. What has been determined to be the one or two supplier input measures important to this project?

17. What has been determined to be the process measure of efficiency?

18. Does the process measure either cycle time, cost, a measure of labor, or the percent value in the current process?

19. Are the measures under consideration continuous or discrete?

20. If any of the measures under consideration are discrete, could they be measured with continuous data?

21. If these discrete measures could be measured continuously, could their transformation to continuous data be done economically?

22. Have measures under consideration been operationally defined yet?

23. If so, do these operational definitions have the bias of the customer in mind?

24. What is the target value for each measure under consideration?

25. How was the target value validated through contact with customers of the process?

26. What are the specifications for each measure under consideration?

27. How was the specification for each measure validated through contact with customers of the process?

28. Are the data collection forms used in this project reflective of the right type of data?

29. Are we using discrete data collection forms when discrete data is being collected?

30. If we are using discrete collection forms, have we established reason codes for the type of defects that will be collected so that we can create Pareto charts?

31. If we are using continuous data, have we created frequency distribution charts such that at least five to seven measurement cells are formed?

32. What criteria was established by the team relative to assuring that the sampling plan is representative of the larger population to be sampled?

33. What criteria was established by the team relative to assuring that the sampling plan is randomly selected of the larger population to be sampled?

34. Which sampling formula was selected?

35. Does the sampling formula reflect the appropriate one for either discrete or continuous data?

36. How did the team define what a unit is for purposes of baseline sigma calculation?

37. How did the team define what a defect was for purposes of baseline sigma calculation?

38. How did the team define the number of opportunities for purpose of baseline sigma calculation?

39. What were the criteria used to determine whether to calculate defects per unit or defects per opportunity?

Analysis

40. What was the team's baseline sigma calculation?

41. Did the team calculate a separate sigma for each CTQ validated with the customer or calculate a cumulative sigma combining all CTQs?

42. What data analysis tools were used to visually display the data collected in the Measure phase of DMAIC?

43. If continuous data was used during the Measure phase, did the team determine through data analysis if the process is exhibiting common cause or special cause variation?

44. If the variation in the process was special cause, did the team determine the process components contributing to the special cause?

45. Regardless of the type of data generated, did the team create detailed, granular micro-problem statements?

46. Is there a logical progression from the data analysis to the micro-problem question(s)?

47. Did the team create a subprocess map?

48. If so, how did the team validate the subprocess map?

49. Were there any changes when the subprocess map was validated?

50. Did the team subprocess all high-level steps in the original "As-Is" Process Map or did they choose only one subprocess step to drill down?

51. How did the team determine the flow of work analysis at the subprocess level?

52. Did the team conduct the nature of work analysis to determine which subprocess steps add value to the customer and which do not?

53. Did the team complete a process summary analysis worksheet?

54. If the team completed a process summary analysis worksheet, what were the primary types of nonvalue-added steps?

55. In determining the primary type of nonvalue-added steps, did the team use total frequency or contribution to cost to the organization?

56. From the process summary analysis worksheet, did the team create micro-problem questions?

57. Did the team brainstorm as many process variables that could explain the micro-problem *statements?*

58. Did the team use a cause-effect diagram to brainstorm the process variables or did the team use some other method?

59. How did the team ensure that all participants participated in the brainstorming?

60. How did the team narrow the list of total process variables that could explain the micro-problem statements or questions (i.e., their hypothesis)?

61. Did the team use basic data collection methods to test their hypothesis?

62. If the team used basic data collection methods to test their hypothesis, what were their findings from this data collection?

63. Did the team use scatter analysis or another more sophisticated method of regression analysis to test their hypothesis?

64. Did the team use a designed experiment or a series of designed experiments to test their hypothesis?

65. If the team used a designed experiment to test their hypothesis, did this validation provide leads for potential solutions to be used in the Improve phase of DMAIC?

Improve

66. Did the team brainstorm as many solutions that could impact improvement in sigma performance?

67. Did the team use an affinity diagram or some other tool to capture their brainstormed solutions?

68. How did the team narrow their total list of solutions down to the most probable list of solutions?

69. Did the team apply the must criteria against their narrowed list of solutions?

70. Which solutions did not meet the must criteria and thus will not be under further consideration for this project?

71. Did the team apply the want criteria to the remaining solutions to prioritize the implementation of those remaining solutions?

72. Did the team identify the key stakeholders who will be affected by their prioritized solutions?

73. Did the team conduct a stakeholder analysis indicating both the current and desired level of support to the prioritized solutions?

74. For key stakeholders, not at their desired level, was an influence strategy developed indicating what the issues were preventing the key stakeholder from occupying their desired level of support?

75. Did the team develop strategies to overcome the issues that result in key stakeholders being resistant to the prioritized solutions?

76. Do any of the prioritized solutions need to be modified or eliminated to gain support from key stakeholders who remain resistant?

77. Has the project team developed an implementation plan for the prioritized solutions that have key stakeholder support?

78. Does the implementation plan include a "pilot" where the prioritized solutions are implemented on a trial basis so that modifications can be made if necessary?

79. Has the project team completed the "pilot"?

80. What did the project team learn from implementing the "pilot"?

81. What modifications to the prioritized solutions are necessary based on what was learned from the "pilot"?

82. Are any unusual resources necessary to implement the prioritized solutions?

83. Does the project team need any management support relative to those resources?

Control

84. Has the team created a new "should be" Process Map?

85. Has the team determined the level of throughput of products or services that go through the new "should be" Process Map?

86. Has the team determined the level of standardization in the new "should be" Process Map?

87. As a result of determining the level of throughput and standardization has the team selected an appropriate technical control tool to assure the solutions sustain over time?

88. Has the team begun the use of the control tool to insure ease of use and understandability among those in the process who will be affected?

89. Has the project team determined the measures that should be monitored in the new "should be" process?

90. Are these measures new to the process participants?

91. If these measures are new, has the project team included in their implementation plan appropriate training of process participants on both how to collect data and use the control tool?

92. Are there any new targets for the measures in the new "should be" process?

93. Are there any new specifications for the measures in the new "should be" process"?

94. Has the project team developed a response plan that captures all prioritized solutions so that if the process goes out of control, a check to ensure these solutions are being maintained is done?

95. Has the response plan been formalized and documented in written form?

$\mathscr{A}pp\mathbb{C}ndix$

The Champion's Responsibilities

■ THE CHAMPION'S RESPONSIBILITY *BEFORE* THE TEAM IS FORMED

➤ *Select the team members.* For champions to be successful in their pursuit of Six Sigma improvement, they must pick their team. This team should be comprised of between five to eight members. They need to be subject matter experts in the process targeted for improvement. They must be the processes "best and brightest," not those that are available for special projects. The team leader must have leadership capability, an affinity for process improvement, and be able to learn the methodology fast enough to then lead his or her team.

➤ *Create the business case for the project.* The business case is a nonquantitative statement that establishes the purpose and direction for the team. This statement should establish the focus of the team, motivate emotion, and motivate behavior. It should state why this project should be done, why it should be done now, and why it has priority over other projects. Finally, the business case should reference the strategic business objectives of the organization that the project is trying to impact.

➤ *Formulate the preliminary problem statement.* The preliminary problem statement is the quantitative statement of what is wrong with the current process. It is preliminary since the project team will complete this statement with their work done in the Measure phase of DMAIC. It should be a statement that is specific and measurable, describes the gap between the current and desired state, states how long the problem has been going on, describes the impact of the problem, and is stated in neutral terms.

➤ *Identify the preliminary scope of the project.* Scope refers to what is inside the parameters of the project team's work and, more importantly, what is outside the parameters of the project team's work. This crucial step in project work is first created by the Project Champion, modified by the project team, and finalized by the Champion during the first weeks of the project team's existence.

➤ *Identify the preliminary goals of the project.* Project goals for first projects typically focus on a 50 percent improvement over the baseline sigma generated by the project team in the Measure phase of DMAIC.

➤ *Allocate the resources for the team to complete its work.* From work areas (known as War Rooms) to computer time, the Champion must provide all the resources to their team to maximize the chances of success for their team.

➤ *Identify the team leader (either a Black Belt or Green Belt).* The team leader will have the responsibilities of assuring that all milestones of the team will be met. This person needs to have good facilitation skills, project management skills, and be able to learn the DMAIC methodology quick enough to act as an informal mentor to other team members.

➤ *Communicate the business case to each team member.* As part of the prework of a good Champion, the business case must be communicated to all team members before their training on DMAIC begins. This includes motivating the team sufficient for them to be excited about what they are about to embark on for the next six months.

➤ *Establish the timeline for the project team to complete its work.* From the Define to the Control phase of DMAIC should take approximately six months, with some teams taking a shorter time and some teams taking longer. This period should include formal review cycles that establish the formal reviews of the Champion.

➤ *Establish the milestones along the way for input from the Champion.* The Project Champion and team leader should meet a minimum of once a week. There will be times that the Champion will meet either with the team or team leader other than once a week but this weekly schedule needs to be established formally before the team begins its work.

➤ *Distinguish decisions requiring Champion input from independent team decisions.* Some decisions will be made by the team exclusive of the Champion. In other cases, the Champion will want input. A preliminary review of the types of decisions that can be done without the Champion and the types of decisions that should be in conjunction with the Champion should be discussed and agreed on before the team begins its work.

■ THE CHAMPION'S RESPONSIBILITIES DURING THE PROJECT TEAM'S EXISTENCE

In order of importance, the responsibilities of the Champion during the team's existence are:

➤ *Validate and finalize the charter.* A pivotal role for the Champion is to validate and finalize the charter. The largest responsibility relative to the charter is to take the input regarding scope generated by the team in their first meeting and determine whether their ideas results in an item being inside the scope of the team or outside. Champions are encouraged to have limited scope in first projects. In addition to learning the Six Sigma methodology, project teams are expected to produce actual results associated with the processes selected for improvement. Champions are always encouraged to limit the scope of projects so that they maximize the opportunity for their teams to succeed. In addition to project scope, the Champion must validate any additional input relative to team membership. Many times, the teams when reviewing the team members will notice a subject matter expert who should have been a part of the team. The suggestions for additional team membership (even if only on an ad hoc basis) should be taken under advisement by the Champion and resolved quickly. To a lesser extent, Champions may be provided with input from the team relative to missing items on the business case or problem statement. Issues raised by the team impact the problem statement as well as the project scope. It is strongly recommended that this validation and finalization of the team charter be done within one week of the conclusion of the project team's first week of training.

➤ *Monitor and approve all project team tollgate work.* A good Project Champion will not over manage their teams. However, they should at a minimum review all work for each tollgate. Some tollgates are so significant that they are stand-alone reviews for the Project Champion. For example, the project charter is of such importance it should be a stand-alone tollgate review for the Champion. In other cases, several tollgates can be combined in a single review. For example, tollgates 2 and 3 of Define can be combined into a single review and approval session.

➤ *Meet regularly with the team leader/facilitator.* One of the most important responsibilities a Project Champion has over the course of the four to eight months the project team exists is to meet with the team leader/facilitator a minimum of once a week. This meeting could last as little as 30 minutes for some meetings. For more formal tollgate reviews, the meeting could be more extensive. However, this weekly meeting is imperative for the ultimate success of the project.

➤ *Remove barriers or roadblocks to the team's success.* Over the course of a team's existence, barriers and roadblocks that call for management attention is inevitable. For example, what if a team member begins missing regularly scheduled Six Sigma meetings. If the team leader/facilitator determines that the team member's manager doesn't support their employee's involvement in Six Sigma, they may directly or indirectly influence the participation of that team member's involvement with the team. This situation would necessitate the Champion approaching the team member's manager with the goal of gaining greater support for the participation of the team member in question. Another example of roadblock removal requiring Champion involvement is if their team is not receiving the necessary support from such functions as finance or information technology. If support from these groups is not sufficient, it is the responsibility of the Champion to assist the team in gaining support from these functions. There are a host of other barriers and roadblocks too numerous to cite here. A good Champion will actively solicit from his or her team leader/facilitator whether there are roadblocks getting in the way of the team rather than just be reactive to requests for help generated by the team leader/facilitator.

➤ *Maintain momentum of the team and keep them on task.* Project teams working on DMAIC will exist four to eight months normally. Any team that exists for that period of time will reach plateaus or become discouraged with the course of their project. If this discouragement or frustration is allowed to fester, there is greater likelihood that deadlines will be missed or performed poorly. It is the responsibility of the Project Champion to maintain the momentum of the team. In some cases, this may call for the Champion to attend the beginning of a Six Sigma meeting and reiterate the importance of the project. Referencing the business case can be of value here. Reinforcing why the project is worth doing, why is it worth doing now, and why this project has priority over other work can help reinvigorate the team members. Many times, the focus of this encouragement will be aimed at the team leader/facilitator who will play more of a day-to-day role in maintaining momentum. In addition, it is important for the Champion to maintain adherence to the milestones that are a part of every project team charter.

➤ *Deal with resistance among the team.* Team members are made up of subject matter experts. Many of these subject matter experts will be selected for their knowledge and involvement of the process targeted for improvement, not their support for Six Sigma. Exacerbating this dilemma are team members who have been a part of a previous quality initiative that has failed. Resistance must be dealt with in a timely, direct manner. Worst case scenarios call for the removal of the team member if resistance cannot be overcome.

➤ *Communicate progress to upper management.* Particularly in first projects, upper management is expecting quantitative results. Rather than waiting for the results of the project and reporting the outcome, a good Champion will communicate progress (or the lack thereof) to upper management periodically through the course of the DMAIC training and implementation.

➤ *Continuing education.* Most Champions receive limited training prior to the launch of their Six Sigma teams. At the same time, Six Sigma project teams over the course of four to eight months will receive more extensive training on the improvement methodology. While the Champion does not need to know as much detail associated with Six Sigma as the team leader/facilitator, Champions who hone their technical skills on DMAIC manage their projects better than those who don't. Therefore, Champions should augment their training with both reading and coaching from others who are content experts. For example, the Master Black Belt in an organization is the Six Sigma subject matter expert. Good Champions will seek out coaching on DMAIC so that they can ask the type of questions that make for better project work.

➤ *Recognize efforts.* In typical first projects, cost savings is the measure that determines the ultimate success or failure of Six Sigma. In the best-managed projects, this may take months after the conclusion of the project team's work. Even when things are going well on a Six Sigma team, this long-term goal may not sustain enthusiasm for the team. Thus, it is the responsibility of the Champion to recognize efforts. This could be as simple as treating for pizza during a Six Sigma meeting or obtaining a free personal day for the team members. Recognition of the team is a critical success factors to maintain the enthusiasm for the project.

➤ *Re-evaluate Scope during the project.* As data is collected and analyzed over the course of the project's existence, Scope may need to be re-evaluated. This usually happens after baseline data collection is available or after the data and/or process has been analyzed. It is not unusual for the data to lead to a logical expansion of Scope. However, expanding Scope, even legitimately, had significant hazards for a Six Sigma team. It is recommended that Scope be expanded on an extremely limited basis. It is far more preferred to identify a second wave project and keep the originally Scoped project. Nonetheless, a formal review of the Scope should be the domain of the Champion during the course of the project's existence.

■ THE CHAMPION'S RESPONSIBILITIES AFTER THE PROJECT TEAM'S EXISTENCE

➤ *Communication of the new process (and results) to the Business Quality Council.* Through the use of the response plan, the Champion is expected to communicate the new process and its associated results to the business quality council. In the case of the Call Center where the solutions were part of another project (and more importantly another process), it is essential that these communications are orchestrated so that the strategic component of Six Sigma (see the *Six Sigma Revolution*, pp. 230–241) is maintained and managed.

➤ *Capture lessons learned.* Regardless of the extent of success or failure of any given team, the Champion should conduct a poll of their Six Sigma project team. In this poll, the Champion should gather data on what went well over the course of the team's existence and what could have been done better. This information could apply to the team's results, its methods of achieving same, or the role of the Champion or the executive team.

➤ *Monitor performance of the new process.* The Champion in more cases than not is also the process owner. As such, the process owner has the long-term responsibility of assuring the response plan becomes standard procedure. When the Champion and process owner is the same person, this transition of monitoring the new process is simple. However, when the Champion and the process owner are different persons, the Champion needs to contract with the process owner about the duration and extent of their involvement in the transition of monitoring and managing the new process and implementation of the response plan.

➤ *Recognize, reward, and celebrate both success and effort.* Particularly in first wave projects, it is imperative that Champions recognize, reward, and celebrate both success and effort. These activities should focus on the collective team. Many organizations sponsor a combination of science fair and banquet. At this gathering, the entire organization can review the storyboards and templates of the various projects. As the day progresses, a banquet is held where the business leader and Champions pay special recognition to the teams. Sometimes special note of individual performance is given. In most cases, the teams are recognized and the lessons learned from the first wave of projects captured.

Index